A stage of their own

For Joel

Sheila Stowell

A stage of their own
Feminist playwrights of the suffrage era

Ann Arbor
The University of Michigan Press

Copyright © Sheila Stowell 1992

Published in the United States of America by
The University of Michigan Press

Manufactured in Great Britain

1995   1994   1993   1992   4   3   2   1

Library of Congress Cataloging-in-publication Data applied for

ISBN 0-472-10334-2

Contents

Acknowledgements

I would like to thank the following institutions for their assistance in the completion of this book. For significant financial support, The Society for Theatre Research (UK), The Social Sciences and Humanities Research Council of Canada, and the H. R. Macmillan Foundation. For extending to me the courtesy of their research facilities, The British Library, The British Newspaper Library (Colindale), The Mander and Mitchenson Theatre Collection, The Fawcett Library, The Garrick Club, The Theatre Museum, The Billy Rose Theatre Collection (New York Public Library at Lincoln Centre), The Fales Library (New York University), and The Harry Ransom Humanities Research Centre (University of Texas at Austin). For allowing me to reproduce unpublished letters of Bernard Shaw and Harley Granville Barker, The Society of Authors, on behalf of the estates of Bernard Shaw and Harley Granville Barker.

I would also like to extend thanks to the following individuals, Air Marshal Sir Leslie Bower RAF (Retd), executor of the estate of Cicely Hamilton, Mabel Smith, executor of the estate of Elizabeth Robins, Jon Wisenthal, David Mayer, Viv Gardner, Chris Dymkow-ski, Frank Walker, Dennis Kennedy, Tirthanker Bose, and David Lemon.

I am particularly grateful to Joel Kaplan for his advice and continuing support.

Material from Chapter 3 has appeared in 'Re[pre]senting Eroticism: The Tyranny of Fashion in Feminist Plays of the Edwardian Age' (*Theatre History Studies* XI (1991): 51–62); a more theoretical consideration of issues raised in Chapter 4 will appear in 'Rehabilitating Realism', forthcoming in *The Journal of Dramatic Theory and Criticism*.

Introduction

'How do they know what is womanly? It's for women to decide that.'
So speaks Ernestine Blunt in Elizabeth Robins's *Votes for Women!*,
her challenge to men and women heralding a battle that was to be
waged over many fronts in the early years of the twentieth century,
as feminists of that period struggled for the right to define themselves and their place within the social and political systems of a
troubled nation. For in spite of nostalgic efforts to cast the period
in a golden afterglow, Edwardian Britain was characterised by
turbulence and uncertainty, as an entrenched 'old' order met up
with the voices of a 'new' century eager for release from what
Samuel Hynes has called the 'ossification of authority.' It was a
period, Hynes continues, in which 'the *forms* of values had become
the values [and] institutions had become more important than the
ideas they embodied' (5). Such hollowness at the heart of the
Empire produced both anxiety and exhilaration, antagonism and
fierce loyalties, as attempts were made upon a number of fronts to
confound such 'forms' with manifestations of a new age. It was
during these years that a women's movement, dispirited after a half
century of legal lobbying for the vote, was revitalised by the formation in 1903 of the Women's Social and Political Union.[1] Innovative
in its highly public, confrontational (eventually violent) tactics, the
organisation offered feminists a new, militant image that helped to
spur women of all classes, talents and occupations to renewed
political and social action. Indeed, agitation for suffrage became
the locus of a wide-ranging critique of a capitalist patriarchy that
purported to explain and contain women by means of the ideology
of 'separate spheres'. Among those who actively challenged the
relegation of women to a 'private', domesticated world were a
number of self-consciously feminist playwrights who used the
overtly 'public' forum of drama as a point of entry to the debate. It
is their work that forms the subject of this book. Recognising that it
was a period that witnessed a veritable explosion in the number of
women dramatists – Julie Holledge estimates that there were over
four hundred writing at the time (3) – my study is selective rather
than exhaustive, focusing upon a group of women playwrights who

sought to exploit in the theatre proper some of the elements of dramatic display so successfully appropriated by the WSPU. Written in response to what they called male-determined or male-imitative playmaking, their endeavour was a conscious attempt to construct an 'authentic' woman's drama. With the exception of Githa Sowerby, about whom virtually no documentary evidence exists, the dramatists looked at were all actively involved in the suffrage movement and, in addition to their full-length work for the avant-garde theatre, contributed to the overtly propagandist drama of the cause itself. Elizabeth Robins, an actor and producer who had done much to champion the Ibsen cause in Britain, was the first of this group to take her chances as a professional playwright. Her *Votes for Women!* (1907) is an intentionally politicised 'tract' which initiated a series of formal experiments by sister playwrights to renegotiate existing genres. A grab-bag of conventions recycled for feminist ends, *Votes for Women!* looks remarkably like a drawing -room play of the 1890s yoked uneasily to Drury Lane city spectacle and Ibsenesque duologue. By adopting forms of drama associated with certain social and aesthetic postures, Robins raised expectations in her audience which she proceeded to frustrate by means of the disruption of each form by feminist voices. Inevitably linked to an inherited (male-determined) tradition of drama, Robins's work uses such points of continuity to underscore feminist positions, most obviously her challenge to separate-spheres ideology and the sexual double-standard it perpetuated. The result was a remarkable play that asked audiences to think not only about the subjects of feminist debate but about the very aesthetic structures to which they had grown habituated. As Shaw had earlier said about the coming of Ibsen, one didn't have to like a play like *The Wild Duck*, but after experiencing it one couldn't look at what had come before in quite the same way (*Our Theatres in the Nineties* vol .1, 165).

The immediate response to *Votes for Women!* was to make theatre itself part of the cause, Robins's full-length experiment in form and content spawning a series of so-called 'suffrage plays', a species of 'agitprop' drama that flourished from 1908 to 1914. In 1908, recognising the propaganda possibilities of the theatre, suffrage supporters in the theatrical professions formed the Women Writers' Suffrage League (WWSL) and the Actresses' Franchise League (AFL), organisations which successfully enlisted dramatic art in the fight for women's rights. The drama composed and performed by the WWSL and the AFL manipulates existing genres and styles, sometimes into obvious arguments for female enfranchisement but also into more generalised portrayals of women's experience. These include both representations of woman's continuing victimisation within the existing social and political system (depictions intended to urge spectators to challenge that system) and celebratory renderings of current and potential accomplishments. Among the former are the grimly realistic dramas of Inez Bensusan (*The Apple* 1909) and Gertrude Vaughan (*Woman with the Pack* 1911) in which hardship, harassment and economic betrayal are shown to be woman's common lot, and suffrage farces such as Cicely Hamilton's *How the Vote Was Won* (1909) and Evelyn Glover's *A Chat with Mrs Chicky* (1912), works which exuberantly ridicule the arguments of anti-suffragists. Hamilton's *Pageant of Great Women* (1909) is the best known of the celebratory pieces, drawing upon England's rich tradition of politicised street theatre and civic pageantry to argue the ability of women in times past and present. Informed by and informing the movement that contained them, these pieces were an integral part of the propaganda machine of the cause, being conceived, written and performed for immediate and specific socio-political ends.

Cicely Hamilton, whose plays and pageants were among the most potent weapons in the AFL/WWSL arsenal, was an articulate speaker for the suffrage cause. Her own more broadly based feminist agenda – she pointedly called herself a feminist rather than a suffragist – found fullest expression in *Marriage as a Trade* (1909), a prose tract that set out to 'relentlessly strip away the romance surrounding marriage' (Intro 1). Hamilton's purpose, as her title suggests, was to examine the consequences for woman 'of the conditions imposed upon her by her staple industry' (17). An insistence upon these same 'trade aspects of marriage' also informs *Diana of Dobson's* (1908), Hamilton's four-act play, ironically called 'a romance'. This Cinderella tale of an exploited shop assistant who marries into the minor aristocracy (via a sojourn on the Embankment) is intended to raise uneasy questions not only about marriage as an institution but about the comedic form that insists upon the desirability of such unions. Grappling with both social conventions and the dramatic structures in which they are mirrored, Hamilton makes plain the embodiment in 'comic' resolutions of society's insistence that women dwindle into wives. Self-consciously redeploying the conventions of 'cup and saucerism' (as popularised by Tom Robertson and the Pinero of *Trelawny of the 'Wells'*) with its romantic championing of cross-class alliances, Hamilton makes uncomfortably explicit the connection between theatrical contrivance and the compulsory nature of 'marriage as a trade'. The romance in romantic comedy is itself problematised, revealed by Hamilton as a device for masking the inequitable nature of marital barter.

What Hamilton did for romantic comedy, Elizabeth Baker and Githa Sowerby did for dramatic realism, appropriating what had become a discrete style and genre as the basis for a wide-ranging feminist critique of the worlds they reconstructed. In both the Hammersmith drawing-room of Baker's Wilsons (*Chains* 1909), and the North Country parlour of Sowerby's Rutherfords (*Rutherford and Son* 1912) we are confronted with bleak, oppressive environments that replicate both the surface details and socio-economic forces of the workaday world. In each, however, such resources are mustered to demonstrate how women (and certain men) are made to suffer at the hands of a tyrannical social and economic patriarchy. Both plays, moreover, challenge the inevitability of such an order through the refusal of their heroines to submit to prescribed domestic roles. In fact, marriage itself, identified by Hynes as 'the most central' and 'inflammatory' issue of the suffrage movement (174) is measured and found wanting, a manifestation in the drama of the pervasive attack upon the institution that characterised the period's feminism. In *Chains* and *Rutherford and Son* – as in *Votes for Women!* – female protagonists reject marriage and 'respectable' family life in favour of an heroic celibacy that allows them to break free of the 'closures' conventionally imposed upon the forms they inhabit.

At the same time, each play, taking its cue from Robins, reworks that *locus classicus* of the New Drama, Ibsen's doll's-house wife slamming the door upon husband and children. Nora's casual lumping together of motherhood and wifedom, Baker and Sowerby suggest, was the product of a prejudiced if sympathetic (male) observer. Each offers a distinct corrective, arguing, as Robins had done, for the greater claims of the child, born or about to be born. Drama, with its ability to expand and truncate time, has always had an advantage in dealing with the theme of generation. For Edwardian feminists the form encouraged a serious re-examination of the issue of motherhood. Which is not to suggest that these women subscribed to the new century's 'cult' of the mother.[2] Indeed, they pointedly refused to celebrate women's procreative function as a solution to what in conservative quarters was perceived to be a declining birth rate, or endorse eugenics as a remedy for what many saw as England's 'degenerate stock'. Rather, their work demonstrates the vexed nature of the 'motherhood' issue, representing both 'the principal element in the definition and regulation of female sexuality and at the same time a source of feminine power' (Tickner 217). These playwrights all agreed that motherhood meant a complete subordination of self to the child's interest, a subordination that could, ironically, provide women with an ability to control men in thrall to patriarchy. Equally importantly, however, they urged both the claims and (potential) power of women who chose not to become mothers, who were not caught up in what male playwrights from Henry Arthur Jones to Bernard Shaw defined as a biological imperative. Indeed, such figures were often turned into social role models which at the same time provided innovative dramatic roles to women actors frustrated with the stage's predominantly conservative presentation of women, what Robins called the 'hack work' of the stage.

The experiments of Baker and Sowerby with realism as a container for feminist ideology, in turn, raise questions about current methodology and critical approaches. Some contemporary feminist critics of the drama have argued that realism in and of itself necessarily endorses or at least tolerates the fictive worlds it represents. To be sure, it may. But as the work of Edwardian feminists demonstrates, both a social and an economic order may be replicated for subversive ends. We cannot ignore the fact that realism in the guise of naturalism developed as a radical, low mimetic response to the glittering make-believe world of society drama, which was seen to be, to quote Jill Dolan's critique of realism, 'prescriptive in that it reifie[d] the dominant culture's inscription of traditional power relations between genders and classes' (84). During the period under investigation here, realism (in the form of naturalism) was championed as a means of challenging the ideological assumptions imbedded in melodrama and the well-made-play. The point is that feminist theatre history cannot afford to theorise a-historically, or for that matter dismiss lightly the continuity of theatrical forms or experience. We need to acknowledge 'the sense in which revolutions originate from within the stylistic paradigm', and the manner in which anti-conventions push against conventions and conventionality as they in turn break into new conventions (States 88, 12). Otherwise, as Austin Quigley notes, we run the risk of 'misunderstand[ing] the nature of the novelty if we ignore as "derivative" elements of plays that are indispensable if their novelty is to function successfully'. We would do well 'to regard both innovative *and* conventional aspects of a drama as necessary and deliberate choices – choices made, each in the context of the other, for particular purposes' (Quigley xi) – in the case of the work examined here, for feminist purposes predicated upon the effort to re-educate perception, to see anew. As a consequence my work has focussed upon genre, upon the specific forms inherited by feminist playwrights of the suffrage era, upon their manipulation of those forms, and upon the symbiotic relationship between such form and its content. In the end, I believe, a generic approach to feminist drama has particular merit because, as Janet Todd has argued in more general terms, 'it makes discernible otherwise hidden ideological constraints and because it opens up the question of aesthetics. Demoted from its high romantic position as a universal truth, art has none the less an aesthetic of sorts, but it is worth considering what happens to the culturally constructed aesthetic when women artists are massively considered and what it implies for a political enterprise' (136). I have also sought to examine these plays within the context of their initial audiences and reception. Particular attention has been paid to the reaction of the feminist press and 'gendered' responses in more mainstream publications.

It follows, that in our attempts to come to grips with this suppressed body of women's writing, we cannot neglect the relationship it bears to the work of both sympathetic and sceptical male playwrights of the period. The differences between writers like Robins, Hamilton, Baker and Sowerby, and conservative figures like Pinero and Jones are obvious enough. The latter, in fact, provided feminist authors with a storehouse of determined antagonists, characters to be upended, from Sir Richard Kato (*The Case of Rebellious Susan* 1894) who lectures a proto-Suffragette about her warped womanhood, to the irate husband of *The Ogre* (1911), who asserts his dominion by literally nailing his breeches to the wall. The playwrights of the New Drama – Granville Barker, Galsworthy, Hankin, Houghton and, of course, Shaw – present a more complex and interesting problem. They were, by their own lights, 'feminist' in their sympathies. All supported female enfranchisement, and, in the case of Shaw and Galsworthy, worked to effect social change through theatrical means. Granville Barker, and again Shaw, were instrumental in getting playwrights like Robins staged in the first place. Both contributed to the text of *Votes for Women!* which was produced and directed as part of Granville Barker's 1907 Court Theatre season. Yet the 'feminism' of such male helpmates differs significantly from that of the women writers whose work forms the core of this study. And nowhere is this more apparent than in their tackling in dramatic form that vast subject referred to as 'the Woman Question'. Whether we look at the themes most crucial for Edwardian feminists – sexuality, marriage, motherhood, female friendship, work – or the presentation of character types – mother, daughter, spinster, wife, working woman – we find a significant divide separating male New Dramatists from their female colleagues. It is a distinction, moreover, that in affecting theme and character also affects dramatic form and social intent, as a rehandling of a subject like marriage, for example, merges imperceptibly into a re-examination of the assumptions supporting traditionally comic endings. I have tried, in the chapters that follow, to illustrate some of these differences – in subject and form – by introducing where they seemed most pertinent particular plays by this group of male writers. It is hoped that such a comparison will not only sharpen our definition of the feminist theatre of the suffrage era, but contribute to a revaluation of the larger field of early modern drama.

I have, in this book, attempted to heed women's voices across the space of a long silence. While laying emphasis upon the historical moment, I have also endeavoured, in the words of Trevor Griffiths, to recover 'a usable past' for a 'lived present'.[3] Brought together by the highly organised struggle for the vote, the women playwrights considered here turned to the stage as a vehicle for feminist agitation; according to E. F. Spence, it was in general 'the woman rather than the man dramatist who appreciate[d] the utility of the stage as a means for seeking reform' (115). Their plays should not be read as efforts at accommodation, if by accommodation we mean simple integration into an existing social and political structure. Some are grim portrayals of the consequences of life for women in Edwardian England, others representations of women's power and potential. As a body, they stand both as a condemnation and a challenge: a condemnation of twentieth-century patriarchy and a challenge to construct feminist alternatives, social as well as theatrical.

Notes

1 This is not to suggest that the last quarter of the nineteenth century was unmarked by feminist agitation. Certain progress was seen to be made in areas such as higher education, property rights and increased professional employment (particularly in medicine) but, as Susan Kingsley Kent has noted, feminism at this time became selectively fragmented, focusing upon discrete and separated reforms (perhaps consciously) as a means of avoiding overwhelming organised opposition (194). The significance of the vote, however, as a symbol both of patriarchal power and of women's freedom therefrom was too obvious to be ignored, and in the early years of the new century a cause languishing in the 'doldrums' was reanimated by the sensational methods of the WSPU.

2 As Hamilton observed, 'Male humanity has wobbled between two convictions – the one, that [woman] ... exists for the entire benefit of contemporary mankind; the other, that she exists for the entire benefit of the next generation. The latter is at present the favourite' (*Marriage* 24). It is a conclusion reiterated by Jeffrey Weeks in *Sex, Politics and Society*: 'What was taking place, indeed, [in the early twentieth century] was a partial shift in the dominant ideology, away from the nineteenth-century stress on woman as wife towards an accentuated (though not of course new) emphasis on woman as mother' (126).

3 Indeed, a certain number of the plays that form the subject of this study have received recent revivals, albeit under amateur or semi-professional auspices: *Votes for Women!* was staged at RADA in 1987; *Rutherford and Son* at the Court (Upstairs) in 1980, and RADA in 1988; and *Diana of Dobson's* at the University of London (RHBNC) in 1988. Of the suffrage plays proper *A Chat with Mrs Chicky* was presented by the Antonio Pinto Players (Bounds Green 1988). Most recently The Theatre Museum, as part of its 'Rough Magic' series, offered an entire programme of suffrage drama, including *The Mothers' Meeting* and excerpts from *Votes for Women!* and *The Apple* (1990).

I

Elizabeth Robins
'What we need is a Battle Cry'

> To women far and wide the trumpet call goes forth, Come fight with us
> in our battle for freedom. This is no ordinary petty conflict, the issue of
> which can be decided by a few strenuous workers indifferently and
> languidly supported. This is a battle in which all must take part; they
> must come ready for active endeavour and for strenuous service; they
> must be prepared not to flinch in the hour of difficulty or under tempo-
> rary reverse, for the battle is not to the weak or to the downhearted, or
> to the indifferent, but to those who resolutely set before themselves the
> determination of victory. (6)

Thus 'The Battle Cry' went forth in October 1907 in the first issue of
Votes for Women, the official organ of the Women's Social and
Political Union, or WSPU as it was commonly known. Founded in
Manchester in 1903 by Mrs Emmeline Pankhurst, her daughters
Christabel and Sylvia and others, as an organisation dedicated to
the enfranchisement of women, the WSPU soon came to the conclusion that the vote could be won only by a shift in tactics away from
the constitutional and legal lobbying that had been practised by a
variety of organisations over the previous half-century.[1] To that
end on 13 October 1905 Christabel Pankhurst and Annie Kenney, a
Lancashire cotton mill worker and WSPU recruit, interrupted a
meeting at the Manchester Free Trade Hall, demanding of the
Liberal speaker, Sir Edward Grey, 'Will the Liberal Government give
women the vote?' They put their question more than once but it
went unanswered. Instead, in Kenney's own words, the 'strong
arms of Liberal stewards dragged us from the meeting and literally
flung us out of doors' (Kenney 35). Attempting to address the
crowd outside, both women were charged with obstruction and
marched off to jail by the police. The episode initiated a policy of
radical militancy the WSPU would pursue for the next decade, a
period which would witness an ever-increasing spiral of violence.

Despite the potential dangers, many women answered the 'Battle Cry'. Among them was American writer and actor Elizabeth Robins, who was later to admit that she 'had little understanding of and no particle of sympathy with the first militant act' (*Way Stations* 21). Robins might have seemed an obvious recruit for the cause. Encouraged by her father to attend medical school (itself an unconventional profession for women at the time) she chose instead a career in the theatre. It was while working on the American stage that she reluctantly married a co-worker who ended their marriage soon after by committing suicide; in true (if bizarre) theatrical style he jumped into Boston's Charles River dressed in a suit of stage armour (Marcus, *Elizabeth Robins* 21). Shortly thereafter Robins, aged twenty-six, departed for England, which was to become her permanent home. It was in London during the 1890s that she played a significant role in bringing Ibsen (with his perceived revolutionary ideas) to conservative British audiences. Having secured performing rights to *Hedda Gabler*, Robins, in partnership with another American, Marion Lea, staged the first English production of that play in 1891, Robins playing Hedda to Lea's Thea. (Lea appeared the following year as Mrs Linde in Janet Achurch and Charles Charrington's 1892 revival of *A Doll's House*.) Two years later Robins presented England with its first *Master Builder*, of which she claimed, 'no other [play] ever seemed so much mine' (*Ibsen and the Actress* 47). It was as Hilda Wangel, she tells us, that 'I suppose I scored my greatest triumph; I certainly remember that as the crowning pleasure of my theatrical life' (*Book News Monthly* 242, quoted by Marcus, *Elizabeth Robins* 153). *The Master Builder* was followed in 1896 by *Little Eyolf*, which contained according to Harley Granville Barker 'perhaps the most tremendous single moment I have ever experienced in a theatre' ('The Coming of Ibsen' 180). In each of these productions Robins was forced to circumvent the actor-manager system. When she tried to persuade the established theatre managers of the value of *Hedda Gabler*, for instance, their response was a variety of 'There's no part for me?' and 'But this is a woman's play, and an uncommon bad one at that' (*Ibsen and the Actress* 16). For a woman otherwise 'condemned to the "hack-work" of the stage ... [which] was what we called playing even the best parts in plays selected by the actor-manager', Ibsen's 'glorious actable stuff' (*Ibsen and the Actress* 33, 31) proved irresistible. To have the opportunity of playing such roles Robins successfully undertook all aspects of stage production. As she described it in the case of *The Master Builder* (co-produced with actor Herbert Waring) '[we] had not only ourselves to think about, we had everybody else's part and clothes to think about, the rightness of the scenery, the lighting, the advertisements, the seating – all the thousand things that make up a production as a whole' (*Ibsen and the Actress* 44).

Perhaps it was inevitable that this independent and capable artist who had, at one stroke, championed the cause of the 'new' woman and the 'new' drama would be drawn to the suffrage movement. Robins's conversion to the cause, she tells us, came on

> a certain memorable afternoon in Trafalgar Square when I first heard women talking politics in public. I went out of shamefaced curiosity, my head full of masculine criticism as to woman's limitations, her well-known inability to stick to the point, her poverty in logic and in humour, and the impossibility, in any case, of her coping with the mob.
>
> I had found in my own heart hitherto no firm assurance that these charges were not anchored in fact. But on that Sunday afternoon, in front of Nelson's Monument, a new chapter was begun for me in the lesson of faith in the capacities of women. (*Way Stations* 40)

Robins joined the Women's Social and Political Union in 1906, remaining a committee member until 1912 when she, along with others, left over a disagreement concerning militant tactics. She delivered her first suffrage speech in the autumn of 1906 and by April 1907 'St. Elizabeth' (as Shaw called her following her emphatic dismissal of his advances) had once more 'marched onto that battlefield ... [of] the stage' (*Ibsen and the Actress* 46), this time as a partisan supporter of the women's movement. Her principal contribution was what she termed a 'dramatic tract', a three-act play entitled *Votes for Women!*, performed at the Court Theatre as part of the third ground-breaking repertory season presented by Granville Barker in partnership with John Vedrenne. 'An innovator seeking a new kind of theatre for the new century' (Kennedy 5) Barker's tenure at the Court was marked by his profound commitment to new and 'vital drama' (Barker's words), the presentation of which demanded experimental acting and production techniques. His was a radicalised form of theatre management and its influence has been immense; according to Barker's biographer, C. B. Purdom 'no theatrical enterprise of this century has left a deeper mark upon the theatrical history of London' (26). Hailed at the time as

London's 'Theatre of Ideas' (*Clarion* 19 April 1907, 3), the Court
introduced Shaw's controversial plays to the stage in company
with works by such playwrights as John Galsworthy, John
Masefield, St. John Hankin and Barker himself, considered by many
at the time to be a more intellectual Shaw. Searching for a suitable
venue for its performance, Robins – 'the first intellectual I had met
on the stage' according to Mrs Patrick Campbell (65) – brought her
innovative feminist drama where it would be looked upon with
particular sympathy.[2] Barker considered himself 'strongly prejudiced in favour of its subject' (from the collection of the Harry
Ransom Humanities Research Center, University of Texas at Austin; hereafter HRHRC) and accepted the piece for almost immediate
production. As Barker put it, 'now is undoubtedly the time for a
tract on the suffrage' (HRHRC).

Under such auspices Robins's 'tract' went forward, insisting, in
the martial language that would become the common coin of the
suffrage movement, upon its share of 'the most effectual weapon in
all man's armoury ... the Power of the Word' (*Way Stations* 29). By
her endeavour Robins hoped to raise woman's voice in that most
public of forums, the theatre, and in so doing begin to fill in the
silence she had felt to be woman's traditional lot. Robins was
profoundly committed to the belief that the feminist movement
was providing women with the support necessary to allow them to
speak with their own voice, that they were no longer absolutely
constrained by a patriarchal hegemony which forced them 'to
imitate as nearly as possible the method, but above all the point of
view, of man' (*Way Stations* 5). Feminists, alive to the political,
social and cultural consequences of being women, had realised,
according to Robins, a place from which they could begin to speak
out of silence, here anticipating the position and perspective of
Anglo-American feminists in the 1970s. In an address to the Women
Writers' Suffrage League, given at the Criterion Theatre on 23 May
1911, Robins insisted upon both the political and the aesthetic
implications of the venture:

> Fellow-members of the League, you have such a field as never writers
> had before. An almost virgin field. You are, in respect of life described
> fearlessly from the woman's standpoint – you are in that position for
> which Chaucer has been so envied by his brother-poets, when they say
> he found the English language with the dew upon it. You find woman at
> the dawn.
> Critics have often said that women's men are badly drawn. Ladies,

what shall we say of many of the girls drawn by men? I think we shall be safer *not* to say. But there she stands – the Real Girl! – waiting for you to do her justice. No mere chocolate-box 'type', but a creature of infinite variety, of curiosities and ambitions, of joy in physical action, of high dreams of love and service, sharer in her brother's '... exultations, agonies,/ And man's unconquerable soul.'

The Great Adventure is before her. *Your* Great Adventure is to report her faithfully. So that her children's children reading her story shall be lifted up – proud and full of hope. 'Of such stuff', they shall say, 'our mothers were! Sweethearts and wives – yes, and other things besides: leaders, discoverers, militants, fighting every form of wrong.' (*Way Stations* 250-1)

In *Votes for Women!* Robins shows how such goals are to be realised, presenting Court audiences with a protagonist meant to supersede the 'chocolate box "type".' While it is true that Vida Levering is 'an attractive, essentially feminine and rather "smart" woman of thirty-two', her good looks are designed to be read as an overt political manoeuvre, a retort to pervasive stereotyping of suffrage women as 'all dowdy and dull' (47). Something of an unknown quantity (she has been living abroad), Levering is 'the kind of [woman, about] whom men and women alike say, "What's her story? Why doesn't she marry?"' (46). The play's subsequent action emerges from just such questions, as Robins transforms the 'tainted' female of popular society drama into a champion of women's rights and social justice. (Levering's name is particularly apt as throughout the play she serves to 'lift' up other women.) Ten years before the play begins, Levering, having taken umbrage at some unspecified offence perpetrated in her father's house, left his 'protection'. An upper-class woman unskilled at any trade, she soon found herself with 'an unpaid hotel bill, and not a shilling in the world'. By chance she met a family 'friend' who 'said he wanted to help'. The result: Levering found herself pregnant and her 'friend', the Honourable Geoffrey Stonor (again the surname is suggestive) who saw before him a brilliant political career, counselled abortion, maintaining that an illegitimate child would make it impossible to win his father over to their eventual marriage. Levering acquiesced, but the 'ghost of a child that had never seen the light ... was strong enough to push [Stonor] out of [her] life' (84). Upon her return to England (this is where the play begins) Levering becomes swept up in the suffrage cause, recognising that it provides the means to fight what she characterises as 'the

helplessness of women' (49). In the course of the play Levering re-
encounters Stonor, now a successful Tory MP ready to marry a
young and beautiful heiress. Inspired by Levering, however,
Stonor's fiancée attends a suffrage rally and is suddenly converted;
she also comes to learn of Levering's 'past' and insists that her
would-be husband make amends. In his subsequent interview with
Levering, Stonor too becomes convinced of the suffrage cause – or
at least realises that it may coincide with his own self-interest – and
at the play's conclusion promises to support women's suffrage in
Parliament.

In the continuing struggle for power to define 'woman' and
locate her place within the political and social hierarchy, *Votes for
Women!* can be read, to adopt Hynes's phrase, as 'a dispatch from
the front, fiercely partisan and militant' (202). Believing that drama
can be more than ideologically complicit, Robins reshapes the
conventions and traditions of the late Victorian stage to present us
with 'corrective' representations of women, both on stage and off.
She adapts for her own purposes the look and form of the well-
made-play, using both 'against the grain' to subvert rather than
reaffirm the values of drawing-room melodrama. Act I reveals additional debts to the Shavian/Barkeresque discussion play, Act II a
reliance on the public displays of Victorian spectacular theatre,
and Act III the influence of what was known as Ibsen's psychological drama.[3] To draw upon such material was perhaps inevitable. To
those like Robins, who believed they were the first to begin to
speak out of a history of silence, there was as yet no discrete tradition of women's theatre upon which to build. Certainly there had
been women playwrights, but what small success they had enjoyed
was mostly due (according to Robins) to their ability to ape the
writing of men, to imitate their method as well as their point of
view. In Robins's words, 'All that is not silence is the voice of man'
(*Way Stations* 4). Or as Lisa Tickner points out in her recent study of
the iconography of the suffrage campaign, 'There was no alternative
tradition of repressed but "feminine" meanings to bring into play, no
ultimate or essential femininity to be unveiled behind the layers of
(mis)representation' (152). Determined as she was to produce
such feminine writing, to free woman's voice as it were from the
strangle hold of male determinism, Robins was nevertheless compelled to rely upon conventions and traditions deeply imbedded in
patriarchal assumptions. It was through a manipulation of these
resources that Robins sought to produce a drama of her own.

Although the composition of *Votes for Women!* was marked by the specific intervention of a number of male writers, Robins seems to have exercised final control over the shape and details of her work. Barker, we know, provided the play with its title. Tentatively called *A Friend of Woman*, an ambiguous term that might be applied both to Levering and (ironically) to Stonor, Barker fastened upon Robins's reference to the work as a 'dramatic tract', recommending that she 'accentuat[e] the description ... by using some obvious political title; this will focus attention on that side of the play which you want to stand out. The best that occurs to me, of course, is "Votes for Women", the motto on the banner in the second act. From a business point of view I should think it's good too' (HRHRC). Barker obviously believed that overtly political drama could be commercially successful. That it could be considered a threat to the government was also on Barker's mind; in a letter to Robins he expressed some concern over potential problems with the Lord Chamberlain's office. Given Barker and Shaw's difficulties in obtaining licences to perform their own political dramas (Barker's subsequently banned *Waste*, concerning an abortion and a rising politician's subsequent fall from grace, shares common ground with *Votes for Women!*) one wonders whether the ultimate granting of a licence to Robins's play was evidence of the Lord Chamberlain's whimsical inconsistency or of a patriarchy so smug as to be unperturbed at the possibility of any real threat from specifically women's agitation.[4]

And yet if the Censor chose not to act, Robins seems to have invited intervention from other quarters. Asked to comment upon an early draft in November 1906, Henry James (a long-time correspondent of Robins who shared her theatrical aspirations) provided copious suggestions – 'half a hundred pages dictated about the lst third of the lst Act' wrote Robins (Gates 204) – although he subsequently defended them as having 'a possible worth as tentative, elastic, plastic only – made to be adjusted, to be arranged and fitted, and *certain*, I felt to have to be rehandled' (*Theatre and Friendship* 264). In an earlier letter, however, he had anticipated a more conventional 'masculine' involvement: 'What I want to do is to *dictate*, for you, in type, some groping ghost of a Scenario' (*Theatre and Friendship* 264). His ambitions were to be thwarted; although Robins was persuaded to shift indoors the play's Act I setting and to reduce somewhat the number of characters, she adopted few of his other suggestions. Instead, she passed the script to Bernard Shaw for his comments towards the end of December 1906, as a result of which the play underwent substantial revision. Shaw's succinct advice, written he says, 'in great haste to catch the post', was concerned with tightening up the stage action and sharpening the play's focus in order to ensure it had 'the swiftness and body of a melodrama' (HRHRC). He suggested compressing the first two acts into a single one by 'cutting out a great deal of small talk' (which resulted in the deletion of a number of characters and relationships), omitting a confused flurry of comings and goings (mostly 'mysterious visits to the library') and focusing more clearly upon Levering's past and its relationship to the suffrage theme. Judging from the prompt copy of the play located at the Fales Library as well as the published text, Robins chose to accept much of the advice.

Shaw's subsequent suggestions on the revised version were not as readily incorporated. On 8 March 1907 after Barker had accepted the play for production, Shaw proposed that Robins cut back on the first act which he felt was 'enormously too long' or alternatively restructure it along the lines of *The Doctor's Dilemma*, rearranging scenes 'so that all the Suffragette part gets thoroughly threshed out at the beginning, and then come to the dramatic part, which, once started, must go on with increasing momentum right up to the climax at the end' (HRHRC). Robins ignored this recommendation as well as his further suggestion of deleting what he considered to be a minor male character in the first act. Granville Barker expressed reservations similar to Shaw's regarding the structure of the first act. While willing to admit that in his own plays he wasn't primarily concerned with 'getting on with the story', Barker nevertheless felt that Robins's lengthy discussion (between women) of a recent suffrage demonstration was too extended a disruption of the forward movement of the act. Robins remained unconvinced, however, and Barker agreed to leave the 'scene practically intact. It was, I saw, most inadvisable to dispense with it' (HRHRC). Barker also reminded Robins that 'a great deal of patter for the crowd [in Act II] will want writing in. Will you do this, or would you rather leave it to me'. Robins did in fact leave it to Barker. As his prompt copy shows, he added pages of meticulously scored stage 'noise', although the crowd 'patter' in the play's published version (used to generate dialogue between speakers and audience) is Robins's own.

As important to Robins as her control over the overall direction of her play was her attempt to (re)define specifically womanly behaviour. Given the strength of the period's 'separate spheres' formulations, which spelled out 'natural' male (work/politics) and female (domestic) areas of endeavour, to compose within what Patricia Stubbs has called the 'non-privatised form of drama' was itself intended as an act of provocation. But such a move from the private and contained world of the realist novel to, for instance, the public forum of the theatre is, according to Stubbs, 'necessary if women are to be freed in literature from the closed world of private experience' (235). To free women from such constraints was one of Robins's objectives in composing *Votes for Women!*, and reflects a major goal of the suffrage movement as a whole, which was insisting in ever more adamant terms upon women's right to engage in the political life of the nation. But it is not simply by writing a stageworthy play that Robins makes her point. The very structure of the drama works as a refutation of the period's deeply-rooted 'separate spheres' position. While Acts I and III take place in what might in another play be the private world of the home, Robins's action occurs in the most 'public' rooms of very substantial houses, Act I in the 'Hall of Wynnstay House' and Act III in the drawing-room of a house in Eaton Square (significantly the young fiancée, Jean Dunburton, enters from her own sitting-room which is attached to but separate from the drawing-room). And the conversation which takes place in these public/private rooms is largely concerned with political issues directly relating to women. In Act I the pressing need for public housing for the poorest of homeless women is discussed (the irony of these women's actual relationship to their 'proper sphere' is underscored) as well as the continuing demand for enfranchisement and direct participation in the law-making process. Act II overtly challenges the argument that woman's place is in the home. It shows a group of suffrage workers at a rally in Trafalgar Square publicly demonstrating women's competence in that arena. And not content merely to emphasise the way that the public world impinges upon the private, Robins engineers the further disclosure of Levering and Stonor's private history during Levering's first public speech on women's (lack of) rights.

Of course Robins does more than challenge contemporary orthodoxy on women's suitability for political life. She is concerned in *Votes for Women!* with offering, as an alternative to a plethora of male-defined women, convincing portraits of woman-defined women in all their 'infinite variety'. The struggle proceeds on two levels – as an actor herself Robins was committed to producing new and exciting roles for women in place of what she had called the female 'hack-work' of a male-dominated theatre. And as a feminist she proceeded on the belief that the sight of innovative (as opposed to 'exceptional' or 'strong') female characters on stage would help to invoke their presence off stage as well, would serve in the language of more recent feminist commentary as 'self-actualising role models'. To that end she created Vida Levering.[5] Pulled from the pages of society drama written by the likes of Oscar Wilde, Arthur Wing Pinero and Henry Arthur Jones, Levering is a reconstruction of the popular 'woman with a past', a dramatic type with its roots in a form that espoused conservative acceptance of morality's double standard. Contrary to convention, however, she is not made to suffer irrevocably for her past; she is not pressed to suicide like the assertive Paula Tanqueray in Pinero's *Second Mrs Tanqueray* (1893) or forced out of respectable society like Mrs Dane in Henry Arthur Jones' *Mrs Dane's Defence* (1900). She is under no compulsion to remain for ever abroad (Oscar Wilde's *Lady Windermere's Fan* (1892)) or retreat to a life of religious contemplation (Pinero's *Notorious Mrs Ebbsmith* (1895)). Robins explodes society drama's conventional portraiture of such a woman, with its invariable valorisation of passive acquiescence to the male view and its condemnation of assertive behaviour. For as long as she wishes Levering remains free to travel in society's circles; as for her 'past', she says in Act III, 'You don't seriously believe a woman with anything else to think about, comes to the end of ten years still absorbed in a memory of that sort?' (80). In a neat inversion of the convention, Stonor's naive young fiancée, Jean Dunburton, becomes in Levering's words 'the Other Woman' (83), whose threat of social disruption and consequent expulsion were traditionally the mainsprings of conservative plotting.

Having stripped the 'woman with a past' of her conventional accoutrements, Robins reinvests her with a future, not the traditional future of the long-suffering heroine, consisting of requited love with the ideal husband in a happy-ever-after marriage, but a future of public service to the cause of female emancipation. And here is where Robins's play parts company with a work like *Mrs Warren's Profession* (1893). Shaw's depiction of Kitty Warren was, as that playwright admitted, a response to the tainted woman of drawing-room melodrama. But in offering a corrective for plays like *The Second Mrs Tanqueray* – indeed Shaw had first considered calling his brothel-keeper Mrs Jarman, one of Paula Tanqueray's aliases – Shaw does not allow Kitty Warren to break free of societal constraints and prejudices. For all his ingenious variations upon the tainted woman, Shaw leaves Mrs Warren in the end both a sentimentalist and trafficker in women's bodies. The point is well put by Vivie Warren who accuses her mother of living one life while believing in another. By contrast, Robins's Levering, as we shall see below, is an attempt to reconstruct the woman with a past as a figure of absolute integrity, one who firmly believes in the life she lives.

Votes for Women! opens in the hall of Wynnstay House, a setting that may have made some of the Court's more avant-garde patrons squirm in their seats. The gathering of 'weekenders' at a country estate had both the look and feel of a piece by Jones or Pinero. Both playwrights were, by 1907, viewed as conservative practitioners of a style of playmaking firmly rooted in the previous decade. The well-made-plays they built for the Edwardians were, like their Victorian progenitors, attempts to reinforce the values of a dominant ideology, using the formalism of Scribe to present what Ian Clarke has called 'an idealised version of contemporary orthodoxies' (28). Robins, however, creates conventional expectations only to frustrate them, her society weekend a means of introducing a thoroughgoing discussion of feminist issues and tactics. Into familiar, for some spectators distressingly predictable, structures, Robins poured a new voice, that of politicised woman, the resulting collision of orthodox form and feminist matter a staged version of a battle shading into all aspects of Edwardian life. Accordingly, at the outset of Act I, the play's protagonist, Vida Levering, is absent from the stage, Robins adopting conventional stage wisdom to make both a theatrical and thematic point – Levering's prepared entry becomes a means of emphasising political inevitability. Instead Lady John Wynnstay enters first, impatient to find her Suffragette friend. When the door opens, however, it is not Levering who appears but a young Conservative hopeful, Farnborough, eager to hitch himself to the Hon. Geoffrey Stonor's rising political star. He readily admits his lack of success with Levering, despite Lord John's subsequent assertion that 'all she needs is to get some "nice" fella to marry her' (45). What we are given here is a definition of Levering from the male point of view; she is discussed in terms of a 'matrimonial prize' albeit a difficult one to win. According to Farnborough:

She only laughs. ... She said she knew she was all the charming things
I'd been saying, but there was only one way to prove it – and that was to
marry some one young enough to be her son. She'd noticed that was
what the *most* attractive women did – and she named names. ... Her
future husband, she said, was probably just entering Eton. (41)

But Farnborough hasn't come seeking matrimonial advice; he
wants Lady John Wynnstay to use her 'influence' to help him
secure a secretaryship to Stonor. Not, he hastens to add, because
she is 'interested in politics qua politics', but because it is a family
matter for her – Stonor 'her nephew that is to be' (42). Lady John is,
in other words, to exercise her 'indirect influence', a concept much
touted by anti-suffragists at the time as a reason for not extending
the franchise to women. According to the argument, women possessed through such influence – criticised by one writer as arising
from 'mere sensuality and passion' rather than 'the high regions of
the intellect' (Blease 203) – sufficient control over their own interests to make it unnecessary to contaminate their femininity by
direct contact with the electoral process. Ironically, given his
adoption of this perspective, Farnborough proceeds to carry on
with Lady John an animated discussion of the forthcoming election
and Stonor's electioneering tactics.

They are interrupted by the arrival of Stonor's elated fiancée,
Jean Dunbarton. In the play's original production she was called
Beatrice, a gesture on Robins's part towards Beatrice D'Este, at
whose birth, Robins tells us, 'there were no rejoicings – because
everyone wished for a son'. Robins goes on: 'Yet what boy of that
noble house made so great a figure in fifteenth-century Italy – what
Prince of D'Este exercised such influence upon art and politics as
this same Beatrice?' (*Way Stations* 245-6). In the published version
of the play the character's name is altered to Jean, after Jeanne
D'Arc, whose purity, militancy and martyrdom were a touchstone
of radical suffragism. Indeed Levering makes the reference explicit
towards the play's close when, gesturing to Jean's closed door, she
asks, 'Who knows? She may be the new Joan of Arc' (85). When she
first enters, however, the Jean of *Votes for Women!* appears as a
conventional ingenue, rich, beautiful and orphaned, eager to bring
herself into conformity with her future husband's views while
quick to recognise her own limitations: 'Well, if I do think with my
husband and feel with him – as, of course, I shall – it will surprise
me if I ever find myself talking a tenth as well' (45).[6]

Within the early moments of the play, then, Robins manages to

present a number of conventional perspectives on appropriate
feminine interests and behaviour. Each, however, is held up only to
be dismantled and replaced with specifically feminist formulations.
Levering's entrance, for example, is immediately preceded by that
of St John Greatorex, a sixty-year-old country magnate and Liberal
MP, with 'a reputation for telling good stories after dinner when
ladies have left the room' (46). He appears as he says to 'protest
Miss Levering being carried off to discuss anything so revolting.
Bless my soul! what can a woman like you *know* about it?' (46). The
topic of conversation? Public sanitation or, as Greatorex puts it,
'God bless my soul, do you realise that's *drains*?' Although a topical
issue through much of the Victorian and Edwardian periods (reflecting the age's 'scientific' preoccupation with health and sanitation), it was apparently a subject fit neither for proper ladies nor
the stage. Levering introduces it to both, providing Shaw with a
topic he would consider three years later in *Misalliance*. Within
such a context, Levering's femininity (Robins insists that she is
attractive and well-dressed) becomes a deliberate attempt to counter prevailing stereotypes of suffrage supporters as 'unnatural'
masculinised women poaching on male preserves, gaunt figures
shorn of their locks, clad in dark, 'mannish' suits, often with
trousered legs protruding under the hems, and feet much in evidence, shod in clumsy over-sized boots. Much of this portrait
rested upon traditional caricatures of the frustrated spinster,
which depicted repressed sexuality manifesting itself in hysteri-
cally fostered manly guises. As such image-making suggests, much
Victorian/Edwardian thought apparently linked a woman's femininity with sexuality, tautologically defining one in terms of the
other. The response of feminists of the period to such image-
making was complex. Like their conservative critics they insisted
upon gender difference, rejecting a definition of 'woman' that was
male-imitative; they did not, in other words, (despite contentions
to the contrary) seek to dissolve gender distinction by the creation
of a single male-determined sex or to argue, like Shaw, 'that a
woman is just like a man' (quoted by Holroyd 170). Neither did they
accept Shaw's view that they must repudiate 'womanliness' to
secure emancipation (*Quintessence of Ibsenism* 130). Rather they
sought to intrude their own version of 'womanliness' into a male-
dominated social and political system, a position given visible
significance by the WSPU's insistence upon what Cicely Hamilton
has described as a 'costume-code', one that attached great impor-

tance to feminine dress and appearance 'whether ... appear[ing]
on a public platform, in a procession, or merely in house or street
about her ordinary vocations' (*Votes for Women* 30 July 1908, 348).[7]
As Hamilton noted, the 'taboo of the severer forms of garment was
due, in part, to dislike of the legendary idea of the suffragette, as
masculine in manner and appearance – many of the militants were
extraordinarily touchy on that point' (*Life Errant* 75).

Given the theatre's major role as a determiner of what was
'womanly' – Shaw went so far as to claim that 'Woman, of whom we
hear so much, is a stage invention' (quoted by Holroyd 170) –
Levering's stage presence is also a calculated rebuttal to drama's
prevailing depiction of the politicised woman, the classic rendition
of the type being Elaine Shrimpton in Jones's *Case of Rebellious
Susan* (1894). A forerunner of the Edwardian suffragette, Shrimpton
is condemned by the playwright as 'a raw, self-assertive modern
young lady, with brusque and decided manner' (120). According to
Sir Richard Kato, QC, a spokesman for anti-feminism and the play's
supposed voice of reason, she 'is a rather ignorant, impulsive girl,
with a smattering of pseudoscientific knowledge, chiefly picked up
from unwholesome feminine novels' (122). *The Sketch* underscored
this reading of Shrimpton, negatively contrasting the 'unfeminine'
'tweed coat and skirt, double-breasted waistcoat and wide-
brimmed felt hat' (10 Oct 1894, 613) that she wears to deliver a
speech on the future of women, with the 'delightful gowns' worn by
the play's other women. Pinero also engaged in the manufacture of
such stereotypes. In *The Weaker Sex* (1884; 1889), for instance, he
attempts to demonstrate by, what William Archer, a friend of
Robins and fellow-Ibsenite, objected to as 'the most barefaced
psychological jugglery, that women were incompetent to take any
serious part in the non-domestic work of the world'. Pinero's proof,
Archer continues, consists of 'showing two middle-aged widows,
prominent in the feminist movement, who accept as their masculine champion a blithering idiot of an M.P., and themselves collapse
into something very like idiocy the moment the prospect of a
second marriage is dangled before their eyes' (*The Old Drama and
the New* 288). Robins constructs the figure of Levering to challenge
the strength of such stereotypes and to claim for women access to
space conventionally associated with male prerogative without
sacrificing any of the womanly attributes so strenuously denied
them by their opponents. But it was to prove a difficult struggle. Of
a later suffrage meeting at the Criterion Restaurant (above the

theatre in which *The Case of Rebellious Susan* had had its pre-
miere), a writer for *The Referee* wrote: 'I sat expecting that Sir
Richard Kato would pop in from the theatre below and would say
what he is saying nightly to the bold Elaine: "There is an immense
future for women as wives and mothers, and a very limited future
for them in any other capacity ... Go home!"' (5 June 1910 in vol. 10
Arncliffe-Sennett Papers). *The Times*'s reviewer of *Votes for
Women!* put smug conventionality into the form of a question,
demanding 'Why, by the way [if she isn't "yearning to be married"],
does Miss Levering take such care to make the best of her good
looks and pretty figure and wear such charming frocks? Is it to
please other women?' (5). He is magnanimous enough to add 'that
the cause would make much more headway than it does if all its
advocates were as fair to look upon, as agreeable to hear, and as
beautifully dressed as Miss Wynne Mathison [who played Lever-
ing]'. In other words feminists were either to be dismissed as
ridiculous imitators of men, or they were to be contained by a
conventional male perspective which interpreted their femininity
as nothing but sexuality, a lure to win men to their point of view.

Defining 'womanliness' within the specific framework of the fight
for enfranchisement was to prove a continuing source of debate, a
situation reflected in *Votes for Women!*. Shortly after Levering appears in the play, the forward movement of the story grinds to a
halt and the characters fall to discussing (in a fashion reminiscent
of Granville Barker) 'that rowdy scene at the House of Commons'
(47), an event that actually took place on 25 April 1906, when
Labour MP Keir Hardie introduced a resolution that sex should be
no bar to Parliamentary franchise. WSPU supporters were in at-
tendance in the Ladies' Gallery behind the grille, and they watched
as the resolution was aimlessly debated and ridiculed by Members
of Parliament. Whispered protests could be heard. Then, as Sylvia
Pankhurst, a founding member of the WSPU,[8] relates it:

> Suddenly one of our women looked round and saw policemen ranged
> against the wall of the gallery behind us. They were there in obedience
> to the Speaker's order to turn us out should we make any more noise.
> The sight precipitated the demonstration; Irene Miller shouted: 'Divide!
> Divide!' as Members do on the floor of the House. 'Divide! divide! We
> refuse to have our Resolution talked out!' The rest of us all joined in:
> 'Divide! Divide!' Theresa Billington thrust a little white flag through the
> grille. We laughed as the police came rushing down over the tiers of
> seats to drag us out. (210)

And literally 'dragged out' they were, articles of clothing lost in the
struggle later deposited in Palace Yard.

The weekend discussants in *Votes for Women!* react to the episode in predictable form. Greatorex dismisses the protesters as 'a
few discontented old maids and hungry widows' (47) – 'Public
nuisances! Going about with dog whips and spitting in policemen's
faces' (55). Billington had in fact used a dog whip to defend herself
from 'some insults not to be borne meekly' when she was ejected
from a meeting held for the future Prime Minister, Asquith, the
previous June (Billington 43). Sexual molestation was not uncom-
monly directed against protesting suffragettes (a name coined to
distinguish members of the radical WSPU from the more law-
abiding protestors of other suffrage societies), and Billington asserted that in the early years of the suffrage struggle it was 'the one
occasion upon which we have been deliberately aggressive' (42).
Christabel Pankhurst, determined to secure arrest at the first militant protest in 1905, had been guilty of spitting: 'It was not a real
spit but only, shall we call it, a pout, a perfectly dry purse of the
mouth' (Raeburn 9). It was enough, however, to constitute assault
upon the police. In *Votes for Women!*, the young Conservative,
Farnborough, is quick to offer violence in return; he proposes
giving the protestors 'a good thrashing' and having them all 'locked
up! Every one of 'em' (55). A society widow, Mrs Heriot, laments
what she sees as the demonstration's 'unfeminine' nature: 'No
decent woman will be able to say "Suffrage" without blushing for
another generation' (47). Significantly, Heriot's statement is made
in the presence of men. Robins arranges matters, however, so that
all the male characters subsequently leave the stage and the
women alone discuss the demonstration. Free from their con-
straining presence, Mrs Freddy Tunbridge, a constitutional suffragist present at the protest (whose earlier attempt to discuss the
issue had been cut short when she 'catches her husband's eye, and
instantly checks her flow of words' (55[9]) argues at considerable
length that the militants have endangered her own 'gradual' approach:

> There we all sat breathless – with everything more favourable to us
> than it had been within the memory of women. Another five minutes
> and the Resolution would have passed. Then … all in a moment – …
>   All in a moment a horrible dingy little flag was poked through the grill
> of the Woman's Gallery – cries – insults – scuffling – the police – the
> ignominious turning out of the women – *us* as well as the – Oh, I can't

think of it without ... Then the next morning! The people gloating. Our friends antagonised – people who were wavering – nearly won over – all thrown back – heart breaking! (57)

This is just the opening needed for Levering's defence of radicalism. No member of the 'Shrieking Sisterhood',[10] another derogatory term used to discredit suffrage activists, she suggests with quiet dignity that the protestors have

waked up interest in the Woman Question. ... Don't you think *they* know there's been more said and written about it in these ten days since the scene, than in the ten years before it. ... I'm only pointing out that it seems not such a bad way to get it known they *do* want something – and 'want it bad'. (57)

To turn to the historical context from which the play emerged, we might ask why certain women wanted the vote so badly that they were prepared to suffer not only ridicule and contempt but also outright violence. Evelyn Sharp suggested at the time that it was because suffragettes recognised 'the political futility of the voteless reformer' (Sharp 129). Like Robins's Levering, they were shocked by the poverty and hardship of many women's and children's lives, a condition to which a number of middle- and upper-class women had been exposed through 'proper' philanthropic work ('making ugly things for the poor' as Wilde's Duchess of Berwick puts it). And at least within the context of *Votes for Women!* it could not be argued that agitation for the vote was 'merely an expression of the bourgeois desire for women's equality within the present unchanged patriarchal and late capitalist system' (Todd 56). The vote was a symbol of freedom, and served as a rallying point for protest, but as Robins makes clear in the play, many feminists pursued changes far more profound. They recognised a direct link between political, sexual and economic oppression, and rejected the possibility of a simple integration into the existing social order.

Adopting in *Votes for Women!* the rhetoric of the suffrage movement, Robins casts the struggle as a war between the sexes:

Lady John ...: We oughtn't to do anything or *say* anything to encourage this ferment of feminism, and I'll tell you why; it's likely to bring a very terrible thing in its train.
Miss Levering: What terrible thing?
Lady John: Sex antagonism.
Miss Levering (rising): It's here.

Lady John (*very gravely*): Don't say that. ...
Miss Levering (*to Lady John*): You're so conscious it's here, you're afraid
     to have it mentioned. (59)

Levering aligns herself with her own sex, and, recognising that her
personal economic independence provides her with a certain
power – 'I belonged to the little class of armed women. My body
wasn't born weak, and my spirit wasn't broken by the *habit* of
slavery' (51) – she engages in a struggle with what she calls 'the
greatest evil in the world', women's helplessness (49). She comes
to Wynnstay Hall to work on plans for a shelter for exploited homeless women, recounting, despite Mrs Heriot's scandalised protests
that it is socially inappropriate, the story of one young girl 'dying in
a Tramp Ward':

> ... she had been in service. She lost the train back one Sunday night and
> was too terrified of her employer to dare ring him up after hours. The
> wrong person found her crying on the platform.... Two nights ago she
> was waiting at a street corner in the rain.... She was plainly dying – she
> was told she shouldn't be out in the rain. 'I mustn't go in yet' she said.
> '*This* is what he gave me', and she began to cry. In her hand were two
> pennies silvered over to look like half-crowns. (50)

Levering's account is based squarely upon a document entitled
'Three Nights in Women's Lodging Houses' (1905), an exposé by
social and religious philanthropist, Mary Higgs, who decided to dress
in 'tramp attire' and experience first-hand the life of homeless women.
Donning 'an old gown and a tawdry hat' Levering follows Higgs's
footsteps 'into the Underworld', her 'fictionalised' speech a confla-
tion of incidents in Higgs's commentary which refers at one point
to a 'very weary' woman with a bad cough who 'had been out late
one night when in service on a gala day, and, having a strict mistress,
she was afraid of returning to her place. A companion persuaded
her to take train to N——' (275), and subsequently to 'another girl,
young and pretty, [who] said she was given in the dark two pennies
silvered over!' (279). In the process of their translation to drama,
these incidents are heightened and sensationalised (death and the
weather are given a role to play) and the female employer becomes
male, it being left to Robins's men to enforce the political and social
status quo. So too the Liberal MP Greatorex refuses to meet a
delegation of women because 'there isn't a weekender among 'em'
(48) and Stonor himself suggests in Act III that his 'conversion' has
as much to do with political opportunism as it does with a real

sympathy for the feminist cause: 'after all ... women are much more conservative than men – aren't they?' (75).

Stonor, like Levering, makes a late entrance in Act I, and his arrival causes a great sensation among the weekenders. But his past involvement with Levering emerges only in the last moments of the act when the 'story' is re-introduced by means of a device from the well-made-play tradition; Stonor identifies Levering's conveniently dropped handkerchief by the name embroidered in its corner. As the curtain comes down his fiancée asks significantly, 'I didn't know her name was Vida; how did you?' (60). Once again, however, traditional expectations are frustrated. For Levering's handkerchief, having served its immediate purpose, does not become like Lady Windermere's fan, Mrs Chevely's bracelet, or Paula Tanqueray's list of ex-lovers, a significant property whose fortunes both provoke and trace the changing relationships of Robins's characters. When the curtain next rises, Robins pointedly abandons what appeared to be the initiation of a carefully prepared chain of incidents – we hear no more of the handkerchief. Instead, we find ourselves relocated, the drawing-room milieu having given way to a suffrage rally at 'the north side of the Nelson Column in Trafalgar Square' (61). Here Robins's starting point is the recreation of public London familiar to patrons of late Victorian spectacular theatre, which replicated on stage such well-known sites as Euston Station (*Silver King* 1882), Piccadilly Circus (*Pluck* 1882) and the Stock Exchange (*White Heather* 1897). A posed photograph of the scene in *Votes for Women!* shows a number of speakers assembled on a raised plinth at the rear of the stage; attached to the base of the column behind them are banners reading 'Votes for Women'. In front, ranged along the foot-lights, is a crowd of representative types reflecting, according to one observer, 'the Chorus in a Greek play more nearly than anything in English drama since *The Knight of the Burning Pestle*, in as much as they gave vent to the gnomic and critical remarks of the ordinary spectator' (Court Theatre 35) The scene was much praised in its own day for its naturalistic effect, ensemble acting, and authentic platform rhetoric. It was 'an admirably managed "living picture" with as realistic a crowd as we have ever seen manoeuvred on the stage' according to *The Times* (10 April 1907, 5) while the critic for the *Clarion* declared:

> There never was anything like it. Here, on a stage little bigger than a suburban concert hall platform we have a representation of a mass

meeting in Trafalgar Square; [apparently there were forty-eight actors on stage] and, though the whole of an act is devoted to the speeches of four agitators and the interruptions of the crowd, the outcome is an illusion of tumultuous excitement, and a scene more compact of laughs and dramatic thrills than any orthodox theatre in London can now show. (19 April 1907, 3)

The Illustrated London News asserted that the scene's 'veritable clash of sex-emotions and intellectual arguments, makes better drama than we have had in scores of problem-plays' (27 April 1907, 622). If it could be criticised at all, according to Max Beerbohm, it was because 'Mr Granville Barker has so drilled the crowd that its reality is overwhelming enough to be almost inartistic' (*Around Theatres* 461).

While Robins's purpose was to compel (successfully it would seem) spectator attention to a suffrage rally, the ultimate appeal of the scene was to the ear. For it was not just public sites but also feminist arguments that were rebuilt upon the Court stage, and in a situation in which Robins could control both her speakers and their reception. The first to address the gathering is a working-class woman 'dressed in brown serge' (apparently modelled upon WSPU member Hannah Mitchell[11]) who argues the case for the 'homeless' and 'overworked' women. The presence of this 'pinched and sallow' figure on the plinth is Robins's acknowledge-ment that working women, too, were part of a movement that did not consist solely, as many tried to assert, of the well-to-do prompted to action either by a narrow self-interest or by a patron-ising view of the economically oppressed. As this woman makes clear: 'People 'ave been sayin' this is a middle-class woman's move-ment. It's a libel. I'm a workin' woman myself ...' (61). (It is worth noting, however, that this is the only speaker not named in the play. Might this not in itself be construed as a specific instance of middle-class insensitivity on the part of Robins?) The 'Working Woman', as she's known, valorises women's maternal and domes-tic roles, arguing that those very capacities need accommodation in the legislative processes of the country. Historian Sandra Holton characterises this seemingly conservative argument as in fact of-fering a 'quite radical challenge to [the period's] restrictive ideolo-gies concerning women' (18). According to Holton,

> ... suffragists did not seek merely an entry to a male-defined sphere, but the opportunity to redefine that sphere. They rejected the characterisa-tion of political life in terms of masculine qualities, and sought to

redefine the state by asserting for it a nurturant role. British suffragists aimed to reform their society by domesticating public life. The most striking aspect of British suffragism, then, is that it did not present feminist goals in terms of equivalence with men but in terms of an autonomously created system of values derived from women's particular experience. (18)

Agnes Thomas's performance of the Working Woman was much praised by the *Sketch* reviewer, who marvelled at her 'superb sincerity' at the same time that he denied her any real political commitment,: I daresay she does not care twopence about Woman's Rights' (22 May 1907). In fact, Thomas, along with Edith Wynne-Mathison, Gertrude Burnett (Mrs Freddy Tundbridge) and Dorothy Minto (Ernestine Blunt) would all go on to join the Actresses' Franchise League. On the speakers' plinth she is followed by the young, obviously middle-class Ernestine Blunt, Robins's fictional rendering of Christabel Pankhurst, whose speech exposes the relationship between economic hardship and sexual exploitation, exploding at the same time the concept of chivalry which was much touted in conservative circles as providing society with the necessary means to protect the status of women:

> Men say if we persist in competing with them for the bigger prizes, they're dreadfully afraid we'd lose the beautiful protecting chivalry that – Yes, I don't wonder you laugh.*We* laugh. (*Bending forward with lit eyes.*) But the women I found at the Ferry Tin Works working for five shillings a week – I didn't see them laughing. The beautiful chivalry of the employers of women doesn't prevent them from paying women tenpence a day for sorting coal and loading and unloading carts – doesn't prevent them from forcing women to earn bread in worse ways still. So we won't talk about chivalry. It's being over-sarcastic. We'll just let this poor ghost of chivalry go – in exchange for a little plain justice. (65)[12]

Blunt precedes Mr Pilcher (Mr Walker in the original production[13]) a Labour Party spokesman who takes the opportunity while speaking for women's enfranchisement to lambaste the 'speaking both ways' Liberals. He is followed by the obviously moneyed Levering who endures the taunts and sneers of spectators in order to explain, in her first public speech (modelled upon Robins's own first suffrage speech of 1906), her view of women's and children's attempts to secure 'a little justice' within that bastion of masculine power, the court of law. As a specific indictment of a judicial process that accepted women's sexual abuse as an aspect of their 'thing-ness' in domestic service (see Meacham 188), Levering re-

counts the story of 'a little working girl – an orphan of eighteen'
convicted of the murder of her child.[14] She had

> crawled with the dead body of her new born child to her master's back
> door, and left the baby there. ... Her master – a married man – had of
> course reported the 'find' at his back door to the police and he had been
> summoned to give evidence. The girl cried out to him in the open court,
> 'You are the father!' He couldn't deny it. The Coroner at the jury's
> request censured the man, and regretted that the law didn't make him
> responsible. But he went scot-free. (71)

The girl, on the other hand, was 'arrested by a man, brought before
a man judge, tried by a jury of men, condemned by men, [and]
taken to prison by a man' (72). Where, Levering, demands, was this
woman's trial by *her* peers? In fact, just such an issue was to be
taken up by the Women's Freedom League (a splinter group of the
WSPU) in the autumn of 1907 when it initiated a number of protests
in the Police Courts:

> When a woman was brought before the Magistrate, a protestor would
> stand and make a set statement. One presented at Greenwich in Novem-
> ber 1907 was as follows: 'Your Worship, before this case proceeds
> further I must rise to protest against the administration by men only of
> laws made by men only, and enforced by men upon women and chil-
> dren. As long as women are denied the elementary rights of citizenship,
> we protest that this is trial by force, and constitutes a very grave
> injustice.' (*Women's Franchise* 28 November 1907 253, quoted by
> McPhee 301)

In the course of her speech Levering happens to notice Stonor,
who had appeared on stage with Jean Dunburton during Blunt's
address. As she looks upon him in the crowd, the private effectively
intrudes upon the public, pushing Levering to a more emphatic
closing statement, one that stresses gender over class alliance:

> I would say in conclusion to the women here, it's not enough to be sorry
> for these unfortunate sisters. We must get the conditions of life made
> fairer. We women must organise. We must learn to work together. We
> have all (rich and poor, happy and unhappy) worked so long and so
> exclusively for *men*, we hardly know how to work for one another. But
> we must learn. ... I don't mean to say it wouldn't be better if men and
> women did this work together – shoulder to shoulder. But the mass of
> men won't have it so. I only hope they'll realise in time the good they've
> renounced and the spirit they've aroused. For I know as well as any man
> could tell me, it would be a bad day for England if all women felt about
> all men *as I do*. (72-3)

Through stage contrivance, Robins is able to make explicit the
modern feminist slogan, 'The personal is political'. Its ramifications
for the characters of *Votes for Women!* are explored in the play's
third act.

Act III is constructed in a series of duologues reminiscent of
Ibsen. Indeed, Ibsen must have been on the minds of many, as
Victorian London's leading creator of Ibsen re-distilled from a
woman's point of view the quintessence of Ibsenism. Again, Robins
is in no hurry to get on with the story; in fact the play's 'formless-
ness' (*Era* 13 April 1907, 13) might be considered by some contemporary feminists as specific evidence of the sex of its author. Sue-
Ellen Case in *Feminism and Theatre* refers to Gillian Hanna of the
Monstrous Regiment who considers 'linear modes as peculiar to
male experience, and insists that her feminist troupe hopes to
refute them'. According to Hanna a woman's 'life and experience is
[*sic*] broken-backed' and 'fragmented' (123), an apt enough description of the disrupted structure of *Votes for Women!*.[15] Accordingly, although Jean separated from Stonor at the end of Act II in
order to find Levering and begin to work for her, the first movement of Act III is concerned with Stonor's electioneering tactics; his
constituency is in trouble and he needs to manufacture some
'political dynamite' if he wants to ensure re-election. He decides for
pragmatic as well as personal reasons (it will please Jean) to
support 'Votes for Women', but before he has a chance to make
clear his political 'conversion', personal matters intervene. Having
pieced together the history of Stonor and Levering, Jean insists
that he make amends in a conventional way: through an offer of
marriage. Stonor is convinced that Levering has 'bewitched' Jean,
another traditional explanation for otherwise inexplicable female
behaviour, but he agrees at Jean's insistence to make Levering an
offer. When Stonor later accuses Levering of being 'mad' she responds with a feminist critique of such labels: '"Mad". "Unsexed".
These are the words of today. In the Middle Ages men cried out
"Witch!" and burnt her – the woman who served no man's bed or
board' (85).[16]

The act proceeds in a series of discussions which explore the
nature of men and women's relationships, the hold of the past on
the present, and the connection between the personal and the
political. In a frank conversation between Levering and Lady John
which takes place when 'there are no men listening' the economic
basis of marriage is acknowledged ('the thing's largely a question

of economics') and the 'old pretence ... that to marry at all costs is every woman's dearest ambition' is jettisoned. As for her past sufferings, Levering has come to see them as part of a larger pattern of female oppression:

> Geoffrey Stonor? For me he's simply one of the far back links in a chain of evidence. It's certain I think a hundred times of other women's present unhappiness, to once that I remember that old unhappiness of mine that's past. I think of the nail and chain makers of Cradley Heath. The sweated girls of the slums. I think of the army of ill-used women whose very existence I mustn't mention –. (80)

In an ironic twist, Levering proposes to turn the doctrine of 'indirect influence' upon its proponents: to 'use [Jean's] ... hold over Geoffrey Stonor to make him help us!' (80). As such this scene stands in stark contrast to other 'forced proposal' episodes of the time. In plays like Wilde's *Woman of No Importance* (1893), Hermann Sudermann's *Magda* (1896) and Stanley Houghton's *Hindle Wakes* (1912) seducers are also compelled to offer marriage to the women they have compromised, and are likewise shunned. But in each of these instances the playwright's central concern is with a generation/value gap that focuses attention upon the relations between parents and their grown children. Robins's interest, on the other hand, lies in the process by which Levering transforms a personal experience into a public and political act.

When Stonor enters to offer 'amends' to Levering, they engage in a heated clash over interpretations of the past. And although the conservative *Era* considered that Stonor's part 'was comparatively subordinate to the female interest ... [as] Miss Robins has taken care to give the women all the best parts in the piece', one female reviewer felt that Robins's 'attitude [was] a strictly impersonal one in the last scene between Vida Levering and Geoffrey Stonor, where the point of view of both is put with almost poignant clearness' (*Votes for Women* 23 April 1909, 582). According to Stonor, Levering deserted *him* after the abortion, making no attempt to renew contact even after his father died less than a year later. From Stonor's point of view his father had been the only real 'barrier' to their eventual marriage, and an illegitimate child would have seriously complicated matters: 'if the child had lived it wouldn't have been possible to get my father to – to overlook it' (76). Stonor, with an obvious eye on his patrimony, overtly endorses the existing order. From Levering's position, however, the 'sacrifice' of the child had the effect of realigning her emotional loyalties: 'happy mothers teach their children. Mine had to teach me. ... – teach me that a woman may do a thing for love's sake that shall kill love' (84). 'The ghost of a child that had never seen the light, the frail thing you meant to sweep aside and forget – have swept aside and forgotten – you didn't know it was strong enough to push you out of my life' (84). Succumbing under a combination of pressure from Stonor and fear of his father – 'how the thought of that all-powerful personage used to terrorise me!' (83) – Levering agreed to an abortion. Her subsequent suffering stemmed directly from her failure to resist that male imperative. She proves powerless over the reproductive process, a 'natural' function much eulogised in the period as eugenicists' ambition to improve the Imperial Race by good breeding combined with an Empire anxious over its declining birth-rate and 'weak-chested youth' to produce an exaggerated emphasis upon Motherhood. It was, however, a Motherhood subordinated, the play makes clear, to the sexual prerogative and self-interest of men,[17] their control over women's bodies a mainspring of feminist rebellion.

The scene can also be read as Robins's feminist response to the conclusion of *A Doll's House*. For she would have agreed with Elizabeth Hardwick with regard to Ibsen's play, that Nora's decision to leave her children '... is rather casual and ... drops a strain on our admiration of Nora. Ibsen has put the leaving of her children on the same moral and emotional level as the leaving of her husband and we cannot in our hearts assent to that. It is not only the leaving but the way the play does not have time for suffering, for changes of heart. Ibsen has been too much of a man in the end. He has taken the man's practice, if not his stated belief, that where self-realisation is concerned, children shall not be an impediment' (46). Juliet Mitchell takes exception to this interpretation, insisting that Hardwick '... in her heart of hearts would stop Nora leaving'. Mitchell argues 'that it is not a question of Ibsen's masculine sensibility predominating at the end, it is a question of the meaning of motherhood in a world where women are unequal. Women do not have economic and hence social and personal independence; they are judged by a patriarchal law' (124). But Mitchell seems to be deliberately missing the point; it is not that Hardwick would keep Nora in her doll's house, only that she would challenge Nora's passive acquiescence to Torvald's easy equation of a woman's duty to husband and children. The point is given dramatic significance in *Votes for Women!* where Robins makes explicit Levering's insistence upon a woman's responsibility to her children that differs from and overrides all other obligations and attachments; in fact Levering goes so far as to advise Stonor at the play's end that 'Jean's ardent dreams needn't frighten you, if she has a child. That – from the beginning, it was not the strong arm – it was the weakest – the little, little arms that subdued the fiercest of us' (87). It could be inferred here that Robins agrees with Ibsen and Shaw – the latter in like terminology insists that 'unless Woman repudiates her womanliness, her duty to her husband, to her children, to society, to the law, and to everyone but herself, she cannot emancipate herself' (*Quintessence* 130) – that without a disavowal of her duty to her children, a woman cannot free herself. They part company, however, over the advisability of such repudiation. For Robins, unlike Ibsen and Shaw, argues in her play that maternal duties (once incurred) take precedence over personal freedom, 'such a deliberate attitude towards the responsibilities of motherhood' marking the work, in Cicely Hamilton's words, as 'essentially feminine' (*Marriage* 114-5). Which is not to suggest, and the point must be stressed, that Robins advocates motherhood for all women, only that she insists upon the paramountcy of its obligations. Social and political agitation belong to those like Levering, who, childless and determined to remain so ('for me there was to be only one'), recognise in such a state 'no excuse for standing aloof from the fight'.[18]

Like *A Doll's House*, *Votes for Women!* ends with a woman's exit. Unlike Nora, however, Levering knows exactly where she is going. Rejecting marriage and motherhood, she chooses instead a life of female alliance and public service to the feminist cause. Stonor remains behind, alone in a deserted drawing-room, awaiting marriage to yet another 'ardent' woman. And if, as a character, he seems 'rehabilitated' by the play's close, it could be said that it is because he has seen the advantage of treating women well – Robins's final argument for continued female agitation.

If the close of *Votes for Women!* can be interpreted in part at least as a redrafting of that of *A Doll's House* from a woman's perspective, Granville Barker's *Waste* should be viewed as a consideration of aspects of *Votes for Women!* from a male perspective. In fact, the two plays offer interesting points of comparison between a self-consciously female and a sympathetic male voice. As already mentioned, *Waste* concerns the effect of an abortion upon the ambitious politician (Barker's Stonor figure) who fathered the child.

Although Barker began to compose the play in April 1906 (almost a year before the staging of *Votes for Women!*) it was not ready for performance until November 1907, during which period he seems to have been influenced by Robins's play. In a letter dated 20 March 1907 Barker had suggested a method of reshaping Robins's central action:

> Should [Levering] not warn [Stonor in Act III] that his uncompromising advocacy of the cause may cost him his seat in the Cabinet at first, anyway that he runs considerable risk if he is going to make a Government Suffrage Bill the condition of his joining? I think one ought to see that he is prepared to stake his political career on the question, and if we don't face the fact that he may go under, we lose interest in him as a human being. (HRHRC)

Robins agreed in production to the addition of a couple of lines to the effect that Stonor would be venturing his political life if he linked women's suffrage to a seat in Cabinet. In that version, Levering exits shortly after informing Stonor that 'I shall be watching you. I shall follow your career with an interest I take in no other man's – And before the next Session's done I shall know whether Woman has found at last – a friend who doesn't betray her' (Gates 191). The curtain falls upon Stonor drafting his telegram of support. Robins rewrote the conclusion for publication, however, her alterations shifting the focus further away from Stonor's career as observed by Levering, towards Levering herself as subject and her future commitment to the feminist cause. The work becomes in other words increasingly woman centred, this despite Barker's suggestions as well as those of Henry James who had observed

> A thing I should have felt of great importance, for instance, would have been to provide somehow from the first for the 'case' of Stonor himself, for his presence, interest and figure, his (male) centrality, which the situation for *its* full interest so much requires; Miss L's (female) centrality gaining so much, as it were, – as these things in a play always gain – by his importance being also strong. (Gates 224)

In *Waste* Barker eventually built the kind of play he wished upon Robins. Henry Trebell, his protagonist, is a politician unwilling to compromise on the Disestablishment Bill he considers his life's work. His public ambition, however, is threatened by a brief liaison with a married woman which results in her pregnancy. Here it is the woman who seeks the abortion, compelled by a 'fear of the burden of her womanhood' (210). Trebell desires the child's birth and

echoes the husband's cry, 'Is the curse of barrenness to be nothing
to a man?' (210). In a neat reversal of *Votes for Women!*, *Waste*
considers the issue of abortion from Trebell's point of view, exam-
ining its consequences, both public and private, for his career and
personal life. Indeed, the pregnant Amy O'Connell – who is pretty
and charming, 'if by charming you understand a woman who con-
verts every quality she possesses into a means of attraction, and
has no use for any others' (163) – is of interest primarily as an
adjunct to Trebell. She is, in fact, silenced for the second half of the
play, dying between Acts II and III. Trebell stands in marked contrast to Stonor, who is untroubled by Levering's abortion and
easily forgets the unborn child in his efforts to advance his political
future. Trebell on the other hand believes that 'the man bears the
child in his soul as the woman carries it in her body' (235) and finds
his future child's death politically and spiritually devastating. He
comes to view his life's work as 'barren' (234) and when he 'turns
inward for comfort … he finds there only a spirit which should
have been born, but is dead' (235). Despite her private suffering,
Levering finds purpose and a reason to live in a public affirmation
of the woman's cause; Trebell finds only death. Like Nora he leaves
the stage with a bang of the door, but unlike Ibsen's heroine, he
leaves to commit the suicide she has come to reject as melodramatic posturing.

Robins intended *Votes for Women!* to be a rallying cry for feminists;
through her protagonist Levering she called to all women (a majority in her matinée audiences) to join in a common cause. Of course
it is difficult to know how many audience members were actually
converted to the feminist movement as a result of viewing the play.
It certainly proved popular – receipts increased with every performance and Vedrenne and Barker, who had originally contracted
for only eight matinées, extended the play's run for two more
matinées and eleven evening performances.[19] In fact, the play was
never really taken out of the Court Theatre's repertoire. Its performances stopped only when the Vedrenne–Barker management
permanently ceased operations in June 1907. Yet despite its popu-
larity with audiences (Christabel Pankhurst noted that crowds
were turned away each day) a number of reviewers expressed
reservations over the play's power to prescribe the desired response. The *Era* critic assumed that people would react according
to their preconceptions, 'with enthusiasm or disapproval or

growls' as the case might be. He added, however, that if it 'does not have the effect of altering opinions as to the question of female suffrage, it will, at any rate, show the woman's side of the question in a fresh light to most playgoers, who are not, as a rule "strong" in philanthropic facts and figures'. Other reviewers doubted the wisdom of Robins dealing with feminist issues other than the vote. The *Times* critic, for instance, wondered whether it was wise to cloud that question with such other matters as seduction, abortion and infanticide. But as the play demonstrates, the demand for enfranchisement represented only one aspect of the struggle for female emancipation. And Robins's commitment to this wider definition of the cause is made plain in a letter read aloud to a luncheon meeting of the WSPU:

> I have decided with respect to the play *Votes for Women* that I will divide a percentage of my receipts between the older Suffrage Society and the Women's Social and Political Union, that younger society which has done so much to bring the question of women's enfranchisement to the position of political and public significance it now occupies. This may not be a matter of much moment in itself, but if it leads others to exercise one of the 'rights' women already possess, the play aforesaid may have one sort of success, if no other. (*Daily Mirror* 23 April 1907 in vol. 1 Arncliffe-Sennett Papers)

Of course *Votes for Women!* did enjoy another kind of success, breaking theatrical ground as it were for other women playwrights and actors bent on using their talents to further the feminist cause.

Notes

1 The best known and largest was the National Union of Women's Suffrage Societies (NUWSS) founded in 1897 as an amalgam of sixteen pre-existing societies, and headed by Millicent Garrett Fawcett.
2 In fact, Robins began the play as a commissioned work for Gertrude Kingston, who released Elizabeth Robins from the contract when it became clear that the political nature of the work was discouraging managers from staging it (Gates 213).
3 In the words of *The Times* (New York) reviewer, the play 'has the tang of Shaw, without his brutality, and that insight into the heart of woman which is Pinero's greatest gift. ... Her first act is leisurely conversation, her second blazes with honest human passion and her third is feminine psychology' (quoted by Marcus, *Elizabeth Robins* 314-15).
4 Certainly when he testified before the 1909 Committee on Censorship, Barker noted that the Lord Chamberlain's play reader had required that he delete any reference to abortion in *Waste*, although, Barker went on to state, 'I had myself produced at the Court Theatre a few months before under the Lord Chamberlain's licence a play the plot of which partly turned upon a criminal operation

which was quite openly referred to on the stage' (quoted in McDonald 79).

5 Originally called Christian Levering, Robins altered the name of her protagonist at the request of Emmeline Pankhurst, who was concerned that parallels might be drawn with her daughter, Christabel.

6 Shaw objected to the casting of Jean Sterling MacKinlay as Beatrice/Jean, insisting that 'she is quite impossible as an ingenue. She is a capable female ... and might be useful in certain parts; but – !!!!!!!!!!!' (Purdom, *Letters* 81). Of course, Shaw seems unable to recognise that it was just such ability beneath the surface of the conventional stage ingenue that Robins was seeking to register. She was, incidentally, happy with the casting.

7 Hamilton also saw a connection between the WSPU's concern with dress and what she called the 'combative impulse', observing that all soldiers 'are inclined to be fussy about their personal appearance' (76). For a further discussion of suffragette dress see Martha Vicinus's *Independent Women* 263-4.

8 Jane Marcus characterises *The Suffragette Movement*, Sylvia Pankhurst's socialist feminist history of the period, as a 'tragic family romance' in which Pankhurst pictures herself as engaged in battle with an increasingly wicked/aristocratic mother and sister. It is a 'drama' that Marcus believes most influenced George Dangerfield's highly theatrical rendition of the suffrage movement as 'comic farce' in his extremely influential and 'hardly challenged' *Strange Death of Liberal England*. It is, according to Marcus, an historical plot that needs reconsideration (Intro *Suffrage and the Pankhursts*).

9 It was Mr Freddy Tunbridge that Shaw recommended deleting from the play. Apparently James had suggested cutting Mrs Freddy, to which Robins responded, 'But I have *got* to have as much of the woman movement as shall put the ignorant in possession of its main facts, and I must to that end have in Mrs Freddy' (Gates 220-I).

10 The term was coined by Mr Smollett in his speech in opposition to the proposed Women's Disabilities Removal Bill of 1875 (*Hansard* 7 April 1875, 449).

11 Mitchell describes her appearance at WSPU meetings as a 'dingy blown sparrow' (142) 'very shabby in my old brown costume' (159). She also tells how Robins used 'one or two incidents which I told her' (163) in *The Convert* (first published by Heinemann in 1907), the novel Robins developed from the play.

12 Cicely Hamilton also takes the opportunity in *Marriage as a Trade* (1909) to attack the 'vaguely nebulous idea of chivalry'. She defines it not as a form '... of respect for an equal but of condescension to an inferior; a condescension which expresses itself in certain rules of behaviour where non-essentials are involved. In very few really essential matters between man and woman is the chivalric principle allowed to get so much as a hearing; in practically all such matters it is ... an understood thing that woman gets the worst of the bargain, does the unpleasant work in the common division of labour, and, when blame is in question, sits down under the lion's share of it. In return for this attitude on her part ... man undertakes to regulate his conduct towards her by certain particular forms of outward deference' (80-81).

13 Possibly the name was changed to avoid unfavourable associations with the brutal working man, Bill Walker, from Shaw's *Major Barbara* (1905).

14 Infanticide was the subject of Elizabeth Robins's other play, *Alan's Wife*, written in collaboration with Lady Florence Bell and staged by J. T. Grein's Independent Theatre Society in 1893. The play is a sympathetic portrayal of a young widow who kills her deformed infant and is hanged after refusing to repent or plead insanity.

15 We should, however, be wary of anachronistic analyses based upon culturally determined definitions of gender. After all, Barker's plays were notorious in the period for just such a 'fragmented' structure. Indeed, Joel H. Kaplan has suggested that Hanna has an unlikely ally in Oscar Wilde's Lord Goring who, in the

last act of *An Ideal Husband*, distinguishes between the lives of men which 'progress ... upon lines of intellect' and that of a woman which 'revolves in curves of emotion'. This view was attacked in a *Votes for Women* review of that play's 1914 revival: 'The fatuousness of such a summing-up of the lives of the two sexes is painfully obvious. The pity of it is that the thoughtless and irreflective, men as well as women, accept these false statements as an epitome of the differences between the sexes, and not as the opinions of two persons who both require a fuller knowledge of the facts of life and a course in logic to improve their reasoning faculty' (3 Jan 1914, 549).

16 The figure of the witch is celebrated in the cartoon on the front page of the 12 April 1912 edition of the WSPU's *Votes for Women*. Christabel Pankhurst, then in Paris hiding from the police, is pictured astride a broom stick dropping messages down to WSPU headquarters at Clements Inn. For another Edwardian feminist discussion of the witch, see Hamilton's *Marriage as a Trade* 88.

17 Christabel Pankhurst would return to this point in 1913 when she insisted that patriarchy's celebration of motherhood properly interpreted, 'really means ... that women are created primarily for the sex gratification of men, and secondarily, for the bearing of children if he happens to want them, but of no more children than he wants' (*The Great Scourge* 20).

18 Rosen has pointed out that an overwhelming majority of full-time WSPU organisers were unmarried, and that unmarried subscribers to the organisation increased from 45 per cent in the years 1906-7 to 63 per cent in the more agitated years 1913-14 (210).

19 See the Vedrenne/Robins correspondence at the Harry Ransom Humanities Research Centre.

II

Suffrage drama

' "One play is worth a hundred speeches"
where propaganda is concerned'

A little more than a year after the successful staging of *Votes for Women!*, and prompted in part by its example, the Women Writers' Suffrage League (WWSL) was formed. Founded in June 1908 by Cicely Hamilton and Bessie Hatton, it included among its charter members Sarah Grand, May Sinclair and Olive Schreiner. Elizabeth Robins served as first President. Its object, as stated in *The Suffrage Annual and Women's Who's Who* of 1913, was 'to obtain the vote for women on the same terms as it is or may be granted to men. Its methods are those proper to writers – the use of the pen' (137). Appropriately enough, the WWSL published a variety of suffrage plays, poems and pamphlets written by members. In addition, the organisation held its own fund-raising events and participated in the massive processions held to display the breadth of support for the suffrage cause. It made its first appearance as an organised contingent in the June 1908 March organised by the National Union of Women's Suffrage Societies, WWSL members (identified by red and white badges crossed with quills) rallying behind an impressive black and white banner designed by artist Mary Lowndes and held aloft by Cicely Hamilton and Elizabeth Robins, among others. Various smaller banners bearing the names of such celebrated writers as the Brontës, Jane Austen and Elizabeth Barrett Browning were also in evidence (Tickner 84). The WWSL went on to join subsequent processions organised by the Women's Social and Political Union (WSPU) in June and July 1910, where dressed in black and white and accompanied by bannerettes displaying the names of famous women writers, its members marched once more behind Lowndes's black and white banner (Arncliffe-Sennett Papers, vol. 10). It also participated in the June 1911 Women's Coronation Procession, a major collaborative effort which joined the forces of the WSPU and more traditional law-abiding societies during a pe-

riod of cautious optimism over the possible passage of a Concilia-
tion Bill which attempted to satisfy competing political interests by
offering quite limited enfranchisement. On this occasion the WWSL
contingent carried a new banner of Justice specially designed by
artist W. H. Margetson (*Suffrage Annual* 136).

1908 also witnessed the formation of the Actresses' Franchise
League, a sister society instrumental in the development of femi-
nist drama. 'Strictly neutral in regard to Suffrage tactics' (*Suffrage
Annual* 10), the AFL was open to anyone involved in the theatrical
profession. Founded by Gertrude Elliott, Winnifred Mayo, Sime
Seruya and Adeline Bourne, its membership included, in addition
to committed activists like Elizabeth Robins, Cicely Hamilton and
Edith Craig, a real range of such well-known performers as Ellen
Terry, Lillah McCarthy, Lena Ashwell, Lillie Langtry, Nina Boucicault, Decima and Eva Moore, Irene and Violet Vanbrugh and May
Whitty. Like the WWSL, the AFL participated in meetings, deputa-
tions and processions, the appearance of its members in the latter
events often the cause of comment by the press. In the case of the
June 1910 March, for instance, the *Daily Express* remarked on the
'vivid contrast' between the sweated workers' contingent and that
of the AFL: 'The sweated workers were faded women, in poor clothes
and hats that knew no fashion. They were boot-machiners, box-
makers, and skirt-makers, who fight yearly with starvation ... Behind
them marched the best-dressed section of the pageant – the actresses. There was Lena Ashwell, in a black silk dress with a black
picture hat, her arms full of pink and white peonies; Miss Decima
Moore, who wore a grey and white striped dress, with a tight-fitting
skirt of the latest fashion that forced her to take tiny steps ... (20
June 1910 in Arncliffe-Sennett Papers, Vol. 10, 50). The 'elegantly
gowned' (*Observer* 18 June 1911 in Arncliffe-Sennett Papers, Vol. 14,
33) AFL contingent was again singled out for notice on the occasion
of the Coronation Procession. Great care had in fact been taken to
ensure a uniformly striking visual effect, with members instructed
to wear varying shades of white if possible, and to fasten across
their dresses scarves in the League's colours of pink and green.
They carried poles decked with pink and green streamers and
marched behind a pink and green banner displaying the traditional
masks of comedy and tragedy (Gardner intro).

According to its mandate, the AFL sought:

(1) To convince members of the theatrical profession of the necessity
of extending the Franchise to women.

(2) To work for women's enfranchisement by educational methods.
   1. Propaganda Meetings.
   2. Sale of Literature.
   3. Propaganda Plays.
   4. Lectures.
(3) To assist all other Leagues whenever possible. (*Suffrage Annual* 11)

Specifically, the AFL recognised that it offered an opportunity to open 'a new field for propaganda'. Following the example of *Votes for Women!*, it saw the potential for 'illustrat[ing] the speeches and pamphlets of the earlier Suffrage societies in dramatic form' (*Suffrage Annual* 10). Accordingly, it opened a play department under the direction of Inez Bensusan who oversaw the writing, collection and publication of suffrage drama. And working in conjunction with the WWSL it staged its first fund-raising matinée at the Scala Theatre in November 1909, the entertainment consisting of music, poetry recitation, dance and a number of short plays, the latter all written by WWSL members.[1]

In fact the AFL and the WWSL experienced a happy marriage; continuing to work together until the cessation of most suffrage agitation after August 1914, they presented a number of plays concerned with feminist issues. These included but were not limited to works dealing with the vote itself (the term 'suffrage drama' referring to the auspices under which these plays were produced, not their specific content). The struggle for enfranchisement provided a convenient middle ground upon which politically committed women of all persuasions could meet. It also encouraged many women to challenge in more far-reaching ways conventional sex roles and to insist upon a woman's right to define herself and her place within a reconstituted social and political system. The authors of these stage pieces, following Robins's lead, turned to existing genres and styles, altering both form and content in the process of writing over conventional dramatic/social representations of womanhood. The plays are for the most part short – consisting primarily of monologues, duologues, pageants and one-act comedies or dramas designed for production as part of an extensive afternoon or evening programme performed before supporters of the cause. As Gardner points out in her introduction to *Sketches from the Actresses' Franchise League*, these plays 'function as affirmative rather than subversive or agitational propaganda'. Their message was meant to be unambiguous and direct.[2]

There is no doubt that the plays written by members of the

WWSL and performed by the AFL were considered by all involved
to be overt propaganda and this inevitably raises the vexed question of their relationship to art. We must, however, be wary of what
Tickner, in a model study of suffrage 'agitation by symbol', calls
'the art/propaganda divide [which] is itself a kind of propaganda
for art: it secures the category of art as something complex,
humane and ideologically pure, through the operation of an alternative category of propaganda as that which is crude, institutional
and partisan' (xi). As cultural artefacts, art and propaganda do not
exist as separate and unconnected areas of endeavour; art like propaganda is necessarily formed from pre-existing conventions and
traditions (to do otherwise is to ensure unintelligibility) which are
imbedded within certain ideological constructs; its meaning is
formed according to that system, and as such it is, like propaganda,
ideologically constrained. This is not to say that art and propaganda
are indistinguishable, only that their differences cannot be reduced to
'a crude division between the ideologically saturated and the ideologically pure' (Tickner xi). There is no doubt that suffrage drama
was written as part of a consciously organised scheme to propa-
gate political doctrine and advocate social and cultural changes
which would contribute to the dismantling of a system based upon
patriarchal oppression. To that extent it is unabashedly feminist
propaganda, and anticipates in some remarkable ways the self-
consciously 'women's theatre' that emerged in the 1960s.[3]

The most spectacular theatrical events of the suffrage movement
were the political processions which grew in size and splendour
from the first Mud March of February 1907, organised by a branch
of the NUWSS and composed of approximately three thousand
women who for the first time took to the streets in order to
advertise their right to enfranchisement,[4] to the June 1911 Wom-
en's Coronation Procession which attracted over 40,000 partici-
pants. Led by an equestrian Joan of Arc in silver armour, the latter
consisted of hundreds of contingents ranging from sweated workers to university graduates and including (as mentioned above) the
AFL and the WWSL. Of the many groups that participated, the
Prisoners' Pageant was one often singled out for comment. It consisted of 'that strange portent, the body of women, seven hundred
strong, who have endured imprisonment in the struggle for citizen-
ship' (*Way Stations* 265). A separate Historical Pageant also much
praised was designed to demonstrate the fact of women's political

power in history, the force of its argument that women's powerlessness was neither inevitable nor historically justified (Tickner
126). Figures represented included the Abbess Hilda, various peer-
esses summoned to Parliament by Edward III, women-governors,
and free women of assorted guilds and organisations (*Way Stations*
266).

Although Tickner detects in such displays 'a late and rather
feeble diffusion of the 19th century flirtation with medieval chivalry' (57),[5] a more direct link might be argued with a tradition of
secular and specifically urban pageantry that stretched back to the
Lord Mayors' shows of the Elizabethans and Jacobeans. Drawing
upon history, mythology and moral allegory for primary matter,
suffrage processions, like their civic prototypes, were emblematic
in method and didactic in intent, instructing viewers by encouraging them to contemplate heroic examples of what could be
achieved. Such spectacles served not only as a visual display of
women's collective desire for the vote (much was made of the fact
that women of diverse classes, occupations and interests walked
side by side), they also functioned as testaments to women's
accomplishments both through the successful organisation of the
processions and through their representation of famous women
from all facets of history.

The same impulse informed the smaller-scaled Pageants written
for performance at suffrage meetings and fund-raising entertainments. The best known of these, Cicely Hamilton's *Pageant of Great
Women*,[6] produced by Edith Craig for the first AFL matinée at the
Scala Theatre on 12 November 1909, offers a display of exceptional
women through history. Praised by Ellen Terry as 'the finest practical piece of political propaganda' (*Votes for Women* 19 November
1909, 117), Hamilton's *Pageant* exploits the stage device of the
'realisation' to recreate a 'suffrage cartoon' by W. M. Margetson.[7]
Like the cartoon itself, the piece presents the allegorical figure of
Woman pleading her case before a female Justice while her hector-
ing opponent Prejudice (played by the sole male in a cast of forty-
seven) raises a number of arguments against women's enfranchisement. Each is answered by means of a parade of women from
history summoned to provide overwhelming, purely visual retorts
to the case of Prejudice. In fact, the only 'famous woman' to speak
is eighteenth century actor Nance Oldfield, who makes her appearance with the group of Artists. This was probably a conscious
decision by Hamilton in recognition of the play's AFL connection as

well as an obvious attempt to exploit the metatheatrical possibilities of the moment. Ellen Terry, who took the role in the play's first production, was allowed to deliver a tribute to herself – she says, 'If you, Sir Prejudice, had had your way, / ... The stage would be as dull as now 'tis merry – / No Oldfield, Woffington, or – Ellen Terry!' (44) – by such means making palpable the connection between past achievement and a living present. The *Pageant*'s affinity with the larger Processions is apparent in the other famous women chosen for inclusion. Among the 'learned women' for instance, summoned in response to Prejudice's claim that women 'scorn learning [and] shun knowledge' is Jane Austen, already commemorated by the WWSL in the 1908 Procession. Abbess Hilda, who would reappear in the Coronation Procession, figures here among the 'saintly women'. And Joan of Arc, 'patron saint' of the movement's most radical wing and equestrian leader of their processions, makes her appearance at the vanguard of the 'Warriors'. Her virginity and gender rendering her the ideal symbol of unsexualised womanliness at the same time that her militancy and transvestism precluded containment by conventional domesticity, Joan of Arc proved an enduring icon and a popular role (model).[8] Confronted by this show of exceptional women, Prejudice ultimately falls silent and 'slinks away'.

I use the word 'exceptional' in this context advisedly, aware that for Elizabeth Robins, at least, 'the Exceptional Woman is one of our chief obstacles' (*Way Stations* 70). According to Robins men have controlled and divided women throughout history by 'dint of labelling "exceptional" those women whose capacity could not be denied'. When women accept such a designation, however, they endorse a system which continues to oppress women as a group. Instead, Robins argues, they should subordinate their individual claim to merit as defined by male opinion in the interests of women's common good. I would argue that this is what pieces like Hamilton's *Pageant* attempt to do. They seek to reclaim these 'exceptional' women as part of a larger feminist movement. Such women are drafted in the pageants and processions as it were, to fight 'shoulder to shoulder' with those actively engaged in a struggle to secure women's rights.

Suffrage pageants and processions drew upon a legendary and historical past to argue the movement's inevitable triumph. Plays proper produced under the auspices of the AFL and WWSL tended to fall into one of two broad categories: gritty social dramas designed to expose women's victimisation within a social hierarchy that habitually de-valued them, and farces which attempted to destroy through laughter the positions of suffrage opponents. Since in each case political argumentation was largely determined by dramatic form, my consideration of these pieces is generically organised. Among the social dramas, one of the earliest and most effective was *The Apple*, first presented at the Court Theatre for a single matinée on 14 March 1909. Its author was head of the AFL play department, Inez Bensusan. Like Robins's *Votes for Women!*, the piece strikes root in the 'problem plays' of the 1890s, uneasy forerunners of the Edwardian 'drama of ideas'. Like the problem play, *The Apple* takes as its subject female sexuality but like the later discussion dramas, it goes beyond the merits of individual cases to consider issues in a broader social context. Subtitled 'An episode of To-day in one Act', Bensusan's play actually depicts what Robins had only recounted: an instance of sexual harassment linked to economic exploitation. Bensusan's heroine, Helen Payson (the name is significant) cries out against the 'sacrifice' of her life for the well-being of her brother, 'the apple' of his parents' eye and play's title:

> I know that every penny that can be saved or squeezed out of the miserable family exchequer goes to support the Apple, instead of supporting *us*! And I consider it's high time the Apple was self-supporting. He's older than Norah or me – he's a man, a strong healthy male thing. What right has he to everything, while we girls are struggling to cover ourselves decently? (32)

Helen works in a city office, Norah (an absent sister) serves as an exploited nursery governess and Ann, the only sister 'unemployed', handles all the domestic duties (given an apparently feckless mother) while she awaits the single 'profession' open to her, marriage. Ann's household work includes 'slaving' for her brother (she is even expected to clean his boots), a state of affairs not uncommon in many working-class families of the day. Lynn Jamieson's study of 'Working-Class Mothers and Daughters in Urban Scotland c. 1890-1915' recounts like practices in disturbingly similar imagery:

> Mary, for example, wryly remarked: 'They were the apple of my mother's eye. Nothing could go wrong with the boys' (she had just described how she and her sisters had to wash the white gloves and polish the

patent leather shoes which their brothers wore 'to the dancing'). Annie made similar complaints with reference to her brother: 'My mother was more lenient with the boys than she was with the girls. She preferred boys of course. My mother used to think boys shouldn't have to do anything in the house, that was a girl's place you know'. (64)

As Jamieson goes on to point out, it wasn't the doing of the housework that offended these women so much as the insistence by their mothers on the male's higher status: 'this experience forced them to see not just gender difference but hierarchy' (64). In Bensusan's play, however, it is not the mother who insists upon this state of affairs, it is the father. Although neither parent actually appears in the play, the mother is only mentioned occasionally (dramatically as well as thematically she proves something of a cypher) while references to the father permeate the play and effectively shape its forward movement.

'Awakened to a sense of the injustice of it all', Helen announces to her sister: 'I'm going to fight for my rights, your rights, equal rights for us all' (32). What has prompted this spirit of revolt? It unfolds that Helen has been sexually harassed at the office, kissed by a married 'family friend' who is also her father's employer. She responds by throwing a ruler at him, quitting her job, and announcing her plans to emigrate to Canada, in the company of other women only. All she asks is a share of the money left to the children by their grandfather. The 'apple', however, lays claim to the fund which he maintains he needs in order to marry well. Ironically his sisters are made to suffer financial hardship so that another woman (conforming to society's views of proper female behaviour) can marry into the family. Helen is 'trying to go straight. Trying to help [her]self, – to fight [her] way', but what can she do? The family friend appears bearing the ruler's mark, 'a large patch of sticking plaster on his forehead', to inform her that all's well at work and she can return tomorrow, return in Helen's words 'to the beck and call of small-minded, self-satisfied men' like her brother. But 'that's where the degradation comes in. The work's all right. I don't mind the work, but it's having to knuckle under to the very men I wouldn't even wipe my boots on in the ordinary course of things, that's degrading' (35). It is worth noting that for Helen the work place simply duplicates the oppressiveness of the home. Both endorse a patriarchal hierarchy; at work the brother simply becomes the boss. In this the play seems to corroborate Jane Lewis's statement (contained within an examination of women's work *c.* 1870-1950) that the 'pattern of male dominance and control at the workplace must be related to power relationships within the family, for it has been hypothesised that male domination of the pre-industrial family work unit ... was carried over into the factory when the workplace separated from the home' (172).[9] Nor does the world of fashion offer an acceptable refuge. Instead of a parade of delightful tea dresses and ball gowns, the common coin of the period's society drama, Bensusan offers us a subtle but telling 'clothes incident': as the play opens Ann is sewing a dress that will allow Norah to attend a party. And so concerned is she that Norah be given the rare opportunity to enjoy herself that she pawns her necklace to pay for the fabric. During their initial exchange Helen expertly fits the gown's bodice directly on to Ann, who cannot then extricate herself. As the stage business makes explicit, she is trapped by clothing itself.[10] For if it is a truism that clothes make the man and the woman – or in the words of one of the Edwardian period's formative sexologists, Havelock Ellis, 'the extreme importance of clothes would disappear at once if the two sexes were to dress alike' (Steele 26) – within a system determined by male privilege (and a male gaze) female dress can serve as a marker of woman's sexualisation and consequent containment.

Helen seeks freedom from a state of affairs that oppresses her with conventional (sexualised) expectations of appropriate female behaviour: 'I don't want your decent husband. I want a little pleasure, a glimpse of life, a taste of the joy of living, a few pence in my pocket, my rights as an individual – ' (37). In fact, Helen is articulating one of the reasons that the suffrage movement proved so attractive to women; its activities were exciting and often enjoyable, bringing, as one suffrage supporter put it, 'a draught of fresh air into our padded, stifled lives' (quoted in Vicinus 253). Equally importantly, it provided companionship and non-sexualised work that recognised women's strength and self-worth. According to Emmeline Pethick-Lawrence, Treasurer of the WSPU:

> In spite of opposition on every hand, in spite of hard work to which there was no 'let up', in spite of occasional violent assault and imprisonment and hardship of every kind, there was a spirit of triumph, laughter and joy that possessed our movement in 1906 and unceasingly for many years to come. There was an intense sense of union and comradeship, lifted into devotion by the common service of a great idea, there was the certainty of ultimate victory, and beside that, there were exhilarating adventures, events and comic interludes every day. (164)

Helen, however, does not run out to join a suffrage society. She attempts to evade the system by fleeing with other dissatisfied women to the supposedly new world of the colonies. Unfortunately such escape proves impossible. The only 'freedom' offered is another form of sexual oppression. Says the so-called friend:

> Freedom? You know what your answer was when I offered you that. ... You thought it brutal of me. So it was. But I'd like to give you a good time. No good-looking girl ought to fight for a living. I've told you this over and over again. Do you suppose I don't understand? I'd like to take you abroad, anywhere you please, – show you how to enjoy life, – let you revel in pretty things, buy you new hats enough to turn your head, – take you to dances, theatres,... (38)

Such, according to Bensusan, are male valuations of women, objects to be dressed up or pressed down as men deem fit. Yet despite her portrayal of Helen's brother as a selfish and inconsiderate brute who is bested by his sister in every verbal skirmish, Bensusan does not paint every man as a villain. In fact the 'family friend' is allowed to state explicitly, 'I'm not a villain in a melodrama, I'm a reasonable human being' (38). As for the head of the family, Helen says, 'I'm not grumbling with Father, he's acting according to his lights I suppose. It's the gospel of the generation that everything must be done for the boy' (32). It is not the behaviour of individual men but the social and political condition of England which accepts such behaviour as reasonable, that is at fault, and through her depiction of women's oppression under that system, Bensusan hoped to encourage her largely sympathetic audience to fight for change. Her play stands as a form of protest, every protest a call to action. The work ends with a telling image; the two men depart having triumphed over potential female rebellion, leaving Ann rattling her pots and Helen turning the wheel of the sewing machine 'with tears streaming down her cheeks' (39). Such a tableau rests upon but also corrects a tradition of so-called 'social realist' iconography which sentimentalised the seamstress as an oppressed but picturesque labourer, engaged as she was in suitably feminine work.[11]

In *Before Sunrise*, a one-act drama by Bessie Hatton, such exploitation is extended to middle-class women of forty years earlier. It is only unfortunate that in Hatton's attempt to evoke 'historical' speech, the dialogue becomes stilted and awkward. The play, first performed at the Albert Hall Theatre on 11 December 1909, is set in

1867, the year that John Stuart Mill made his historic motion in Parliament to amend the Representation of the People Bill so that the word 'person' should replace that of 'man'. The proposed amendment was defeated but it began a period of agitation for female enfranchisement that would continue to gather momentum into the twentieth century. Like Bensusan, Hatton is concerned to demonstrate women's oppression within a system constructed to protect male interests. In *Before Sunrise* the son is entitled to the best of educations ('To Rugby he goes and later to the University') while it is enough for the daughter that 'she can play and sing nicely, write a neat ladylike hand speak a little French, sew and embroider' (61). When the daughter shows signs, however, of demurring to the marriage proposal of an extremely wealthy, hence most suitable, suitor, she is forced to acknowledge her lack of education which leaves her, like Vida Levering, incapable of earning any other kind of living. Although she is, like Helen in *The Apple*, drawn to a life of female companionship, her parents refuse to allow it, insisting instead upon her marriage to a man who has 'run a course of low, common profligacy' (64). Hatton explores from a woman's perspective the central situation of Pinero's *The Profligate* (1887; 1889). In the latter play a dissolute man about town successfully marries a sweet young thing; although he suffers from guilt over his past escapades, audience resistance to his tormented suicide was such that the play's conclusion was rewritten and he was forgiven. Such was not the case for the 'tainted' woman of the piece. Janet Preece, the young woman seduced by the play's profligate, must abandon a love match and emigrate to the colonies when her past is discovered.

In *Before Sunrise* the daughter's emotional and physical well-being is sacrificed in the interests of ignorance touted as innocence. Such an attitude, the play makes clear, protects men's licentiousness at the cost of women's health. In attacking the period's notorious 'double standard' that required, many feminists argued, the compulsory enlistment of women in the service of male sexuality, a service they condemned as both degrading and dangerous, Hatton anticipates by a few years Christabel Pankhurst's campaign against male sexual vice as manifested in 'the Great Scourge' of venereal disease, a battle characterised by the incendiary slogan, 'Votes for Women and Chastity for Men'. Like Bensusan, however, Hatton does not lay the blame upon individual men, although it is true that the male characters in her play are overbearing, selfish, insensitive and in the case of the future husband, Bullock, diseased as well. Women's oppression is, in the words of one female character (and note again the use of 'restrictive' clothing) 'the fault of the false conditions under which we live. Our minds are enveloped in moral stays, just as our bodies are pinched and tortured to take on an unnatural and ugly shape' (64). *Before Sunrise*, described by the reviewer for *Votes for Women* as an 'extremely touching' play 'in which the helpless position of the mid-Victorian girl was very forcibly shown' (27 January 1911, 270), is a cry for women's education;[12] through it comes enlightenment, protection and independence from a condition many feminists characterised as sex-slavery.[13]

Another play concerned with educating women to their oppression within the existing social and political system is *In The Workhouse*, written by WWSL member Margaret Nevinson and produced by Edith Craig's Pioneer Players[14] at the Kingsway Theatre on 8 May 1911. Nevinson had, at Craig's request, adapted the play from a sketch she had earlier written entitled 'Detained by Marital Authority'. The composition of the piece was, she maintained, motivated by a desire 'to show the parlous condition of twentieth century womanhood under the unjust Gilbertian muddle of unisexual legislation' (ll). Like Hatton, Nevinson overtly attacks morality's double standard: 'I have attempted to illustrate from life some of the hardships of the law to an unrepresented sex, the cruel punishment meted out to women, and to women only, for any breach of traditional morality, the ruin of the girl, the absolute immunity of the male ...' (21). Set in a workhouse ward, the play uses a seven-member, all-female cast, with every character dressed according to regulation in the ill-fitting blue cotton gowns of paupers.[15] It unfolds, during the course of the women's conversation, that Mrs Cleaver, 'a respectable, middle-aged matron', is being detained in the workhouse because her husband does not choose to leave. And as long as this 'drunkard' wishes to stay she too is obliged to remain, despite the fact that she is a dress-maker both able and willing to earn her own living. Her plight is heard with sympathy from the other inmates, and Penelope, 'a handsome, voluptuous woman, about thirty', offers her own solution to the problem of sexual inequality. With 'a drunken beast of a father, as spent 'is time a-drinking by day and a-beating mother by night' (53), Penelope learned young the less desirable side of marriage and has deliberately chosen to remain unmarried. As such she is, under the law, sole guardian of her five children although she does manage to collect child support from the various fathers. Mrs Cleaver, on the other hand, acknowledges, 'I ain't got no responsibility for my children, being a married lady wit the lines' (i.e. marriage licence) (49). According to activist Dora Montefiore it was just this circumstance that convinced her that she was a suffragist. When her husband died and she was informed by her lawyer that 'In law, the child of the married woman has only one parent, and that is the father' (30), she responded in terms that echo Penelope: 'If that is the state of the law, a woman is much better off as a man's mistress than as his wife, as far as her children are concerned' (30). As Penelope prepares to leave the workhouse with her newborn, she announces to the others including the detained Mrs Cleaver, 'I'm going back tomorrow to my neat little 'ome, which my lidy-help is minding for me, to my dear children and my regular income, and I can't say as I envies you married lidies either your rings or your slavery' (65). Like Robins, Nevinson does not present working-class women only as victims to be rescued through middle-class political intervention. In *In the Workhouse* Penelope successfully negotiates man-made laws to secure her independence, and in so doing stands in marked contrast to Mrs Cleaver who is obviously victimised as a result of her acquiescence.

What Galsworthy's *Justice* did for the issue of solitary confinement, *In the Workhouse* did for that of the forced detention of wives. Nevinson concluded that at least partly as a result of it, the law was altered less than two years later, ostensibly on the precedent of the 1891 Jackson case in which the Court of Appeal had ruled that a husband has no legal right to kidnap his wife (225-6). The play also aroused considerable controversy at the time of its performance. Although praised by critics for the *Pall Mall Gazette* ('There is nothing to approach it in directness and force') and *Reynolds Magazine* ('I found it interesting and convincing') most reviewers 'were very shocked and apparently blushed in the corridors in shame and confusion at the "plain-speaking"' (Nevinson 224). *The Standard* wrote that 'the masculine portion of the audience walked with heads abashed in the entr'acte; such things had been said upon the stage, that they were suffused with blushes' (225). Apparently women were not such sensitive plants; in fact Nevinson records that Mrs Pankhurst and Mrs Despard, both leaders in the suffrage movement who had been roused to work for the women's cause as a result of their experiences as Poor Law Guardians, agreed that 'far from exaggerating, they knew things were worse in reality' (225).

A Woman's Influence, written by actor and commercially successful farceur Gertrude Jennings, was staged by the AFL as part of the WSPU's Women's Exhibition at Prince's Skating Rink in May 1909. It too is concerned with exposing women's suffering and degradation, in this case through an examination of the practice of 'indirect influence', one of the issues specifically addressed in *Votes for Women!* two years before. The play's single male character, Herbert Lawrence, is a well-to-do pleasant young man but, as one of the play's feminists says to his wife, 'You've got the money and the brains, he's got the vote' (70). The wife, Margaret, stands as a representative of the feminists' version of the womanly woman. She is 'a grave, beautiful woman of 27 or 28' and although married with children nevertheless remains financially independent of her husband, earning her own living as a writer. She is also an active member of the suffrage movement and is supported in that work by her secretary, 'a pleasant, comely young woman, with very neat hair and a decided manner'. Both women resent their voteless condition, believing it hinders them from securing social change which in the play manifests itself as an attempt to improve the appalling working conditions of women at a local factory. Conventional middle-class female intervention in the form of individual philanthropy is rejected as a solution – when her husband suggests that she send a cheque, Margaret responds that money isn't enough, 'it's their whole social condition that's wrong' (69).[16]

Such sweated factory workers fall outside the reach of the 'separate spheres' formulation which excluded women from the work force:

> ... What are these poor women to do unless they work? This one, Annie Matthews, has been deserted by her husband, she brings up and supports his children, by making shirts at 1*d*. an hour. Liza Green works inside the factory, standing for eight hours, though her baby is only a week old. Mary Ball, wage-earner for the household, husband drinks – she does a man's work for the Factory at Hill Rise, but because she's a woman she only gets half the wage. (71)

This might sound like an instance of middle-class condescension to the poor with lower-class women perceived as requiring rescue from irresponsible and brutish working men. Yet the play's purpose in citing such instances is to anatomise an economic and social system capable of change – hence the need for the vote, which is advocated for *all* women. Even the hard-pressed Mary Ball collects signatures in her neighbourhood for a suffrage petition and asserts, 'it's not men as can help us any more, it's women – it's ourselves, and that's the truth' (72).

Another visitor to the house, Mrs Perry, 'a pretty babyish little woman of thirty-five', with 'no settled home to go to, no children to care for', demurs, advising Margaret to 'coax her husband into helping her' (71) with her causes. When Margaret declines to use such means, Mrs Perry decides to attempt the task herself. In preparation she 'powders her nose, and puts her hair straight, makes a face at the door, sits by table, leans her head on her hands, pretends to cry' (72), her actions underscoring feminist Catherine Gasquoine Hartley's contention that 'it is not the purifying influence of women ... but an unguided and therefore deteriorating sexual tyranny that regulates society' (quoted by Kent 164). By such 'indirections' Mrs Perry successfully 'influences' Margaret's husband who agrees to approach his Member of Parliament regarding working conditions at the factory – until, that is, Mrs Perry discovers that her income is invested in the very factory in question. Unlike Trench in Shaw's *Widowers' Houses*, she is not initially outraged that her money is invested in a morally reprehensible concern. Instead, agreeing with Lawrence that 'if you start monkeying with wages, shares go down' (73) she urges him in her own self-interest to 'absolute silence' and inaction.

A Woman's Influence is meant to serve as a demonstration of the pernicious effects of indirect influence – to expose, in the words of the *Votes for Women* reviewer, its 'naked hypocrisy' (20 May 1909, 724) – and to argue for a different, more accountable form of female political involvement:

> ... the sin and misery that lie underneath it all, the helplessness of Woman using her one weapon, sometimes beautifully, sometimes merely frivolously (like to-day), sometimes with degradation, but always – always the same weapon. Ah, if you men would only give us another one, the use of our intelligence, so that we could realise that we are reasonable creatures, fit to be heard equally with man, not parasites. (74)

The husband learns the error of his ways and agrees to help the Woman's Movement, the play ending with a conventional plea for men and women to work together. Yet it is perhaps curious that a play that proved quite popular with suffrage audiences should conclude, despite Mary Ball's claim that women must help themselves, by suggesting that women must appeal to men for what they lack.

Gertrude Vaughan's *The Woman with the Pack* proves something of a generic experiment, combining the emotive force of topical realism with the universality of allegory – borrowing, in fact, a technique familiar to its audiences from the movement's pageants and parades. Described as 'A Sketch in four scenes and two tableaux', the piece was performed on 8 and 9 December 1911 by the AFL as part of a WSPU Christmas fête. The play, which the reviewer for *Votes for Women* maintained might have been called 'The Making of a Suffragette' (15 Dec 1911, 175), although Claire Hirschfield has more recently objected that it is 'guilty of rhetorical overkill' (4), concerns an upper-class young woman who balks at the uselessness of her life which is hemmed in at every turn by conventional views of appropriate womanly behaviour. Philippa Tempest cannot take a degree at Oxford although she passes the same exams as her brother nor can she practise at the Bar if she pursues her longing to study law. Instead she is expected to marry a man who 'hasn't a single mental muscle in his whole composition' (41). Objecting that she 'shall have to promise to obey him ... and he might not always be right' (32) she refuses the match.[17]

In the play's second act Vaughan portrays an extreme instance of exploitation, that of a mother and her children forced to make match-boxes at home for less than subsistence wages. Such 'homework', as it was euphemistically called, is described by Clementine Black in *Sweated Industry and the Minimum Wage*, where she recounts in excruciating detail the elaborate procedures that had to be gone through 144 times to produce $2^{1}/4d$ of income (5). While they are engaged in such debilitating work at the opening of Vaughan's second scene, Bill Higgs, the drunken husband, enters and takes the family's last halfpenny, and then because there is no supper on the table punches his wife. He is interrupted by Philippa Tempest who rushes in as if to hit him. Backing away, he justifies his actions, claiming 'I've the right to; the law's on my side' (59), the truth of his assertion underscored by periodic columns in *Votes for Women* and *The Common Cause* (NUWSS) which juxtaposed the light sentences meted out for violence against women with the disproportionately heavy sentences passed for crimes against men and property.

Also lodging with Higgs is a young unmarried woman being coerced into prostitution by an employer who pays her starvation wages. Although it might be fair to characterise this as an instance of what Weeks identifies as the late-Victorian reformers' portrayal of young prostitutes as 'victims of individual evil men', his linking, in what has become almost kenning-like fashion, of 'passive' with 'victim' as well as his subsequent objection that 'this sort of approach ignored the very origins of prostitution in the economic system' (88) is surely untenable. For Vaughn stresses the character's resistance to prostitution as well as the clear connection between it and patriarchal capitalism. In the play's original version, selections of which were published in *Votes for Women*, the young woman struggles but finally succumbs as a direct result of her employer's economic stranglehold;[18] in the published text, however, she successfully resists, Vaughan seemingly rewriting the scene in order to avoid implying that all starved working women are eventually driven to sell their bodies. Of course this 'poor girl' is only rescued from prostitution by Vaughan's well-to-do heroine who, when confronted with the scene, exclaims in a declaration of female solidarity, 'I won't hesitate any longer! I see it all now. It's for this that women are fighting. This is why they go to prison. ... Something must be done' (71). Tempest immediately rushes out to join a Suffragette raid on Parliament Square. In this the play seems to correspond to Tickner's analysis of the use of prostitution in the suffrage campaign. She writes that,

> The sisterhood invoked in a recognition that (middle-class) womanly women and exploited (working-class) women could struggle together against male sexual licence and oppression had about it a distinctly philanthropic sense of condescension. But it was at the same time the only means by which suffragists could exercise their moral authority to contest the undoubted fact of male sexual power. In doing so they simplified the complexity of contemporary sexual ideologies and practices, which were themselves in the course of codification and change, and made the prostitute a passive victim in their representations as they claimed she was in life a passive victim of economic circumstance and men's lust. (225)

Of course a number of the plays examined here demonstrate that feminists were also prepared to argue marriage as a (legitimised) form of prostitution imposed upon victimised women of all classes.[19] By such means a camaraderie in oppression (and resistance to it) was realised that emptied such an alliance of the taint of condescension.

In the final scene of the play we learn that Philippa Tempest has been imprisoned as a result of the suffragettes' march and made to endure forcible feeding. This method of dealing with women who used the hunger strike to protest their treatment in gaol was introduced in September 1909 as a means of preventing the early termination of sentences (the government unwilling to have martyrs on its hands, had been releasing hunger strikers when they grew seriously weak). Sylvia Pankhurst was one of those to suffer forcible feeding, and has captured its indignities in a passage that makes plain the sexual nature of the violence offered. The process, which would have been familiar to the play's intended spectators and helped shape their response to Vaughan's allusions, is best conveyed to contemporary readers by citing Pankhurst's account in detail:

> [Six wardresses] flung me on my back on the bed, and held me down firmly by shoulders and wrists, hips, knees and ankles. Then the doctors came stealing in. Someone seized me by the head and thrust a sheet under my chin. My eyes were shut. I set my teeth and tightened my lips over them with all my strength. A man's hands were trying to force open my mouth; my breath was coming so fast that I felt as though I should suffocate. His fingers were striving to pull my lips apart – getting inside. I felt them and a steel instrument pressing round my gums, feeling for gaps in my teeth. I was trying to jerk my head away, trying to wrench it free. Two of them were holding it, two of them dragging at my mouth. ... A steel instrument pressed my gums, cutting into the flesh. I braced myself to resist the terrible agony. I wrenched my head free. Again they grasped me. Again the struggle. Again the steel cutting its way in, though I strained my force against it. Then something gradually forced my jaws apart as a screw was turned; the pain was like having the teeth drawn. They were trying to get the tube down my throat. I was struggling madly to stiffen my muscles and close my throat. They got it down, I suppose, though I was unconscious of anything then save a mad revolt of struggling, for they said at last: 'That's all!' and I vomited as the tube came up. (443)

Although forcible feeding was condemned by many as cruel and brutal torture, the government did not desist in its use. In the protest iconography of the period the practice became the subject of a famous WSPU poster by A. Patriot (Alfred Pearse) entitled the 'Modern Inquisition'. Published in January 1910 to coincide with the General Election, it portrays a victim being forcibly restrained by four women and one man while another man feeds her through

a tube inserted into her nose. Forcible feeding was not so graphi-
cally depicted in suffrage drama; perhaps it was felt that too realistic a re-creation of the practice on stage would be beyond the
acceptable bounds of Edwardian theatrical decorum. Whatever the
reason, Philippa Tempest is forcibly fed off-stage between the
play's scenes. Like many of its actual sufferers (some of whom
would most likely have been present at the play's performance) it
is a torture she is willing to endure for 'a future with no woman
overburdened, no man cruel, no child unhappy' (55). It is quite
clearly a future characterised by women's and children's release
from male oppression. The allegorical figure of weighed-down but
resilient Womanhood who gives the play its title, and who was
described by *Votes for Women* as 'the incarnation of the woman's
movement' (31 May 1912, 561), responds, 'O, God of Battles! Steel
my soldiers' hearts' (56). The play concludes with a tableau of
Philippa Tempest dressed as Jean of Arc surrounded by a group of
dancing and singing children. Men are entirely absent from this
final scene of celebration.

If suffrage 'drama' moved audiences by grim portrayals of oppressed womanhood, suffrage comedy set out to puncture the
arguments of anti-suffrage opponents. Its weapon was exuberant
satire directed at gender stereotypes, often operating through sex-
role reversals. The best known of these plays – indeed the most
familiar piece in the suffrage repertoire – is *How the Vote was Won*.
Originally a short story by Cicely Hamilton (published by the
WWSL in 1909), it was adapted for the stage by Hamilton herself in
collaboration with Christopher St John (Christabel Marshall),
translator of Hrotswitha and co-editor with Edith Craig of Ellen
Terry's *Memoirs*. It was performed at London's Royalty Theatre on
13 April 1909. Like Aristophanes' *Lysistrata*, the play concerns a
women's strike although in keeping with Victorian prudery and
following a long tradition in English farce, which habitually
resituated French bedroom encounters in English dining or draw-
ing-rooms, it avoids the issue of physical sex. Women here do not
deny sexual favours; on the model of striking trade unionists (an
increasingly familiar phenomenon for the Edwardians) they simply
withhold their labour. Accepting the conventional dictum that
places women in the home to be supported there by men who
alone venture into the public world of the work-place, all women in
the play throw up their jobs and move into the home of their

nearest male relation.[20] The decision to focus on women as productive members of the work-force rather than as objects of male
sexual gratification may also have been influenced by the feminist
movement itself which was waging an on-going battle to define
women in terms other than sexual.

How the Vote was Won focuses on the plight of Horace Cole, a lowly
clerk who with his wife, Ethel, lives in a cheaply furnished house in
Brixton. An adamant anti-suffragist, Horace insists that 'English-
men can't be bullied' by suffragettes. He is made to see the error of
his ways, however, under the onslaught of his female relations, all
coming 'to demand support and the necessities of life from their
nearest male relative' (24). The cross-section of Edwardian womanhood that parades through Horace's house in a low mimetic version of the *Pageant of Great Women* renders ridiculous a literal
reading of the adage that all women belong at home. In fact, as a
result of the play's action the text is finally rephrased as the 'appalling problem of maintaining millions of women in idleness' (24).[21]

The first women workers to strike are the usually 'invisible'
domestic servants who functioned as just so many cogs in the
machinery of household domesticity; Martha, who is supposedly
'simply devoted' to Ethel, but who remains literally unseen in the
play, goes without saying good-bye while Lily, 'a shabby little maid-
of-all-work' who has no male relations at all leaves Horace's home
to join the long line filing into the workhouse. As Winnifred, a WSPU
spokesman shouts, 'we shall hit men as ratepayers even when they
have escaped us as relatives!' (24).

Horace's home is soon inundated. Agatha arrives first. 'A weary-
looking woman of about thirty-five, she wears the National Union
colours and is dowdily dressed' (27). Like Levering in *Votes for
Women!*, she was raised as a lady with no education to fit her for
employment. At eighteen, however, she was forced to earn her own
living as a governess, one of the few acceptable professions for
middle-class women. She too likens her situation to slavery, adopting (as Penelope does in Nevinson's play) a metaphor popular in
the feminist writing of the period to describe women's place in the
social and political hierarchy. Agatha is followed by Molly, 'a good-
looking girl of about twenty ... dressed in well-cut, tailor-made
clothes ... and carrying some golf-clubs and a few books'. Molly is
the author of a 'scandalous' book according to Horace, who disap-
proves of her writing for money and who has called her 'sexless'
because, able to support herself, she refused to marry an 'awful

little bounder'. Madame Christine, 'dressed smartly and tastefully, age about forty, manners elegant, smile charming, speech resolute', enters next. A distant relation of Horace's, she runs 'a profitable dressmaking business in Hanover Square' (29).[22] Maudie Spark, the black sheep in the family, follows, wearing 'a hat of huge size'. She has disgraced herself in Horace's eyes by pursuing a career in the music-halls. Despite his disgust at her choice of careers, however, Horace is not prepared to have her forsake it in order to become yet another dependent. As with Molly, his squeamishness at her choice of occupations is shallow and hypocritical (he is after all quite willing to attend the theatre). His moral sensibility is simply shocked at the prospect that Maudie's career offers her the possibility of a less constrained way of life. The last female relation to put in an appearance is Aunt Lizzie, 'a comfortable, middle-aged body of a type well known to those who live in the less fashionable quarter of Bloomsbury. ... Her features are homely, and her clothes about thirty years behind the times' (30). A motherly type who terrifies Horace, she supports herself by keeping lodgers, considered at the time a suitably 'womanly' occupation for lower-middle and working-class women. Word soon arrives that the entire country is in chaos, and the play ends as Horace, decked in various suffrage ribbons, rushes out to join an all-male rally advocating 'Votes for Women' while the women 'stay, quiet at home' (23).

It is worth noting that the most confident and financially successful of Horace's relations are Molly and Madame Christine. Both are self-employed and both, it is made clear, make more money than Horace. Unlike Mrs Warren's profession in Shaw's play of the same name (1893; 1902), their career choices are not socially culpable (other than that as women they should not be working at all) and unlike Vivie Warren their rejection of marriage for a life of work and female companionship is not compromised by a grim and chilly Puritanism; in *How the Vote Was Won* these women are celebrated. The poorest and most down-trodden on the other hand, Lily and Agatha, are directly dependent upon male employers for whom they perform conventionally female tasks: they cook, clean house and teach the children. The message of *How the Vote was Won* is clear enough. Any situation for women which involves overt dependence upon men is not only psychologically debilitating, it is also economically precarious. When financially pressed, Horace is much more willing to advocate votes for women than to provide their support.[23]

The play proved popular, many critics finding it both clever and witty. According to the *Pall Mall Gazette* for instance, 'the story is funny enough, but the way in which it is told is funnier still ... The fact that it is so acutely controversial is not at all against it – is, in fact, a virtue rather than a defect, for the Theatre of Ideas is upon us' (quoted by Spender 20). This is not to say that all reviewers were sure of its power to convert. The *Stage* noted that 'the sentiments expressed in *How the Vote was Won* seemed to arouse conflicting feelings, and perhaps it is a little risky to present this skit with a purpose before a mixed audience' (13 May 1909, 20). The *Era*, on the other hand, while questioning the probability of the piece, was willing to acknowledge that 'it certainly seems likely to have the effect intended', although it added an interesting caveat: 'whether the men would not prefer to be deserted by the fair sex rather than be governed by them is a problem yet to be considered' (17 May 1909, 21).

Another successful suffrage comedy which satirised conventional views of appropriate female behaviour is Evelyn Glover's *A Chat with Mrs Chicky*,[24] first performed at the Rehearsal Theatre on 20 February 1912. The play consists of a 'conversation' between an anti-suffragist, Mrs Holbrook, and her brother's charwoman, Mrs Chicky. While Mrs Chicky cleans around her, Mrs Holbrook tries to convince her to sign her anti-suffrage petition. It becomes clear, however, as the play progresses that Mrs Chicky is in fact a suffrage supporter who easily bests Mrs Holbrook in discussion. The play is important not only because it successfully satirises the anti-suffragists, but because it presents a portrait of a working-class woman who is not a victim. Dramatically, Mrs Chicky herself springs from a long line of knowing servants that stretches from Roman New Comedy to Shaw (and beyond). She is also fashioned as a political response to complaints that the suffrage movement was a middle-class organisation functioning in the interests of that class only. Like the Working Woman in *Votes for Women!*, Mrs Chicky presents the suffrage case from the working-class perspective. And the stage business goes a long way to making her point. While a seated Mrs Holbrook articulates (in a nice reversal of arguments) the elitist position of the anti-suffragists, Mrs Chicky (a widow who works to support her family) chars. The irony of their respective positions is brought home in Mrs Chicky's final impassioned speech:

The first time I 'eard a lady at a street corner sayin' as women orter 'ave
votes, I listens for a bit 'an I says 'I'm on this job' I says. I says 'She
knows. She's talkin' gorspel. She aint sat in no drorin'-room an' *read*
about us' I says. 'She knows'. ... She didn't waste no time tellin' women
out workin' to keep body an' soul together as they orter be queens of
their 'omes! She didn't go talkin' about a man's 'ome for all the world as
if 'e orter knock at the door an' arsk 'is wife's leave every time 'e wanted
to get inside it! ... She didn't waste no time tellin' sweated women drove
on the streets – women 'oo's 'usbands give 'em a drib 'ere an' a drab
there when they're sober, an' the childrin goin' 'alf-naked – women 'oo's
'usbands take up with another woman, an' 'I'm afraid the lor can't 'elp
you my good woman' says 'Is Wushup, in nine cases outer ten – women
'oo get drove to despair with facin' their trouble alone while the man
'oo's brought 'em to it gets scot free – women 'oo'll take on their
'usband's job when 'e's ill, to keep the 'ome going', an' get eight or ten
shillins docked off for the same amount of work cos they aint men – she
didn't waste no time, I say, jorin' to women like that about the splendid
way their int'rests are protected already! She *knew*. (112-13)

And how did middle- and upper-class supporters know of such
matters? Another suffrage comedy takes as its subject this very
question. *10 Clowning Street*, written by Joan Dugdale, a Secretary
of the AFL, and performed in December 1913, examines the consequences of Prime Minister Foljambe's proposed Women's National
Service Bill. Operating on the assumption that 'the women at the
bottom of this agitation are the unmarried ones; those at a "loose
end",' Foljambe's bill, worked out 'scientifically' he claims, with the
help of the Eugenics Society, obligates every single woman over the
age of twenty-one to enter into some kind of employment. As a test
case the Prime Minister has sent his three anti-suffrage daughters
out to work:

> Isabella, the eldest, confessed she had always longed to be a parlour-
> maid, and has gone off in that capacity to one of the Labour Members;
> Judith developed a sudden passion for laundry work, and is in the
> Snowdrop Laundry at Stonehenge; while Enid is measuring ribbons
> behind the counter in Birmingham. (181)

In the course of their brief work experiences, all three are sweated,
bullied and insulted. They return to 10 Clowning Street (in a manner similar to the women's arrival in *How the Vote was Won*) ardent
suffragettes ready to engage in the most militant activities in order
to secure the vote. Echoing Mrs Chicky, Judith demands of her
father, the PM, 'What do you know about women's work and its

conditions?... You know nothing about it, so you have no business
to legislate for it. Why, I know a thousand times more than you now
... I'm thankful I've had my week's misery. It's opened my eyes;
taught me what women have to go through when they're not
sheltered behind padded front doors like ours' (182). Threatened
with the prospect of his three daughters in Holloway Gaol, the PM
finally agrees to support a government measure extending the
franchise to women.

Like many other suffrage comedies, the play satirises conventional sex-role stereotypes. The men are portrayed as complacent,
self-centred political opportunists with no real belief in the positions they adopt. As Isabella says to her Labour Member employer:
'I told him he ought to stop talking about Social Reform when he
kept a slave in the house' (185). This particular comment reflects
the disenchantment of many feminists of the period (particularly
the WSPU) with the Labour movement, which was divided at best
over its support of female enfranchisement. Of course, the Liberals
do not fare much better: the Hon. Geoffrey de Haughten, one of the
PM's private secretaries, 'is so slow and unbusinesslike, that if one
did not know that his father had won fame as the "Tory Renegade
Peer" one would wonder what qualifications had secured him his
post' (173-4). Featherstone, the PM's other secretary, grumbles
that his work might keep him from his golf game. The women, on
the other hand, once exposed to the appalling working conditions
of many of their own sex, become actively committed to their
cause.

10 Clowning Street reveals a certain similarity to Shaw's propagandist piece, *Press Cuttings*, written in the spring of 1909 for the
London Women's Suffrage Society, but banned by the Censor on
the basis that 'General Mitchener' and 'Prime Minister Balsquith'
were too obviously modelled upon Kitchener, Balfour and Asquith.
Shaw's play is, like *10 Clowning Street*, set in the rooms of a high
government official, the action consisting of the besieging of the
beleaguered General and PM by a delegation of women. Unlike
those in *10 Clowning Street*, however, these women are anti-suffragists, and in typical farcical fashion, parodies of the type. Mrs
Banger in a reversal of anti-suffrage imagery is the manly woman
seeking to do battle with the suffragettes, 'those gentle pretty
creatures who merely talk and cross-examine ministers in police
courts and go to prison like sheep, and suffer and sacrifice themselves'. Conversely, Lady Corinthia Fanshawe is an exaggeration of

the womanly woman seeking to influence men through the exercise of her female wiles. Yet in spite of his sympathy with the Cause, Shaw indulges here in conventional sexual stereotypes; as Holledge observes, there is 'a marked difference in [Shaw's] treatment of the sexes: the men are ludicrous because of their political prejudices while the women are ridiculed for being ugly, aggressive predators' (68). *Press Cuttings* also differs from women's suffrage drama in that it is as much concerned with the issue of compulsory military service and England's hysteria over possible German invasion, as it is with feminist questions. In fact, in keeping with popular dramatic convention, the play ends with the prospect of marriage between its various main characters. This is certainly a departure from women's propagandist theatre which celebrates women's self-sufficiency, often advocating independence from marriage as an institution increasingly associated with degradation and slavery. Such a position was anathema to conservative forces during the period who saw marriage and family as mainstays of social and political stability.

The most clear-cut use of sex-role reversal in suffrage comedy is found in the monologue *Jim's Leg*, written by L. S. Phibbs and published in January 1911.[25] A contemporary reworking of the farmer and his wife folk-tale, it tells the sad story of Jim, who, having lost his leg in a drunken altercation with a motor bus, is forced to stay at home doing his wife's work while she takes over his job (for less pay) as a bottle-washer at a brewery. His wife, in what Holledge considers to be an unintentional parody of East-End life (62), describes in gleeful detail his bumbling attempts at the job; she concludes, however, that it '... was the makin' of Jim. 'E began to see for the fust time in 'is life what a woman's work meant, and by the time 'e could go back to 'is bottle washin', 'e was a changed man. 'Andy 'e could never be, and sometimes I wished 'e'd lost an arm instead of a leg – 'e'd 'ave missed it less. But one night 'e 'opped along of me to a Sufferagette meeting and comin' out 'e says, says 'e, "Esther", says 'e, "I'm a goin' to be a Sufferagette myself" (171). If the play confirms a gender-specific division of work it also insists, in the face of a tradition which dismissed it as a non-occupation, that housekeeping and childcare be granted status as labour, reflecting a position adopted by a number of suffrage supporters. In fact, a document entitled 'The Women's Charter of Rights and Liberties' (1910), by Liberal suffragist Lady McLaren, advocated under the heading of 'Earnings' that:

A wife who devotes her whole time to housekeeping and the care of the children shall have a claim upon her husband during his life, and upon his estate after his death, for a sum calculated on a scale not exceeding the wages of a housekeeper in her station of life, provided she has not received any other personal allowance. Such sum shall not however exceed one half the amount saved during the marriage. (quoted in Garner 116-17)

Although, as Garner points out in his study of the suffrage movement, the charter was never formally endorsed by any suffrage society, it certainly aroused widespread discussion among members of various organisations (14). And despite the fact that the WSPU executive dismissed the charter because it was not specifically concerned with female enfranchisement (52), it is worth noting that it was the WSPU newspaper, *Votes for Women*, that published *Jim's Leg*.

Elizabeth Baker's *Edith*, a one-act comedy included as part of a matinée entertainment hosted by the WWSL at the Prince's Theatre in February 1912, also inverts conventional expectations of proper male and female endeavour. Like other more substantial works of the period including Granville Barker's *The Voysey Inheritance* (1905) and Pinero's *The Thunderbolt* (1908), it is constructed around a disputed or compromised inheritance. This particular comedy focuses upon the will of a Mr Stott, a man who made his fortune in trade and maintained his family, much to their humiliation, in a home above the shop. Contrary to the family's expectation that the estate will go to the son, Gerald, who loathes the business and intends to sell it immediately, the daughter, Edith, is made 'boss of the whole show' (13). The only family member not present when the will is read, Edith left the family home years ago to manage a small milliner's shop whereupon everyone except the late Mr Stott lost touch with her. This 'mere girl' who 'couldn't be cleverer than Gerald' soon arrives and puts paid to such conventional undervaluations of women, although at least one critic objected to 'the easy, and therefore, not over-glorious triumph' of Edith by means of 'the crude device of making the male characters of the cast such poor and commonplace creatures' (*Stage* 15 Feb 1912, 16). 'A handsome woman, young and quite at her ease, in very becoming mourning', (21) Edith immediately takes charge, without however sacrificing any of her femininity; according to the *Era*, 'Miss Jeannette Steer [as Edith] ... was very refined and ladylike' (17 Feb 1912, 13). It unfolds that she now owns a number of shops

throughout England and has major plans to bring Stott's business
into the twentieth century: 'The trade is a bit low down after what
I'm used to, but it's a little gold mine in its way, and you wait and
see what I'll do with it. Poor dead Dad … was getting a bit old for the
times' (26). Like Madame Christine in *How the Vote was Won,* Edith
has achieved financial success and independence through self-
employment. Interestingly, both women deal in women's clothing,
which in the context of comedy provides them with a means of
liberation from overt male control. In this respect, an illuminating
comparison may be drawn with with St John Hankin's *The Last of
the De Mullins* (1908), a three-act 'play without a preface' whose
heroine is a successful self-made milliner. The significance of Janet
De Mullin's undisputed achievement is, however, diluted in this
play by a conventional (and coercive) glorification of Motherhood.
For Janet is a successful mother first, whose exuberant sexuality is
celebrated, and whose failure to marry is excused, by her fulfilment
of the eugenicists' dream of a fine son. There is no room in Hankin's
world for a Madame Christine or Edith, unsexualized women whose
success is not haunted by the spectre of the 'incomplete' spinster
'growing [in Janet's own words] faded and cross and peevish' (83).

Despite their differences in structure and subject matter, the various suffrage processions, pageants, dramas and comedies share a
common and overriding concern with altering the inferior status of
women through both short-term political and long-term social
change. Paradoxically, they sought fuller inclusion in their country's political and social system as the most effective means of
dismantling the sexist aspects of that system. The dramatic works
obviously tackle this matter from differing perspectives and by
different tactics. The pageants for instance use historical and allegorical representations both to celebrate and to reclaim for the
feminist cause women's past achievements, while the social dramas agitate for reform through critical portrayals of women's current oppression in areas of topical concern. The comedies in turn
explode the arguments of the opposition which insisted upon a
narrow and severely circumscribed definition of appropriate womanly conduct, offering in their place an expansive interpretation of
suitable female endeavour. Suffrage theatre satisfied other more
professional needs as well, providing new material for female actors frustrated by the prevalent stage conception of women which
they considered to be conventional and unconvincing.[26] It also

provided an opportunity for professional women writers to compose plays for performance safe from the limiting strictures of the commercial theatre. In such a supportive environment playwrights found themselves free to approach dramatic forms and themes from a feminist perspective. Stress was placed upon the collective nature of the enterprise and if a price was exacted in terms of individual aggrandisement the reward promised to be great. In what might be characterised as the overly optimistic words of Elizabeth Robins,

> ... if no single fame emerges to-day as notable as that of certain figures towering out of the past, intelligent women know that the sum of feminine achievement is for the first time a factor in that *Welt politik* which is the shaping of public opinion. We see clearly that, working shoulder to shoulder as we have never worked before, women are laying the foundation of a power which is to change the course of history. (*Way Stations* 73-74)

Notes

1 The plays performed were *The Pot and the Kettle* (Cicely Hamilton and Christopher St John), *Master* (Gertrude Mouillot), *The Outcast* (Beatrice Harraden and Bessie Hatton) and *A Pageant of Famous Women* (Cicely Hamilton and Christopher St John,the latter a pseudonym for Christabel Marshall).

2 So much so that when Eva Moore played a sketch written by her husband called *Her Vote* concerning 'a "fluffy" young woman who, after persuading everyone she meets that it is "their duty" to attend a big Suffrage meeting, does not go herself, because her "young man" has taken tickets for a fashionable ball', a complaint was registered that 'Eva Moore preferred Kisses to Votes'. She was asked either not to do the play again or to resign; she chose to resign although she rejoined the League at a later date, 'still reserving the right to myself to play in any play, without the assumption that I was working anti-Suffrage propaganda' (Moore 95).

3 The latter is also political and didactic; it strives to demonstrate to women the ramifications of their social, political, cultural and economic inequality as a means of encouraging them to fight for change. And like its forerunner, such drama is primarily concerned with confirming, or rendering explicit, views already held by its mostly female audience. It too speaks mostly to the converted. It does so, according to Janet Brown, through four basic patterns: sex role reversal; use of historical figures as role models; satire of sex roles; and the direct portrayal of women's oppression (140). Such techniques and strategies also inform the work of the propagandist playwrights of the WWSL and AFL. It is an unfortunate irony that this body of writing was unknown to the feminist authors of the 1960s who unwittingly accepted as 'fact that [until they began to write] feminist drama simply did not exist' (Natalle 16). As recently as 1984, Helene Keyssar, in her study of *Feminist Theatre*, makes the same claim, insisting that 'it was not until the last decade that playwrights in significant numbers became self-consciously concerned about the presence – or absence – of women as women on stage' (1).

4 It was called the 'Mud March' in acknowledgement of the less than ideal weather conditions that prevailed. By deciding to appear publicly in the streets at this time these women issued an obvious challenge to conventional definitions of appropriate feminine behaviour.

5 Tickner also discusses what she considers to be more overt influences from both Labour and State. I would argue however that the 'state ritual, which refined and developed the public image of the British monarchy in the heyday of `invented traditions' between 1877 and 1914 [and] labour-movement activities from May Day celebrations to the ritual welcome of released prisoners' (56) were, like the suffrage pageants, informed by a tradition of pageantry which had existed in Britain for centuries, flourishing in the late sixteenth and early seventeenth centuries, and for various reasons again answering the needs of a number of organisations in the late nineteenth and early twentieth centuries. For further information on the early history of English pageantry see David M. Bergeron's *English Civic Pageantry 1558-1642*.

6 Other examples of suffrage entertainments which rely upon the use of historical and/or allegorical figures are *The First Actress* (Christopher St John), Kingsway Theatre, 8 May 1911, *The Reforming of Augustus* (Irene Rutherford McLeod), Rehearsal Theatre, 15 January 1910 and *An Allegory* (Vera Wentworth), Rehearsal Theatre, 25 April 1911.

7 The realisation, or recreation on stage of a recognisable work of art was a theatrical device popular throughout the nineteenth and early twentieth centuries. For an exhaustive study of the convention see Martin Meisel's *Realisations*.

8 So popular in fact that when the *Pageant* toured the provinces and actors were sought for the various roles, occasional altercations arose with 'entirely unsuitable' would-be Joans (Hamilton *Edy* 43).

9 Hamilton argues in a similar vein: 'Because her work as a wife and mother was rewarded only by a wage of subsistence, it was assumed that no other form of work she undertook was worthy of a higher reward; because the only trade that was at one time open to her was paid at the lowest possible rate, it was assumed that in every other trade into which she gradually forced her way she must also be paid at the lowest possible rate. The custom of considering her work as worthless (from an economic point of view) originated in the home, but it has followed her out into the world' (*Marriage as a Trade* 96).

10 As Jane Marcus records, Elizabeth Robins made the same point when she noted 'that the Paris fashion house of Worth had invented the "hobble skirt" at exactly the moment when the suffragettes were striding toward freedom' (*The Convert* xi).

11 As Tickner shows, the same impulse informed the 1909 'Votes for Workers' poster of W. F. Winter which depicts a worn and middle-aged woman dressed in heavy brown serge working at a sewing machine (50b). The poster was joint winner of the Artists' Suffrage League poster competition of that year.

12 Cicely Hamilton also took the opportunity to descry 'this condemnation to intellectual barrenness [which] is the strongest proof of the essential servility of woman's position in the eyes of man' (*Marriage* 48) Women's education, she contends, 'unlike her brothers', was not directed towards self-development and the bringing out of natural capabilities, but towards pleasing some one else' (41). Like Hatton she condemns the 'conspiracy of silence' which has kept women ignorant or innocent of the 'risks' which men's 'loose living' may have for them and their children (54). Many read the entry of women into the medical profession as a means of correcting this situation, providing the opportunity for women to enlighten women about sexually transmitted diseases. Interestingly, the *Common Cause* claimed in 1910 that over five hundred women doctors

supported the suffrage movement as compared to fifteen who were against it (quoted by Kent 133).

13 According to Sheila Jeffreys, pre-war feminists considered the institution of 'a system of "sex-slavery" for women' to be the consequence of the form taken by male sexuality (47) while Kent states that for many such feminists 'the rights of husbands to force sexual intercourse and compulsory childbearing on their wives established a condition of "sex-slavery"' (92).

14 The Pioneer Players was founded in March 1911 by Edith Craig and gave annual seasons of subscription performances until 1921. Its last production was Susan Glaspell's *The Verge*, Regent Theatre, 29 March 1925. The Pioneer Players had two main objectives: '1. To produce plays dealing with all kinds of movements of contemporary interest. 2. To assist societies which have been formed all over the country in support of such movements, by helping them to organise dramatic performances, it having been asserted that 'one play is worth a hundred speeches' where propaganda is concerned' (taken from the programme for the Third Subscription Performance, Savoy Theatre, November 26, 1911). *In the Workhouse* was part of the First Subscription Performance, which also included Christopher St John's *The First Actress* and Cicely Hamilton's *Jack and Jill and a Friend*.

15 Cicely Hamilton played one of the inmates in the play's first production.

16 The pernicious effect of charities upon the impulse for social change is recounted by Robins: 'A common excuse for not doing something for the Cause is that same honourable-sounding one of "Charities". I am reminded in this connection of an American working-girl who was sent to ask a certain rich woman, of well-known liberality, to help the funds of a Trade Union to which the girl belonged. The lady offered no objection to the principle of Trade Unionism, and she listened to the story of the work this particular body was doing, kindly enough – but to all appeals for help returned the one answer, that she `had her charities' – her Working-Girls' Clubs, her Friendly and Rescue Societies, and the rest – till at last the girl, heart-sick at her failure, burst out with: "Don't you see what we are trying to do is to get rid of the need of your charity?" "But no!" the working-girl said, in telling about the interview, "there's lots like her. They've got the charity-habit. It is the stuff that sends 'em to sleep!"' (*Way Stations* 68).

17 In this *The Woman with the Pack* pre-dates a controversy which erupted in January 1912 when two suffrage supporters proposed to delete the promise 'to obey' from their marriage service. Debate ensued as to the legality of such a proceeding and the couple ultimately capitulated, allowing the clergyman to include the offending phrase although the bride afterwards denied repeating it (see the *Daily Mail* 12 Jan 1912 and the *Daily Chronicle* 15 Jan 1912 in vol. 16 of the Arncliffe-Sennett Papers).

18 In the same scene, Philippa Tempest also makes a plea for consumer activism: 'The people I blame are the people who pay such wretched wages, and those who will have the miserable sweated things Fanchette made' (67). In this she echoes the Women's Co-operative Guild who in the previous decade had begun campaigns to encourage consumers to avoid sweated goods (Liddington 41). It was an issue also taken up in Edith Lyttelton's three-act play, *Warp and Woof*, Camden Theatre, 6 June 1904, produced by Mrs Patrick Campbell who took the lead role as Theodosia Heming, a sweated seamstress. At the play's climax, Heming berates a group of society ladies whose unreasonable demands for ball-gowns exacerbates appalling working conditions: 'We could do the work if you gave us time. But here's her ladyship angry because we're behind with the gown. When did she order it? Only this morning. You don't know what that means, you ladies. I don't believe you want us to work till we're ill and silly and dazed – you're too kind. But that's what happens. You never see us – we're away upstairs

in the workrooms. There we are always stitching – cold often, when you're warm round your fires – hot, stifling hot, when you're in your cool rooms – stitching when you're all fast asleep. ... Oh, don't any of you fancy your gowns are made of silk and satin only – our life and strength goes into them too' (113-14).

19 See Kent's *Sex and Suffrage in Britain* for an extensive analysis of the equation drawn between prostitution and marriage in much feminist writing of the period.

20 It is a position seriously propounded by Hugo De Mullin in St John Hankin's *The Last of the De Mullins* (1908): 'The only form of independence that is possible or desirable for a woman is that she be dependent upon her husband or, if she is unmarried, on her nearest male relative' (70).

21 According to the 1901 census, over four million women (meaning all females over the age of nine) in England and Wales admitted to working while slightly more than nine million women claimed to be unemployed (see Meacham 95).

22 This may be a comic allusion to Lucile (Lady Duff Gordon) whose highly success- ful dressmaking establishment was located first at 17 and then 23 Hanover Square. Lucile, who dressed such a well known anti-suffragist as Margot Asquith, also designed the costumes for *The Liars*, one of Henry Arthur Jones's many endorsements of conventional femininity. In fact in 1909, the year that *How the Vote was Won* was written, Lucile was designing productions for George Edwardes of the ultra-conservative Gaiety.

23 Hamilton makes the same point in *Marriage as a Trade*: 'Theoretically he [the head of the household] might hold fast to the belief that woman's sphere was the home and nothing but the home. Actually he might object to the monetary outlay incurred if that belief was acted upon. The father of five strapping girls (all hungry several times a day), who might or might not succeed in inducing five desirable husbands to bear the expense of their support, would probably dis- cover that, even if home was the sphere of woman, there were times when she was better out of it' (126).

24 The play was recently revived in London (March 1988) by the Antonio Pinto Players. Other suffrage plays by Evelyn Glover include *Showin' Samyel*, a mono- logue in which a working-class wife recounts how she converted her husband to the suffrage cause simply by sitting quietly exercising her 'silent inflooence' and doing nothing else, and *Miss Appleyard's Awakening* (Rehearsal Theatre, 20 June 1911) in which Miss Appleyard becomes a suffrage supporter as a result of an interview with an anti-suffragist.

25 Other suffrage comedies which rely on sex-role reversal include *Lady Geraldine's Speech* (Beatrice Harraden), first performed at the WSPU's Prince's Skating Rink Exhibition in May 1909 and *The Better Half* (Alison Garland), which was produced at the King's Head, 6 April 1913 by the AFL. *Lady Geraldine's Speech*, with its parade of eminent women in Edwardian guise (there is a doctor, painter, pianist and professor) was primarily concerned with establishing new role models for women which, by celebrating potential accomplishment in areas traditionally associated with male endeavour, challenged a definition of the sexes which habitually discounted women. *The Better Half*, which takes place in a fictive country where women alone govern and men engage in suffrage agitation, is described in some detail in Claire Hirshfield's article, 'The Suffragist as Play- wright in Edwardian England'.

26 In fact, 'that the stage conception of women is conventional and inadequate' was a topic set for discussion at one of the AFL members' meetings (Gardner intro). A *Votes for Women* reviewer also objected that 'There is not one play on the London stage at the present time which takes any account of women except on the level of housekeeping machines or bridge players – the actual or potential property of some man, valuable or worthless as the case may be' (8 Oct 1909; quoted in Holledge 70).

III

Cicely Hamilton
'Marriage as a Trade'

The writing and performance of suffrage drama held many attractions for women playwrights and actors bent on freeing themselves from what they conceived to be the stranglehold of male definition. Yet that said, it must be acknowledged that any attempt to construct a more permanent feminist theatre within the boundaries of the suffrage movement was ironically precluded by the movement itself, which considered feminist drama as an advertising and fund-raising adjunct to the more pressing work for the vote. Which is not to say that the idea of a women's theatre company was completely neglected. Prompted by the success of its theatrical productions but frustrated by the ephemeral nature of such endeavours as well as by the continued lack of opportunity for women within the commercial theatre, the head of the AFL play department, Inez Bensusan, established just such a Women's company in 1913, its first season financed by share subscriptions (like Robins's Ibsen series) purchased primarily by women engaged in all aspects of the women's movement. The experiment was a financial and organisational success, all shareholders realising 'a substantial return on their £1 shares, as the net profit was £442, and shareholders received 11s 6d (57 1/2 per cent) in the £' (*AFL Annual Report* 1913-14, 14). Interestingly, however, the plays chosen for presentation were by men, Bjørnson's *A Gauntlet* and Brieux's *Woman on Her Own (La Femme Seule)* – an irony that resulted at least in part from the concentration by women playwrights of the time on 'one-act, small cast plays' (Holledge 94). And certainly the aesthetic limitations of suffrage drama are readily apparent; brevity and clarity of meaning were virtues encouraged at the cost of a more ambitious and ultimately richer full-length drama. It is painfully apparent that rejecting the professional theatre to write and stage propaganda plays for the converted invited easy marginalisation. Unfortunately, a women's theatre company that would also produce women's plays never became a reality; perhaps Bensusan's company would have gone on to do so but its second season scheduled for the autumn of 1914 did not materialise, falling instead an early casualty of the Great War. Throughout the period, women playwrights who wanted their full-length works produced had to seek venues within the existing commercial system.

Of course working for London's West End theatres was not without its problems. In a WSPU pamphlet of 1907 Elizabeth Robins described the dangers commonly awaiting women authors who attempted to write for more wide-ranging audiences:

> Let us remember it is only yesterday that women in any number began to write for the public prints.But in taking up the pen, what did this new recruit conceive to be her task? To proclaim her own or other women's actual thoughts and feelings? Far from it. Her task, as she naturally and even inevitably conceived it, was to imitate as nearly as possible the method, but above all the point of view, of men. ... What she is really doing is her level best to play the man's game, and seeing how nearly like him she can do it. So conscious is she it is *his* game she is trying her hand at, that she is prone to borrow his very name to set upon her title-page. (*Way Stations* 5-6)

Robins is writing here in general terms. In a later work she provides a specific instance of such 'manly imitation' in the person of Mrs Craigie, a turn of the century writer who published under the name of John Oliver Hobbes. Craigie's first play, *The Ambassador,* was successfully staged by George Alexander at the St James's Theatre in 1898, and followed in turn by three additional full-length plays before her early death in 1906.[1] According to Robins,

> The published life of the gifted 'John Oliver Hobbes' shows [an] inability to see her own sex except through the eyes of men, among the first three men of her choice, Byron! Her flattery of men is flagrant, by her own account. Her subservience to their criticism, and their direction, beyond a doubt, clipped her bright wings and weighed down her originality, no less than her native wit. (*Ancilla's Share* 101)

It should be understood that Robins's criticism stems as much from Craigie's political views as from her literary works – the one of course obviously influencing the other. Craigie was an anti-suffragist who on one 'unfortunate' occasion in 1905 took part in a debate on the advisability of including women as jurors. Craigie argued in Spencerian terms against inclusion, declaring that [women's] nature did not contain a proper element of justice, that they were by nature unfair, though their unfairness, in some instances, was a source of fascination. Where would men get sympathy, she asked, if women were impartial? Experience showed that women were not intended to govern; and art rightly represented the woman impersonating Justice as being blindfolded, because a woman could not be trusted to see straight. (*Life of John Oliver Hobbes* 30)

Such a position was anathema to Robins, whose own opinion of the state of Britain's judicial system is registered in *Votes for Women!*. Such abasement of her own sex by a sister writer could only be interpreted by Robins as 'masculine', the product of a woman overcome by male sensibility.

Craigie's fate, as characterised by Robins, was one that a number of women playwrights struggled consciously to avoid. Foremost among these was Cicely Hamilton, whose *Pageant of Great Women* and *How the Vote Was Won* proved popular items in the suffrage repertoire. Like Craigie (and Robins herself[2]), Hamilton concealed her sex when her first play, 'a somewhat gruesome one-act', *The Sixth Commandment*, was staged in 1906, it being conventional wisdom that plays by women were more likely to receive a bad press.[3] And 'certain it is that the one or two critics who had discovered that C. Hamilton stood for a woman were the one or two critics who dealt out hard measure to her playlet' (*Life Errant* 60). Nevertheless, in subsequent work Hamilton made no effort to masquerade as a man, asserting in her autobiography that 'the change – if change it were – was brought about rapidly as an indirect result of the suffrage agitation' (61).

Hamilton was, like Robins, a prominent participant in the suffrage movement. An early recruit of the WSPU, she left that organisation in 1907 as a result of a dispute over internal organisation to become a member of the Women's Freedom League, a splinter group formed under the presidency of Charlotte Despard. Despite her significant contribution to the cause of female enfranchisement, however, Hamilton claimed to be motivated more by feminist than specifically suffragist concerns:

... I never attempted to disguise the fact that I wasn't wildly interested in votes for anyone, and ... if I worked for women's enfranchisement (and I did work quite hard) it wasn't because I hoped great things from counting female noses at general elections, but because the agitation for women's enfranchisement must inevitably shake and weaken the tradition of the 'normal woman'. The 'normal woman' with her 'destiny' of marriage and motherhood and housekeeping, no interest outside her home – especially no interest in the man's preserve of politics! My personal revolt was feminist rather than suffragist; what I rebelled at chiefly was the dependence implied in the idea of 'destined' marriage, 'destined' motherhood – the identification of success with marriage, of failure with spinsterhood, the artificial concentration of the hopes of girlhood on sexual attraction and maternity ... (*Life Errant* 65)[4]

Such views dominate Hamilton's work, finding their most forceful expression in *Marriage as a Trade* (1909), a piece of polemical writing which Showalter describes as being 'on the brink of a feminist criticism' (225).[5] As its title suggests, *Marriage as a Trade* is an attempt to debunk the more romantic connotations of that institution through an examination of its 'trade aspect', Hamilton's extended use of the commercial metaphor evidence of Kent's contention that feminist use of such an idiom 'dispelled the notion of a clear separation between public and private, demonstrating instead the public nature of all domestic life, even the most intimate aspects of the marital bond' (85). The work focuses upon the extent to which 'woman' is a social construct, 'the product of the conditions imposed upon her by her staple industry' (17): 'Vicious or virtuous, matron or outcast, she was made and not born' (44). It examines the unhappy consequences for women's mental and physical well-being of their manipulation into 'the regulation pattern of wifehood' (45), and confirms the ideology of the suffrage movement in its assertion that 'the human female is not entirely composed of sex' (102). The book launches an attack upon the hysterisation of the female body as Michel Foucault would come to call it, condemning the artificial reduction of women to sex, and celebrating celibacy and spinsterhood as alternatives to the subjugation and dependency that marriage and motherhood entailed.

As one specific element in her discussion, Hamilton considers women's place in art and literature. Adopting much the same position as Robins, she argues that

Art, as we know it, is a masculine product, wrought by the hands and conceived by the brains of men; the works of art that have forced themselves into the enduring life of the world have been shaped, written, builded, painted by men. They have achieved and we have imitated; on the whole, pitifully. (107)

It is Hamilton's contention that much of women's art is 'artificial', 'not a representation of life or beauty seen by a woman's eyes, but an attempt to render life or beauty as man desires that a woman should see and render it. The attempt is unconscious, no doubt; but it is there – thwarting, destroying and annulling' (112). Hamilton maintains, however, that a woman can at least attempt to counter such training albeit at great cost: 'even in the comparatively few instances where she recognises what her training has done for her, when she realises the poor thing it has made of her, and sets to work, deliberately and of firm resolve, to counteract its effects upon her life and character, it may take her the best part of a lifetime to struggle free of her chains' (110). Such was to be the pattern of Hamilton's own life.

Rebelling at a young age 'against the compulsory nature of the trade of marriage' (*Marriage* 55) and coming as she did from an impecunious middle-class family, Hamilton was early confronted with the prospect of having to provide for herself. Although she initially struggled with a pupil-teacher's job in the Midlands, she soon rejected such suitable women's work in favour of a new life in the theatre. Finding that she did not conform to the conventional type of female beauty defined by actor-managers, however – 'My face, unfortunately, was not of the type that induces theatrical managers to offer engagements on sight' (*Life Errant* 32)[6] – she was forced to earn her living touring the provinces with second-rate companies whose staple fare was melodrama, her meagre salary augmented by work as a hack journalist. Her most successful stage performance was as Mrs Knox in Shaw's *Fanny's First Play* (1911), a part that came her way through her activities in the suffrage movement. During a rehearsal of *Pageant of Great Women*, Hamilton was apparently noticed by Lillah McCarthy, who subsequently offered her a part in her production of Shaw's piece (which incidentally includes among its dramatis personae an active suffragette) at the Little Theatre, where the play went on to became 'a truly obstinate success' (*Life Errant* 83).[7] But if Hamilton realised the part as a result of her suffrage activities, the play's two-year run had the effect of drastically curtailing such activities: 'at the hour when meetings usually begin I had to be in my dressing-room, making up to go on the stage' (*Life Errant* 84). Unfortunately, Hamilton's stage success came after she had virtually given up performance for composition. Although she professed to a growing literary ambition, she also realised, like many women actors of the period, that middle age and acting were often incompatible, and as that particular age approached, she turned to writing full-time.[8]

Her first attempt at a full-length play was *Diana of Dobson's*, a comedy about a sweated shop assistant, 'who, on the strength of a small legacy, makes a Cinderella-like appearance in the world that does not toil or spin' (*Life Errant* 61). Her unexpected inheritance allows her to live as a woman of means for one brief month at a resort in the Swiss Alps, during which time she is wooed by both Sir Jabez Grinley, the owner of a chain of drapers' shops which cater to the lower middle class, and Captain Victor Bretherton, a ne'er-do-well who, finding it impossible to live 'on a miserable six hundred pounds a year', is encouraged to court Diana on the basis of her supposed fortune. She refuses the former and both rejects and is rejected by the latter when she discloses the true state of her affairs. Her legacy quickly depleted, she returns to England and a life of increasing destitution. Finally evicted from her lodgings, she is forced to haunt the Thames Embankment where she once more encounters Bretherton. Stung by her taunt that he would 'throw up the sponge in a week' (53) if he had to earn his own living without help from friends or relations, he has attempted to do just that with a singular lack of success. Convinced now that his income is not 'a miserable pittance' but rather enough for two, he proposes again and Diana accepts.

Upon its completion Hamilton sent the manuscript to the Kingsway Theatre, which under the management of Lena Ashwell (also an active member of the AFL) had undergone a pink and white chocolate-box type of refurbishment reminiscent of Madame Vestris's earlier prettification of the Olympic. Like Granville Barker at the Court, Ashwell was determined to establish a theatre that would produce new plays by promising English playwrights. *Diana of Dobson's* was the eleventh play in a pile of twenty-five that Kingsway play reader Edward Knoblock was scouring for possible production. He reacted to the script with an enthusiasm – 'Nothing can compare with the joy of finding a really good, human, crisp, amusing manuscript' (*Round the Room* 91) – that Ashwell shared, and the play was signed for almost immediate production. It was an astute business decision; this 'delicious comedy' as Ashwell described it, proved a commercial success. Opening on 12 February 1908 it ran for 143 performances and was withdrawn only because Ashwell, who played the title role, opted for a period of rest before the commencement of her provincial tour (*Era* 16 Jan 1909, 17). The play was revived the following year for a further 32 performances.

Although Ashwell required few alterations to the script, she did

request a change of title.[9] Hamilton had originally called the play
The Adventuress, in obvious reference to an exchange between
Diana and Bretherton in Act III:

> *Bretherton.* ... Oh, hang it all, I know I'm no match for you in an
> argument. But however much you may sneer and jeer at me, you
> must know perfectly well that your conduct has been that of an
> adventuress.
>
> *Diana (lightly).* An adventuress! So I'm an adventuress am I? Doesn't this
> rather remind you of the celebrated interchange of compliments
> between the pot and kettle? (51)

The title is also, however, a challenge to a dramatic stereotype
which had its roots in melodrama. In fact, so prevalent was this
particular type of female villain (a type that Hamilton herself had
specialised in as an actor) that Jerome K. Jerome includes a section
on her in *Stageland*, a series of tongue-in-cheek profiles of figures
from that genre. According to Jerome, the Adventuress of melodrama signifies 'black-hearted and abandoned womanhood' (35)
which translated means that she is a clever business woman who
dresses too well. She almost always has a terrible secret that, when
revealed, wreaks havoc with her marital machinations, and she
stands in marked contrast to the heroine, a passive figure of nobil-
ity and self-sacrifice. She is, in other words, evil step-sister to the
victimised but always angelic Cinderella. The 'mental nausea' suffered by Hamilton in response to 'the utter sloppiness of the
admired type of heroine' (*Life Errant* 57), however, resulted in her
endowing Diana with some of the characteristics normally associated with the stage adventuress. According to Ashwell, 'Diana is by
nature a Bohemian, and, like all Bohemians when they are poor, in
a perpetual state of revolt. And when she is thoroughly put out, she
says a great many nasty and bitter things about the powers that be'
(*Pall Mall* 8 Feb 1908). She is also assertive and willing to initiate
action, and as such stands in marked contrast to the prevailing
social as well as dramatic ideal of womanly submission.

   This is not to suggest that *Diana of Dobson's* launches a full-scale
attack upon patriarchal culture. If Robins's *Votes for Women!* proclaims itself a 'dramatic tract', Hamilton's *Diana of Dobson's*
presents itself as 'a romantic comedy'. Ashwell described the piece
as 'very, very light' and Hamilton maintained that she 'had no
serious object in writing [it]' (*Pall Mall* 8 Feb 1908). Yet the play
does not lack a critical perspective. Hamilton added in the same

interview, 'I am hoping that the story may prove interesting to the general public, who do not know as a rule much about the lives of shop-girls, and the want of consideration with which some of them are treated by their employers'. Ashwell noted that 'the authoress can hit hard when she likes, and some of the scenes are written in a spirit that can only be described as exceedingly sarcastic and satirical' (*Pall Mall* 8 Feb 1908). To borrow Shaw's phraseology when talking about his own plays, Hamilton uses devices of romantic comedy to coat the propagandist pill. As the *Era* critic wrote, the play 'is produced quite apropos of the agitation against living in and of the cry for female suffrage. It voices very boldly the revolt of the modern woman against her subjection, her craving for interest in life, her hatred of monotony, and her desire for a "good time"' (15 Feb 1908, 17). In both her re-definition of well-known dramatic female types and her attention to the plight of a group of women-workers, Hamilton displays a feminist perspective informed by issues raised within the growing women's movement. Rejecting what she considered to be the servile and imitative nature of most women's art, she strove instead to produce work that expressed a distinctly female point of view: 'My conception of woman is inevitably the feminine conception; a thing so entirely unlike the masculine conception of woman that it is eminently needful to define the term and make my meaning clear' (*Marriage* 19). *Diana of Dobson's* is just one instance of Hamilton's struggle to define 'woman' apart from the attributes traditionally foisted upon her by a patriarchal ideology. In doing so she inevitably relies upon dramatic conventions rooted in that ideology, deliberately recasting them, however, according to her feminist perceptions.

In the case of *Diana of Dobson's*, Hamilton harkens back to a tradition of light comedy initiated by Tom Robertson in a trayful of 'cup-and-saucer' plays written for the Bancrofts in the 1860s. Part of a larger-scale reaction to the excesses of much mid-Victorian theatre, Robertson's genteel comedies display 'a cleverness in investing with romantic associations commonplace details of life' (*Athenaeum* 23 Jan 1869). His most successful piece, *Caste* (1867), a Cinderella story of cross-class alliance, relies upon delicately rendered romance to side-step the potentially sticky moral and social problems it raises. Unlike the play's other working-class figures, the heroine, Esther, displays a lady-like gentility that justifies the Hon. George D'Alroy's love and desire to raise her to his station. As he says, 'Caste is a good thing if it's not carried too far. It shuts the door on the pretentious and the vulgar: but it should open the door very wide for exceptional merit' (183). The 'exceptional' Esther, miscast for life among the working class, is rescued through romance, her princely soldier carrying her off to a life of ladylike ease in a very fine house.

In *Trelawny of the 'Wells'* (1898) Pinero had struck a late-Victorian variation upon *Caste*, enlisting the earlier play's formal structure, romantic plot and delicate tone in a reconsideration of the problem play of misalliance and rehabilitation. *Trelawny of the 'Wells'* concerns another working woman's translation into respectability through an impending marriage into the aristocracy. But whereas in the problem plays of the period, such cross-class liaisons are doomed by the aggressive social conventions they violate, in *Trelawny of the 'Wells'* the issue is evaded and the marriage sanctioned by means of an aesthetic attitude that unites romance with theatre history. In a 'Robertsonian tribute to Robertson' the reunion of Rose Trelawny and Arthur Gower is engineered to take place during a rehearsal of what in the context of the play is seen as the 'innovative' cup-and-saucer comedy of reforming playwright Tom Wrench/Robertson (see Kaplan 'Chairs').[10]

In Hamilton's hands, the romance of such genteel Cinderella comedy becomes a feminist issue, and *Diana of Dobson's* serves as a practical demonstration of 'the business-like aspect of love in woman, the social or commercial necessity for sexual intercourse ... usually ignored by an imitative feminine art – because it is lacking in man, and is, therefore, not really grasped by him' (*Marriage* 113). According to Hamilton women are generally less romantic than men by virtue of their commercial interest in matters of sexual attraction (*Marriage* 28), and this affects their reaction to as well as participation in romance:

> It is because her love has always been her livelihood that woman has never been inspired by it as man has been inspired. And it is just because it is so business-like that her interest in love is often so keen. For instance, her customary appreciation of a book or a work of art dealing with love, and nothing but love, is the outcome of something more than sentiment and overpowering consciousness of sex. To her a woman in love is not only a woman swayed by emotion, but a human being engaged in carving for herself a career or securing for herself a means of livelihood. Her interest in a love story is, therefore, much more complex than a man's interest therein, and the appreciation which she brings to it is of a very different quality. (*Marriage* 117-18)

A latter-day Cinderella, the Diana of the play's title was thrown destitute upon the world following the unexpected death of her father. Like most middle-class girls of the period, she was never trained to earn her own living and, lacking either a husband or other means of support, eventually finds herself at the premises of Mr Dobson's high-class drapery emporium. Having pushed Cinderella into the industrial age, Hamilton locates her in an institutionalised dormitory where, along with four other would-be Cinderellas, she retires after slaving all day under the wrathful eyes of Mr Dobson and his forewoman, Miss Pringle, an Edwardian variation on the traditional evil stepmother.

Diana of Dobson's begins, appropriately enough, in darkness (light itself is a costly commodity at the Dobson's establishment and its use regulated by rules and fines), a situation relieved by the groping hands of a female shop assistant. Locating the gas jet, she turns the light up on 'a bare room of the dormitory type ... [with] everything plain and comfortless to the last degree' (7). As the many illustrations of the set show, five small beds are ranged against the up-stage wall to which, during the course of the act, five tired and worn women repair, talking as they undress. Such potentially titillating stage business might be thought curious from a feminist writer who expressed her rage 'that character, worth, intellect were held valueless in woman, that nothing counted in her but the one capacity – the power of awaking desire' (*Marriage* 131). And certainly some reviewers considered the scene 'a little daring' or potentially 'shocking'. The critic for the *Stage* objected that 'it was an obviously make-believe going to bed, an insincere business with no bearing on the play, introduced merely for whatever sensational appeal it may have in itself' (13 Feb 1908 23). Bearing in mind, however, Hamilton's contention that women specialise in personal adornment as a matter of business and not from 'overflowing sexuality', such stage action should be judged as a public disassembling of the female sex-object, a visual dismantling of her various parts. We are meant to witness women's professionalism in the quick and efficient manner in which they discard the puffs and switches, ribbons and collars, waists and skirts that translate them into suitable representatives of attractive womanhood. This may be what motivated the *Stage* reviewer's objection since he goes on to complain that 'these different stages of undress do not happen to be made pretty'. Other critics appreciated the scene's 'professional' aspect. One characterised the women's movements as

'mechanical' (*Illustrated London News* 22 Feb 1908, 266) while another commented that 'There is nothing approaching the improper
in this episode, though we see half a dozen tired shop assistants
getting into their bed clothes after revealing secrets of the
unmaking of various forms of coiffure, which only a woman would
have the audacity to attack' (*Illustrated Sporting and Dramatic News*
7 March 1908, 19). In the words of critic H. M. Walbrook, 'if any
flippant reader imagines that by booking a seat at the Kingsway
Theatre he will get a view of something rather scandalous and
improper – well, all we shall say is, Let him book his seat! He will
deserve his disappointment' (*Pall Mall* 13 Feb 1908, 4). This process of de-eroticisation is also encouraged by the absence of any
male viewers on stage. Women, at least within the context of the
play's initial scene, cease to be objects of a dramatised male gaze.
In fact, men are completely excluded from the action of the first act,
allowing Hamilton to register women's voices safe from male inter-
ruption.

What kind of women are condemned to a joyless round of
overwork followed by 'rest' in a bleak and overcrowded dormitory
that manages to be quite literally only a bed-room? Those, the play
makes clear, without money or matrimonial prospects. Miss
Smithers, who enters first, 'is well over thirty, faded and practical
looking' (7) and considers herself an inmate for life. Past the conventional age for a marriage proposal (the only apparent means of
escape), she has reconciled herself to never having a home of her
own: 'Me, bless you – no such luck. I'm one of the left ones; I am left
high and dry. I made up my mind to that long ago' (7). Existing as
she does in a society that couples women's employment with low
pay, low status and little if any opportunity for advancement or
intellectual challenge, she is condemned to a monotonous round of
unceasing drudgery where dismissal follows hard on complaint.

Miss Smithers is speaking to fellow inmate Kitty Brant. 'About
twenty, pretty, but pale and tired' Kitty has secured her release
through romance; she is to be married soon, and as we would
expect, the commercial aspect of the subject is foremost in her
mind – her marriage is desirable, first because it frees her from
oppressive work conditions, and second because it affords her the
opportunity of 'having a little home' of her own. Fred, the prospective groom, is dealt with in one line, praised because he 'has always
been very careful and steady, and has got a good bit put by' (8).
Given the extreme undervaluation of women in so-called 'paid'

work, unpaid domestic labour can begin to appear the lesser of two evils. We would be forgiven for suspecting that Kitty enters 'the housekeeping trade in order to live ... [which] is not always quite the same as entering the housekeeping trade in order to love' (*Marriage* 27). Kitty is a comedic version of the 'haggard, underpaid girl' Hamilton mentions in *Marriage as a Trade*, who 'cries to another, in a burst of bitter confidence, "I would marry any one, to get out of this"' (27). So it might appear would Diana. As she says in a later exchange with Kitty:

> *Diana.* You're going to have done with it, Kitty. In three months' time you'll be married. However your marriage turns out, it will be a change for you – a change from the hosiery department of Dobson's.
> *Kitty (hurt).* Di——
> *Diana.* ... Oh, I didn't mean to be unkind, Kit. You're a dear, and if I'm nasty to you it's only because I envy you. You're going to get out of all this: in three months' time you'll have turned your back on it for good – you'll have done with the nagging and the standing and this horrible bare room – and the dining-room with the sloppy tea on the table and Pringle's sour face at the end of it. Lucky girl! But I haven't any prospect of turning my back on it, and it doesn't seem to me I ever shall. (13)

Diana, who is already twenty-seven or twenty-eight years of age, looks forward to a life like Miss Smithers's, one of continuous 'grind and squalor and tyranny and overwork' (11):

> The delectable atmosphere of Dobson's will follow me about wherever I go. I shall crawl round to similar establishments, cringing to be taken on at the same starvation salary – and then settle down in the same stuffy dormitory, with the same mean little rules to obey – I shall serve the same stream of intelligent customers – and bolt my dinner off the same tough meat in the same gloomy dining-room with the same mustard-coloured paper on the walls. And that's life. (13)

Quite unlike Miss Smithers or her fairy-tale model, however, Diana does not bear her subjection with passivity. She rails long and loud against her victimization. Unable to cultivate a sufficiently humbled persona, she suffers continual rebukes from both Dobson and Pringle, resulting in innumerable fines for 'unbusinesslike conduct' which reduce her already meagre salary further. Nor should it be thought that Diana's complaints about 'living in' are exaggerated for dramatic effect. Although the play is conceived as a 'romantic comedy', Hamilton's depiction of the life of sweated female shop-assistants is rooted in well-documented fact.[11]

'Home' for such women was a dormitory, described by the reviewer for the socialist *The Clarion* as 'a unique blend of barrack, Dotheboys Hall, and workhouse' (16 Feb 1912, 7). Although strictly bare and institutional, any attempt by residents at decoration was absolutely forbidden. According to the rule of one such establishment, 'No pictures, photos, etc., allowed to disfigure the walls. Any one so doing will be charged with the repairs' (Black 49). The rooms were crowded, inadequately ventilated, and many lacked proper bathing facilities. The food, often insufficient and of poor quality, was prepared according to a menu of unvarying monotony, and served in dining-rooms that were too often infested with bugs. Yet despite such appalling living conditions, a female shop assistant was expected to be quite literally on her feet from 8 o'clock in the morning to as late as 11 o'clock at night for a salary of approximately £15 a year (Diana earns £13 at Dobson's), with which sum 'she had to clothe herself, pay laundry and keep herself during holiday time' (*Common Cause* 19 May 1910, 89). As Diana puts it, she must live 'on thirteen pounds a year, five bob a week, with all my clothes to find and my fines to pay ... Five bob a week for fourteen hours work a day – five bob a week for the use of my health and strength – five bob a week for my life. And I haven't a doubt that a good many others here are in the same box' (12). Such a salary was of course susceptible to reduction from innumerable fines. Chargeable offences numbered from a minimum of 50 at one establishment to a maximum of 198 at another. They covered every aspect of a shop assistant's on and off hours: 'Gossiping, standing in groups, or lounging about in an unbusinesslike manner, fine 3*d*. Assistants must introduce at least two articles to each customer, fine 2*d*. Unnecessary talking and noise in bedrooms is strictly prohibited, fine 6*d*. For losing copy of rules, 2*d*. For unbusinesslike conduct, 6*d*' (Black 54-5). Such were 'the long train of woes that lay in wait for the over-worked, under-fed, and shut-in women' (Black 54) compelled, like Diana and her companions, to live a life of 'shop servitude'.[12]

In *The Madras House*, a comic drama produced as part of the Duke of York's repertory (1910), Granville Barker also addresses the difficulties of the 'living in' system, providing us with a convenient companion piece to test feminist perspectives and sensibilities. Although ostensibly a sympathetic play about both women's sexuality and their place in society, on closer scrutiny it reveals itself to be an exploration of the subject male's crisis of identity.

When we enter a draper's establishment in Act II, one stop on Philip Madras's documentary-like odyssey through Edwardian London, it is because Philip, the 'observer-hero' (Morgan xxv) is co-owner.[13] Certain problems exacerbated by the 'living in' arrangement are addressed in 'the waiting room – the one in which employee sits in shivering preparation for interviews with employer' (36), where Philip struggles to come to some understanding of his employees' positions regarding the pregnancy of an unmarried resident which has become controversial because she refuses to disclose the father's name. The scene is dominated by Philip both dramatically and thematically. And while it is true that the act considers the issue of women in the work-place as well as their financial relationship to men, it is given definition through Philip's presence (he serves after all as the tenuous link between the play's four acts), its content filtered through his baffled gaze. For despite his best efforts, the women in *The Madras House* remain curiously inscrutable, an apparently unknowable factor in Philip's equation for living.

But if Barker's *Madras House* differs from Hamilton's *Diana of Dobson's* in its overt adoption of the male perspective (which seems incidentally to pay tribute to the position of many Edwardian suffragists that only women can truly understand women and the matters that concern them[14]) it does exploit the earlier play's episodic construction with seemingly disparate scenes linked by the protagonist's presence. But even here the works differ significantly as Barker's distaste for plot-line (his notorious refusal 'to get on with the story') stands in marked contrast to Hamilton's reliance on a Cinderella narrative to plot out Diana's 'romantic' journey.

It is no fairy godmother, however, who magically transports Diana away from 'the treadmill grind'. Instead, according to a popular Edwardian dramatic convention, she receives a letter from a solicitor informing her that she is to receive an inheritance. Not exactly a princely sum, the £300 legacy is nevertheless a windfall in Diana's eyes. It means independence, providing her with a temporary way out of Dobson's that does not (like its alternative, marriage) entail subjection and potential degradation. For Diana money is power, 'Power to do what you like, to go where you like, to say what you like' (16). Which is exactly what she does. Discounting her fellow-workers' caution, she opts in true Edwardian fashion to 'waste' her money. While it lasts, she triumphs:

... I'll know what it is to have a royal time – I'll deny myself nothing. I
have had six years of scrape and starve – now I'll have a month of
everything that money can buy me – and there are very few things that
money can't buy me – precious few. (16)

Diana realises Helen Payson's dreams. She wins the legacy that
Helen loses to the Apple, and plans with it an act of radical frivolity,
a continental excursion that will for a single month free her from
having to endure the 'fat white face' of Dobson. 'For one month',
she tells us, 'I shall have done what I chose – not what I was forced
to. For one month I shall have had my freedom – and that will be
something to remember' (17). Diana, in fact, decides to become her
own fairy-godmother, and outfits herself accordingly for the good
life, never forgetting the temporal limits that are usually placed
upon such fairy-tale solutions.

When the curtain rises on Acts II and III, the dingy dormitory of the
first act has been metamorphosed into the posh sitting-room of a
Swiss hotel, the ill-fed and over-worked inmates into bored and
indulged members of the social elite, a poor and resentful Diana
into a merry widow of apparently substantial means. To facilitate
her translation into high society Diana invents, in a comic variation
on the 'woman with a past', a dead husband who allows her all the
social freedoms of marriage with none of the obligations. Enjoying
her new found independence, 'Mrs Massingberd'[15] proves a great
hit among the various well-to-do tourists, her determination 'to
enjoy everything – even [the] revolting soup' (26), a refreshing
change from their practised ennui.[16] If she were a conventional
melodramatic adventuress, seeking by means of her masquerade,
social acceptance and a 'good' marriage, her success would seem
guaranteed. As a figure of conspicuous (and tasteful) consumption,
she certainly stimulates the 'romantic' interest of Sir Jabez Grinley
(he surreptitiously fingers the stuff of her gown), a recently knighted
self-made man who began his 'career as a brat of a boy running
errands' and has amassed a fortune selling goods to lower middle-
class women at 'a halfpenny cheaper than they can get it anywhere
else' (31). In an exchange with a distinctly Shavian flavour,[17] Diana
(from a highly ironic vantage point) discusses 'economics' with her
former employer, who readily admits to keeping down expenses by
sweating workers. When Diana objects – 'Oh, that's the way to
make money – to get other people to work for you for as little as

they can be got to take, and put the proceeds of their work into
your pockets' (31) – he accuses her of being 'sentimental', a pretty
thing in a woman so he says, but out of place in the 'commercial
war' which is business. Like Shaw in *Widowers' Houses*, Hamilton
allows the capitalist trade 'villain' to justify himself, so much so
that in the eyes of one critic 'we have a story for the employed as
against the employer, in which the latter, even with the authoress
on the other side, comes out on top' (*Illustrated Sporting and Dramatic News* 7 March 1908, 19). Yet even this businessman is prepared
to take his mind off business occasionally, and in Act III he abruptly
proposes to Diana, urging, in terms familiar to Shaw's Sir George
Crofts, his case according to economic merit:

> ... most women would consider it a good offer – an offer worth
> considering.
> *Diana.* I have no doubt of that.
> *Sir Jabez.* Forty thousand a year, to say nothing of the title. It's brand
> new, of course – but –
> *Diana.* ...You wouldn't like me to accept you for what you've got.
> *Sir Jabez* (*doggedly*). I'm not so sure that I shouldn't. (42)

Such an 'unbusinesslike' refusal by Diana might be thought curious
from a character whose author insisted upon the economic imperative of marriage. But we must not forget that *Diana of Dobson's*
is a romantic comedy and although Hamilton argues that a woman's
interest in romance has a commercial or business aspect – marriage being interpreted by her as a 'process of barter' with a woman
exchanging 'possession of her person for the means of existence'
(*Marriage* 27) – she maintains from the outset that a woman's
interest is not limited to economic considerations but is in fact
'double-motived'. In other words physical attraction, love, sentiment also have a place. Such a view offers an interesting gloss on
Sir Jabez's neat bifurcation of sentiment and business into separate
compartments, since Hamilton would argue that while marriage is
assuredly a business matter for women, a financially advantageous
marriage without love (or for that matter a love match without
adequate money) is the stuff of tragedy. It is a position she gives
dramatic significance to in a play entitled, appropriately enough, *A
Matter of Money*, produced first at the Royalty Theatre, Glasgow
under the title *The Cutting of the Knot* (13 March 1911) and then by
Edith Craig and the Pioneer Players at the Little Theatre on February 9 and11, 1913.[18] 'A painfully depressing' piece (*Stage* 13 Feb

1913, 18), it 'brings out with much power an unromantic aspect of the popular drama of husband, lover and wife' (*Sketch* 19 February 1913, 204), that 'unromantic aspect' being Hamilton's insistence upon the love/money nexus. The play's protagonist, another ill-educated woman of the middle class hopelessly unequipped to earn her living in any other way, remains married to a man she loathes but cannot afford to leave, channelling her 'thwarted energies' into an affair with a poor, married doctor. When her husband – who despises his wife in turn but refuses to agree to a separation out of 'lust of mastery and the pleasure of holding and hurting' (11) – learns of her affair and confronts her with his knowledge in what was praised as a skillfully contrived cat-and-mouse scene, she promptly leaves him and the 'slavery' of that life for what she romantically envisions will be 'open and un-ashamed flight with a man who loved and was loved' (110). Unfor-tunately, her country doctor must confess a 'sordid financial complication' (216) – he hasn't the means, nor apparently the inclination, to flee: 'he had to pay in hard cash for his pleasant kisses, and the woman to whom he had given them in secret had learned how he grudged the payment – had learned that the price she set on herself was a price he esteemed too high' (216). Without support, financial and other-wise, the heroine, by her own estimate 'quite a useless person [who's] never done a day's real work', chooses suicide at the level crossing.

Although *A Matter of Money* was generally praised by reviewers, male critics objected to the characterisation of their sex, taking particular umbrage at Hamilton's portrayal of the play's doctor which they regarded as a maligning of male professionalism. The *Era* for instance, which interpreted the play as a study of man's culpability, objected that 'the two principal male characters are miserable wretches: scarcely fair samples, and the conduct of both at times is most improbable' (15 Feb 1913, 15). The *Stage* hazarded that Hamilton's 'design probably was to show how mean, base, selfish, cowardly and generally despicable men are' (13 Feb 1913, 18). Only the (female) reviewer for *Votes for Women* discerned no gender bias. In her view 'the men and women concerned behave as real men and women probably would in real life, setting at naught all those theories of existence in obedience to which, if obedience were possible, they would have behaved quite differently' (14 Feb 1913, 287). Not so, urged the critics for the *Sketch* and the *Stage* who were curiously insistent that the doctor would have resisted temptation, 'particularly seeing that the sin in the case of a doctor is peculiarly heinous' (*Sketch* 19 Feb 1913, 204), 'tending, as it does, to undermine one's confidence in the medical profession generally' (*Stage*).

Of course heinous sin and a tragic denouement are not the stuff of romantic comedy, and in *Diana of Dobson's* the heroine is free to reject her moneyed suitor, who has 'the heartlessness to grind a fortune out of underpaid work-girls' (42), because she does not like him. And his is not, after all, the only proposal she receives in the elegant sitting-room of the Hotel Engadine, where, according to the *Dramatic Mirror*'s review of the September 1908 New York production, she 'makes the men fall in love with her' (undated clipping, NYPL). In a nice variation on her own theory, Hamilton projects what she characterises as women's 'double-motived' interest in romance and marriage upon a male character, although it is significant that it is Victor's match-making aunt who first insists upon his need to marry for money. Succumbing to her pressure, the extravagant Captain Victor Bretherton, who seems incapable of supporting himself on an unearned income of £600 a year, stumbles out his confession of love to the widow Diana on the promise of her seeming fortune. And despite Victor's accusation to the contrary, Diana does not behave as a conventional adventuress-cum-woman-with-a-past. She does not, like a Lady Audley or a Mrs Dane, manoeuvre him into a marriage proposal only to have her scheme exposed by the play's hero or raisonneur. In fact, there is no need for their obligatory cross-examinations. Before she is prepared to entertain Victor's offer (she considers it unspoken in the meantime) she reveals herself, like Levering in *Votes for Women!*, as a 'woman with a future'. Unbidden, she confesses to being in truth a penniless spinster 'who has so far degraded herself as to work for her own living' (52). When Victor adopts the part of outraged innocent, however, Diana rounds on him 'with an energy a fighting Suffragette might envy', according to Walbrook (*Pall Mall* 13 Feb 1908, 4), condemning his hypocrisy as well as the utter uselessness of his life and concluding with an attack upon the values of his class that a number of reviewers characterised as a form of stage 'socialism':

> ... for the life of me, I cannot understand how you and your like have the impertinence to look down on me and mine? When you thought I had married an old man for his money, you considered that I had acted in a seemly and womanly manner – when you learnt that, instead of selling

myself in the marriage market – I have earned my living honestly, you consider me impossible. (52)

Such Fabian sympathies as they were described by the reviewer for *Reynolds* – he saw the play as a 'Fabian tract' containing 'a bit of Bernard Shaw's parasite theory' (16 Feb 1908) – are subsumed however by the play's preoccupation with gender. The act ends with a challenge that will result in another merging of male into the specifically female experience of the play as Diana dares Victor to live as she has lived:

> ... try the experiment for yourself. Stand with your back against the wall as I've stood for the last six years, and fight the world for your daily bread on your own hand.... You simply couldn't do it – you'd throw up the sponge in a week. (53)

In a condescending passage that reveals his own anti-feminist bias Walbrook describes the effect of the act's conclusion: 'Victorious Femininity gathers its rustling skirts around it and sweeps triumphantly from [Victor's] presence; and down comes the curtain upon Act III, amid a cheer from the men in the theatre and an ecstatic clapping from the ladies, who have enjoyed seeing one of the tyrants (audi Mrs Pankhurst!) put in his place!' (*Pall Mall* 13 Feb 1908, 4).

For the play's final act, the posh drawing-room of Acts II and III has been translated in turn into 'that place of ill-omen, the Thames Embankment' (*Illustrated London News* 22 Feb 1908, 266). We have, it would appear, traced Diana's theatrical odyssey from naturalistic drama through society comedy to arrive in the realm of what one reviewer characterised as 'transpontine melodrama'. And certainly the sight of 'the Thames Embankment in the small hours of a November morning' (55) conjured up an extensive tradition (literary and pictorial as well as specifically theatrical) which coupled that locale with grim scenes of desperation and suicide 'which disturbed the imagination of the age' (*World* 19 Jan 1909, 97).[19] It is not, however, a helpless, homeless Diana we detect amid that ragged pile of human misery asleep on an Embankment bench. It is Victor, only recently descended to 'the hopelessly unemployed class' (55), who is being prodded along by Police Constable Fellowes. The very Robertson-ian meeting of old soldiers that follows (Fellowes was in Victor's company of the Welsh Guards) provides Victor with an opportunity to explain why he is 'masquerading on this Embankment in these delectable garments' (56). He has not, as Fellowes, immediately assumes, suffered "eavy financial losses'; rather he has taken Diana up on her challenge.[20] Perhaps Hamilton took an exchange between characters in Jones's *Masqueraders* (1894) as fodder for her own plot:

> *Dulcie.* ... Nell, Mr Remon has an odd notion that this world isn't real.
> *Helen.* The cure for that is to earn half-a-crown a day and live on it.
> *David.* Oh yes, I know. Work is real. (82)

So Victor discovers, although lack of work rather than work itself would more accurately describe his experience of the real world. As he says to Fellowes:

> ... How on earth does a man set about earning his own livelihood? I don't mean a man who has been through a Board School and has had a trade at his fingers' end, but a man who has muddled through Eton and Oxford and had practically no education at all? From my experience of the last few weeks, I should say that all trades were closed to the man whose education has cost his father more than five hundred a year. (57)

What Hamilton is attempting to do here is expose a well-placed man of the period to the common experience of his middle- and upper-class sisters, whose so-called 'education' left them equally incapable of earning an independent livelihood. Her efforts were not universally appreciated. In fact, a number of critics seemed genuinely distressed at what they perceived to be Victor's singular behaviour. The reviewer for *Reynolds*, for instance, dismissed it as 'too absurd', adding, 'Why didn't he fit himself for a trade, or business, or profession as he could easily have done? His conduct is sheer lunacy' (16 Feb 1908). Walbrook could explain it only by insisting ironically, given Victor's desire to experience it, that 'this is not real life. In the world of fact Victor would have obtained a berth somewhere, or his friends would have done it for him' (*Pall Mall* 13 Feb 1908, 4). As for Diana, who we learn later is in like straitened circumstances, Walbrook is charitable enough to add that 'with her gifts of speech, presence, and general capability, [she] would surely have found a situation as a companion, or, at the worst, as a general servant'. It is difficult to know whether these reviewers were more disturbed at Diana's decision to 'waste' her legacy or at Victor's determination not to spend his. In the words of the *Illustrated Sporting and Dramatic News*, 'if they were a couple – not absolutely born fools – with sufficient mind to modify their actions, one would say that it is as unreasonable for a man with six hundred pounds a year to starve because a woman has lectured him, as for the woman herself who has known the tyranny of genteel poverty, to throw away the equivalent of twelve years' earnings in a month's "burst"' (7 March 1908, 19). But perhaps this reviewer has betrayed a more fundamental objection. It might be said that what really distressed him as well as others was not so much Victor's decision to strike out on his own, but that he was prompted to do it by a woman, worse yet (as another critic points out), by a woman who 'has vanished out of his life. ... He is martyr- ising himself for an idea – or for the angry word of a girl whose own position was not unimpeachable' (*Stage* 13 Feb 1908, 23).

Of course, Diana does not disappear for ever from Victor's life. The long arm of coincidence intervenes, and while Victor struggles to sleep, she re-enters to take a seat on the far corner of his bench. Her appearance is strangely altered, the attractive Paris frocks of the second and third acts replaced by the costume of the habitu- ally unemployed: 'a shabby hat and coat, a short skirt, muddy boots and woollen gloves with holes in several of the finger- tips'(58),[21] her life's possessions wrapped in 'a small brown-paper parcel'. One is reminded of Vida Levering's cry in *Votes for Women!*: 'Some girls think it hardship to have to earn their living. The horror is not to be allowed to' (51). Given such a scenario, one could be forgiven for anticipating a sensational melodramatic conclusion in which a despairing woman resolves to end it all with a grim leap off the Embankment.[22] But Hamilton rejects sensationalism in favour of more restrained comedy. We see not abject poverty but Cinderella after the stroke of twelve. This does not mean that Hamilton's protagonist adopts the passive and acquiescent man- ner of, for instance, Robertson's more conventional stage-hero- ines; even in the face of adversity Diana maintains an energetic and confrontational 'sub-acid' style. Nor does the 'invertebrate' Victor, whose chronic weakness drew a mutter of disapproval from critics, suddenly develop the stature of the heroic manly man. The play does not end with a melodramatic windfall; neither Diana nor Victor realises a sum vast enough to finance the way of life they enjoyed in the Swiss Alps. Victor simply takes another look at his circumstances and realises that far from being 'a miserable pit- tance, hardly enough ... to live upon', his £600 a year is 'not only enough for *one* to live upon—it's ample for *two*' (62).[23] Diana is also invited to take a second look at Victor when, in an inversion of

attitudes, he offers her 'proprietary rights in a poor backboneless
creature who never did a useful thing in his life' (62). And given that
Diana of Dobson's is the work of a playwright consciously attempting to write from a woman's perspective, it is not surprising that
the protagonist goes on to demonstrate a 'business-like' attitude
which Hamilton argues in *Marriage as a Trade* is an aspect of love
for women generally ignored in that bulk of women's writing that
merely mimics men's work. Accordingly, when Victor proposes
Diana responds in a way that exposes her 'double-motived' interest
in matrimony:

> *Diana (turning on him almost fiercely)*. Captain Bretherton – I'm home-
> less and penniless – I haven't—tasted food for nearly twelve hours –
> I've been half starved for days. And now, if I understand you aright –
> you offer to make me your wife.
> *Bretherton*. You do understand me aright.
> *Diana*. That is to say, you offer me a home and what is to me a fortune.
> *Bretherton*. And myself.
> *Diana (laughing harshly)*. And yourself – please don't imagine I forget
> that important item .... (62)

With no other trade readily available to her, Diana accepts marriage, although in deference to the demands of the genre (as well as
the box-office?) Hamilton's 'Cinderella' apparently enters 'the
housekeeping trade' in order to love as well as to live. I qualify the
latter statement because in the eyes of one reviewer at least,
Diana's love for Victor is not self-evident: 'It is not Miss Ashwell's
fault that the audience does not know exactly what to think of the
girl and her masquerade. ... The position would be simplified if it
had been brought out that Diana is in love with Bretherton. The
author does not free Diana from the suggestion that she is a selfish,
hard, and not over-scrupulous young woman' (*Stage* 13 Feb 1908,
23). As far as this critic is concerned, Diana might well be an
adventuress after all.

Similar suspicions greeted the heroine's decision to marry in
Hamilton's later comedy, *Just to Get Married*, which was successfully produced by AFL member Gertrude Kingston at the Little
Theatre, opening on 8 November 1910.[24] Like *Diana of Dobson's* this
play is concerned with the compulsory nature of marriage, not,
however, from the perspective of a penniless working woman but
rather from the position of a woman who is part of 'that small but
prominent class which will not educate its girls and fit them for

earning their own living, and yet is unable to provide them with sufficient income to live independently in the comfort to which they have been accustomed' (*Englishwoman* 1910, 214). Georgiana Vicary, Hamilton's poor and orphaned protagonist, has been raised by well-to-do relations to be 'a helpless incapable': 'What can I do – nothing, except dress myself and put my hair in pins at night and keep my eyes open for a likely husband' (68). Although she envies an unmarried friend gainfully employed in London – a woman who 'doesn't have to cadge around for a man to keep her' (75) – it is a life that Georgiana, 'a victim of our social organisation' (*Athenaeum* 12 Nov 1910, 601), cannot emulate. Brought up with tastes too fastidious for a working life that entails 'pigging it in a three pair back on a pound a week' (76), Georgiana has been raised to be utterly dependent upon others. Accordingly, Hamilton's unfortunate spinster of twenty-nine is desperately conniving (with the aid of her 'manoeuvring, beguiling, scheming' relations) to wrangle a proposal out of the man she considers to be her last hope.[25] Like Diana, she is outfitted for the part she is to play, only in Georgiana's case her 'nice new expensive frock was a [marital] speculation'. So too the new hats, Georgiana's aunt having 'stuck at nothing that she thought might possibly make [her ward] more attractive' (13); clothes, it would appear, make the marriageable woman, but it is a constructed figure, the play reveals, of humbug and degradation (55). The husband-to-be finally does propose and this 'perfectly useless woman', as she calls herself, accepts because 'I wanted to get married – because my relations wanted me to get married. Because every woman is expected to get herself a husband, somehow or another, and is looked on as a miserable failure if she doesn't' (56). Unfortunately, her prospective husband really loves her and Georgiana, uncomfortable with his amorous effusiveness and guilt-ridden by her own mercenary interest, breaks off the engagement and resolves to flee to London. In a final act much indebted to *Diana of Dobson's*, a transformed Georgiana makes her appearance looking like a 'second-hand scarecrow': 'her long cloak is splashed and caked with mud, and the feathers in her hat are out of curl and soaked with rain' (70). A coincidental meeting *à la* Diana and Victor follows as Georgiana's despondent suitor finds her waiting on the train platform. Hamilton departs from the *Diana of Dobson's* model, however, by insisting that her heroine 'plot' herself into marriage. In a conclusion meant to disturb by its self-conscious juggling of theatrical contrivance,

Georgiana proposes to her erstwhile-rejected fiancé: 'It's awful, it's impossible, it's unwomanly, but you'll never ask me again, so I must ask you – because I care....' (85).

It was a 'happy ending' that provoked critical debate. One critic confessed that he had left the theatre after the first act, it being 'perfectly obvious what would happen next. The engaged people would marry, the man would discover his wife had accepted him "just to get married"; there would be a period of discomfort and suspense; and in the end the wife would fall in love with her husband' (*Saturday Review* 12 Nov 1910, 607). 'It was a breach of theatrical decorum,' he declares, 'that she did not.' Others less witty objected that the conclusion was weak and unconvincing, rather perfunctorily tacked on to what was in truth 'the tragedy of the undowered poor relation, who looks to marriage to secure her independence' (*Era* 2 November 1910, 23). Marjorie Stratchey, on the other hand, a critic for the *Englishwoman*, found Georgiana's last-moment avowal of love 'perfectly plausible', in fact dictated by the demands of the play's genre: 'To have sent off the unhappy Georgiana to starve in London, or to have dragged her back to her insufferable relations, would have been like stuffing seaweed into a bisque on the plea of realism' (1910, 214). Although for Stratchey, the play's *idée mere* had 'stuff in it for a tragedy, and a very sombre tragedy', the 'social reformer' in Hamilton was better served by comedy, which 'may with impunity – even with advantage – be didactic'. 'Had she written a tragedy', Stratchey concluded', 'she would have been accused of exaggeration and undue pessimism', a reasonably accurate description of the critical response to *A Matter of Money*. Finally there were those who suspected Georgiana's love for the hero, although according to the reviewer for the *Sketch*, such doubts about the heroine's sincerity rendered the conclusion of *Just to Get Married* 'cruel, cynical and legitimate' (16 Oct 1911, 170). It was, in other words, a problem play masquerading as comedy with aesthetic contrivance signalling social compulsion.

Diana of Dobson's, which enjoyed a generally more favourable critical reception, nevertheless engendered a like debate over its purpose and genre. Some reviewers praised what they considered to be Hamilton's 'ingenious blend' of social criticism and romance to produce a 'thinking-man's' comedy. The *Illustrated London News* urged play-goers to attend a work that would make them 'think and laugh' (22 Feb 1908, 266) while the *World*, adopting a more conde-scending tone towards London audiences, insisted: 'It is a complete success in that it holds the unsophisticated with its "roe-mance", while the more hardened playgoer is amused and interested by the clever touches which serve to hide the framework: by the humour, the satire, the study of character, the criticism of life' (19 Jan 1909, 97). Others suspected the veracity of the play's conclusion but condoned it as part and parcel of Hamilton's fairytale format. The redoubtable critic for the *Stage* on the other hand insisted upon seeing the play by the light of naturalist theatre and looked forward to a bleak future: 'The audience, at the back of its mind, must have a vague uneasiness about the suitableness of the match and the likelihood of happiness. The married pair, too, will have to reckon with Bretherton's family, especially with the aunt, ...' (13 Feb 1908, 23). A more intriguing complaint was lodged by two reviewers who argued that Hamilton's play had in essence betrayed the labour cause. According to Walbrook, until the end of the third act *Diana of Dobson's* 'is a rather roughly composed tract on the harsh conditions of labour and ignominy of pampered laziness', but the fourth act 'arbitrarily as well as sentimentally' dismisses these issues and their ramifications by opting to save Diana through marriage to a man and his adequate unearned income. The critic for the *Illustrated Sporting and Dramatic News* goes further. He maintains that although the play is intended to argue the rights of labour against the abuses of capital it actually makes the opposite case by failing to portray 'capital ... [as] unreasonable and labour sensible and worthy' (7 March 1908, 19).

To insist however that the play suffers because it *does not*, in melodramatic fashion, divide labour and capital into clearly demarked camps of good and evil or because it *does*, in melodramatic fashion, side-step such issues by means of a limited and specific solution, is to ignore Hamilton's choice of genre as well as the play's feminist component. For the attack in *Diana of Dobson's* upon class and capitalism is inexorably bound up with the play's comedic demonstration of Hamilton's claim 'that the narrowing down of woman's hopes and ambitions to the sole pursuit and sphere of marriage is one of the principal causes of the various disabilities, economic and otherwise, under which she labours ...' (*Marriage* 22). Hamilton is concerned with depicting the consequences for women of a patriarchal hierarchy which treated them as mere adjuncts to men and, by insisting that their proper role was marriage and proper place the home, saw no reason to educate them to earn their own livelihood. If, however, a woman failed to secure said husband and home and was forced to support herself, immediately rendering her social position uncertain, she found that virtually all work available to her was intellectually and emotionally unrewarding, low in status and notoriously ill-paid, 'the custom of considering her work as worthless (from an economic point of view) [which] originated in the home, ... [having] followed her into the world' (*Marriage* 96). Hamilton argued that women as a class were both socially and economically handicapped in a culture that privileged men. Within such a culture money gave power, as Hamilton is at pains to demonstrate in *Diana of Dobson's*, providing women with an independence from men otherwise unrealisable. Unfortunately, most women lacked such moneyed power and were, by various strategies of a patriarchal system, largely prevented from realising it (one is reminded in this regard of the discriminatory inheritance legislation of the period). With most of the work available to them absolutely unrewarding and many better occupations barred to them through custom, regulation or lack of education, women had little choice but to consider 'marriage as a trade'. It is a credit to Hamilton's craftsmanship that in the last act of *Diana of Dobson's* she is able to exploit the conventions of romantic comedy (which dictate some form of marital resolution) to offer a feminist critique upon marriage as romance, one that demonstrates her contention that 'a woman in love is not only a woman swayed by emotion, but a human being engaged in carving for herself a career or securing for herself a means of livelihood' (*Marriage* 117). Hamilton concludes her play with a literal cup-and-saucer tableau of the happy couple enjoying sandwiches and coffee perched on a bench on the Thames Embankment. Yet this final image, too, is problematic. Can we take at face value Hamilton's display of male chivalry (it is, after all, Victor who fetches the coffee) or must we view with an ironic eye her final resolution? One could certainly argue that the taint of domesticity has merely followed Diana to the river's edge.

Notes

1 These plays were *The Wisdom of the Wise* (St James's, 22 November 1900), *The Bishop's Move* (Garrick, 7 June 1902) and *The Flute of Pan* (Shaftesbury, 12 November 1904). In addition, her one-act play, *A Repentance*, was produced at the St. James's on 28 February 1899. None of these plays enjoyed the critical acclaim awarded *The Ambassador*. In fact *The Flute of Pan* closed after only twelve performances and Craigie was so incensed by what she considered

unfair press notices that she arranged a free single performance at which time she polled the audience on their reaction to the play. The verdict was 1,200 against the play's first night condemnation with many accompanying statements of approval while 8 registered qualified disapproval.

2 Robins published her first novels under the name of C. E. Raymond and her first play, *Alan's Wife*, was produced anonymously.

3 So prevalent was the view that critics were biased against women writers that Gertrude Kingston at the Little Theatre adopted a policy of withholding all authors' names.

4 Hamilton insisted that she 'became a feminist on the day I perceived that – according to the story [of Lucrece] – her 'honour' was not a moral but a physical quality. Once that was clear to me my youthful soul rebelled; it was insulting to talk of 'honour' and 'virtue' in a woman as if they were matters of chance ...' (*Life Errant* 282).

5 Curiously, however, given Hamilton's position on the feminist/suffragist divide, Showalter claims that 'she bogged down in her efforts to connect women's literature to the specific goal of the vote' (225).

6 Hamilton was also thrown out of work on two occasions to be replaced by a manager's mistress: 'no fault was found with the playing of my part, but it was wanted for other than professional reasons, and therefore I had to go'. She goes on to elaborate upon what she calls 'the intrusion of the sex-element into the business relations of men and women ... To a much greater degree than men, women are engaged by their employers for reasons which have no connection with fitness for their work; because they have the right shape of nose, the right shade of hair, or a particularly pleasing smile' (*Life Errant* 47).

7 *Fanny's First Play* was among the most successful of Edwardian productions, running for 622 performances (Trewin, *Edwardian Theatre* 156).

8 In her autobiography Lena Ashwell notes that 'All the heroines [of that period] were young. Heroes might be any age, but the older women were merely backgrounds to the drama. Now that it is not always easy to distinguish between a mother and daughter, and women of sixty or more can, and do, look half their age, it is hard to believe that forty was considered old, and that 'too old at forty', practically a new cry about men, had been for long the slogan for women' (81).

9 According to Knoblock, '*Diana of Dobson's* had originally a somewhat misleading title. We searched about for another one. The heroine being called Diana, we thought it might be good to join it up with the name of the shop at which she worked' (*Round the Room* 91).

10 The Cinderella story proved accessible to Shaw as well, who produced his own Fabian reconstruction of the romance in *Pygmalion*, written six years after *Diana of Dobson's*.

11 In order to assure the accuracy of her stage picture, Hamilton requested that Margaret Bondfield, organiser for the Shop Assistants' Union (and later Britain's first woman cabinet minister) read the play before it went into rehearsal to determine if any factual errors had been made. Bondfield suggested only two changes, one concerning the proper amount of a fine for burning gas after 11 o'clock at night, and the other regarding the reckoning of wages (apparently women's salaries were calculated by the year and not by the week as Hamilton had thought). Not surprisingly, the Shop Assistants' Union considered the play a useful piece of propaganda and invited Hamilton to speak at their meetings.

12 There was agitation throughout the period for legislation which would improve the working and living conditions of shop assistants although nothing much came of it prior to the War. The plight of women shop assistants was used by the suffrage movement as another example of women's need for the vote: 'Many shop women do not receive pay sufficient for their work, they are badly fed and

housed, and no regard is given to their physical or moral health; they have no votes to give, and therefore Members of Parliament do not concern themselves about their condition' (*Common Cause* 19 May 1910, 89).

13 In Margery Morgan's words, 'the dramatist lays out the world he sees documentary-fashion, to suggest the simultaneous existence of contrasted groups within the great Edwardian middle class' (Intro xxv-vi).

14 In an article entitled 'A Plea for the Shop-Girl', for instance, the suffrage writer concludes: 'Only women can understand how their fellow-women suffer, and can bring plainly before the country the hardships of a shop-girl's lot, and by striving to obtain a vote, gain means to legislate for better conditions. I am sure that when all right-thinking men realise that only women can deal with questions respecting women's sufferings and hardships they will support the women's franchise' (*Common Cause* 19 May 1910, 89).

15 I am indebted to Viv Gardner for the suggestion that Hamilton's choice of the surname 'Massingberd' for Diana might have been intended as an acknowledgement of Mrs Massingberd, who founded the Pioneer Club in London in 1892. According to David Rubenstein, 'From its inception the club was intended as a home for women of advanced views ... Members were expected to hew a path through the jungle of prejudice and outdated ideas, guided by their own convictions and uninhibited by the constraints of convention. If any single institution could claim to be the home of the new woman it was the Pioneer Club' (222).

16 Diana's thrill at seeing the Swiss Alps mirrored Hamilton's own pleasant memory of her 'first sight of the Alps from a railway window in the pale grey of morning' (*Life Errant* 58). Hamilton was undoubtedly one of those romantic but hopelessly 'unsophisticated Cook's tourists', taking her 'five guineas' worth of lovely Lucerne' who are ridiculed by the 'ornamental class' in the play.

17 At least one reviewer attributed the authorship of *Fanny's First Play* (originally produced anonymously, thereby mirroring the action of the play) to Hamilton.

18 Although Liz Whitelaw records that *A Matter of Money* was published by Lacey's (*sic*) (French's) in 1911, it is a claim I have been unable to verify. There seem to be no copies of the playscript in existence. Searches through the Lord Chamberlain's Plays at the British Library, at the Ellen Terry House (which also houses records of Edith Craig's Pioneer Players), and at the Fawcett Collection, as well as inquiries to Air Marshal Sir Leslie Bower RAF (Retd), executor of Cicely Hamilton's estate, failed to unearth any copies. The catalogues of the British Library and the Library of Congress do not list the play. My account of the work is derived from contemporary reviews, newspaper precis, and the novel (1916) version of the play.

19 For a consideration of the Thames Embankment as 'the locus classicus of self-determined death' both real and fictive, see John Stokes's *In the Nineties* 139-143.

20 In fact, it was not unknown in the period for the curious to 'experience' poverty. According to Pember Reeves in her study of the London poor, various middle-class people chose to live on 3*d* a day in order to demonstrate that it was possible for a working man to do so as well. Reeves is rightly critical of such 'experiments' which did not require the well-to-do person to actually live among the poor, or to cut down expenses, other than for food, to the lowest possible level (*Round About a Pound a Week* 143-4). Apropos this point, Ashwell refers to three young women actors who decided to experience starving on the Thames Embankment so they could depict it more realistically on stage. Accordingly, 'after a good supper at the Carlton and having provided themselves with a bag of buns, they sat through the summer night, enduring the pangs of hunger, gazing at the Thames' (*Myself a Player* 120).

21 Diana's various changes of dress (and address) serve as a comedic demonstration of Vida Levering's account of how she exchanged her fine dresses for 'an old

gown and a tawdry hat' in order to really experience the plight of poor, homeless women: 'You'll never know how many things are hidden from a woman in good clothes. The bold, free look of a man at a woman he believes to be destitute – you must feel that look on you before you can understand – a good half of history' (*Votes for Women!* 50).

22 In fact, in an interview before the play opened Ashwell was asked, 'I see that the Thames Embankment is chosen as the scene of the last act. That has rather a grim suggestiveness, taken in connection with the fact that Mr Norman McKinnel plays the part of a policeman. I hope Diana is not driven to attempt suicide and is rescued only by the strong arm of the law?' (*Pall Mall* 8 Feb 1908).

23 Such an income would put Victor and Diana squarely into the realm of the middle class. Statistics for the last quarter of the nineteenth century placed a 'profess-ional man or tradesman' earning £500 a year into the 'upper middle class' (Best 90).

24 The play ran for 31 performances and was revived in January 1911 for another 30 performances.

25 The same week that *Just to Get Married* opened, Hubert Henry Davies's *A Single Man* appeared at the Playhouse and given that Davies's play deals in comic fashion with the efforts of a forty-year-old man to marry, the two works invited comparison. One of those vying (unsuccessfully of course) for the hand of Davies's bachelor is a conventional stage spinster whose lack of success is due, according to one reviewer, to Davies's 'masculine dislike of her' (*Athenaeum* 12 Nov 1910, 601). But 'strip [that spinster] ... of her nauseous affectations, her ridiculous poses, and her general atmosphere of theatrical fake, and you have Georgiana Vicary, the very real woman who dominates Miss Hamilton's comedy' (*World* 15 Nov 1910, 726).

IV

Elizabeth Baker
'You're married ... You're settled'

In certain recent feminist theatre criticism, realism is presented as a 'conservative force that reproduces and reinforces dominant cultural relations' (Dolan 84). In offering audiences a 'seamless illusion', it is argued, realism precludes interrogation, portraying an arbitrary but self-serving orthodoxy as both natural and inevitable. As such, realism becomes tainted and counterproductive, of use only to those who would endorse a bourgeois hegemony with its consequent enshrinement of domus, family and patriarch. This position raises a number of problems, beginning with its assumption of a simple and direct relationship between reproduction and reinforcement. While genres or styles – realism has been claimed as both – may not be politically neutral, they are surely capable of presenting a range of ideological positions. Why may not realism's recognisable worlds be used to challenge or condemn as well as mystify and naturalise social relations? Indeed, from Ibsen and Shaw to Osborne, Orton and Hare, male playwrights have been quick to recognise the efficacy of replication in attacking normative ideology. In fact, historically those forms of theatre that have most actively endorsed the authority of Church and State – the medieval morality play and Stuart masque come immediately to mind – have been both hieratic and emblematic. This is not to ignore the possibility that 'too much furniture, or walls that [are] too tight, [can] create the effect of an unchangeable world, a "fated" world' (States 90); it is merely to insist that realist drama is not necessarily the expression of a coherent (unassailable) view of the world; it is rather a tool, or variety of tools, for shaping social perception. Kent's general comments on the language of early feminist discourse are apt: 'the language of fact and concrete reality was meant to expose, by contrast, the emptiness of idealised depictions of womanhood and the marital state' (85).

The second problem I have with current attacks upon realism is an apparent reluctance to allow for historical positioning. The contrast, for example, Dolan draws between Brecht's 'exercise in complex seeing' (good) and the 'seduction of the illusionist [i.e. realist] text' (bad) sounds remarkably like Shaw's claim in the 1890s that his own keen-eyed 'realism' (good) could correct the unthinking complicity of 'romantic [i.e. illusionistic] drama' (bad). As Bert States has observed of productions of Brecht, an observation that holds true for Shaw as well, 'It is not the stage illusion that is undercut, or even the illusion that the stage represents a certain kind of "Nature"; what is undercut is simply the conventional system of current theatre' (95). Furthermore, as States elaborates, 'the 'arbitrary' mode of representation does not, in itself, assure the basis of a "critical" theatre. It may, indeed, have been the best kind of theatre for Brecht's project, but this is a little like saying that iambic pentameter was the best kind of language for Shakespeare's. Brecht's theatre, like Shakespeare's, is what he left us and one can draw no conclusions about its form being the best or the correct one for his and similar projects' (97). Push Brecht into a period like our own, in which audiences have come to expect, rather than be unsettled by, his bag of alienation tricks and you have the structural 'disruptions' of *Mahagonny* amusing wealthy audiences at New York's Metropolitan Opera. Indeed, one is as likely today to encounter elements of Brecht's 'epic theatre' on Broadway or in London's West End as in the alternative performance spaces Jill Dolan praises. The point, in both cases, is that while dramatic and theatrical styles may be developed or adopted to naturalise or challenge particular positions, dramatic forms are not in themselves narrowly partisan. They may be inhabited from within by a variety of ideologies.

What strikes me as particularly germane about the work of Elizabeth Baker and Githa Sowerby (considered in the next chapter) is that both employ stage realism as a means of indicting the societies they depict, exploiting what Austin Quigley has identified as 'the tension in natualism between replicating the surfaces of the world and revealing underlying forces in the world' (124). Baker's use of realism as a container for her feminist ideology may be illustrated by *Miss Tassey*, first staged at the Court Theatre on 20 March 1910, and revived by Miss Horniman at the Court on 22 May 1913. A starkly realist piece, *Miss Tassey* paints a 'grim little picture of the living-in system ... with all its malignant conditions and abuses' (*Stage* 29 May 1913, 23). Set in 'bedroom No. 65' of yet another drapery establishment, it explores the tragic potential of such a life only hinted at in Hamilton's *Diana of Dobson's*. Its action – characterised by the *Era* as 'lack of incident' (26 March 1910, 13) – consists of the transformation of a black-garbed shop assistant into a scarlet and white pierette whose object is to arouse her lover and facilitate her escape from the extreme exploitation of her employment. Such calculated resort to clothing's erotic appeal in the play (an interesting inversion of the undressing scene in Hamilton's play), with its concomitant suggestion of prostitution/vice, underscores the interconnectedness of women's economic and social oppression within a male hegemony that leaves them no discernible option.[1] The economic imperative for such erotic display challenges a reading that explained such appearance as proof of women's 'overflowing sexuality', to use Hamilton's ironic phrase, a challenge made more explicit through the suicide of a co-worker which takes place in the background of the play's 'dress-up'. The Miss Tassey of the play's title is a forty-five-year-old spinster who apparently 'missed her chance' at matrimony, and has just been dismissed from her job as a result of her age and infirmity (the latter a direct consequence of the conditions of her employment). Faced with a bleak future of increasing deprivation, she chooses death by drug overdose.[2] Through its juxtaposition of the two incidents, Baker's play stands as an obvious challenge to the period's conservative 'system of reading that linked female desire for clothes to vice' (Valverde 181); in *Miss Tassey* effective manipulation of such finery is shown as a means of economic survival, the accusation of 'vice' redirected by the play against a system that compels women into the service of male sexuality. The effects achieved through the work's concentrated and (largely sustained) singleness of purpose make their own best case. They would, moreover, stamp Baker as the movement's most consistent realist voice.

Like Robins and Hamilton, Baker worked for the suffrage movement. Apparently sympathetic to the National Union of Women's Suffrage Societies, her name appears on the list of subscribers included in the NUWSS's 1909-10 Annual Report. She was also actively involved with the WWSL, her one-act play *Edith* (see Chapter II) being performed as part of a fund-raising event organised by that League in 1912. Like its companion pieces in the suffrage repertoire, *Edith* represents an attack upon conventional stage portraits of women as either passive heroines or assertive villain-esses defined primarily in terms of their relationships with men. Shaw of course had already begun to experiment with assertive heroines in the 1890s, although in his plays such characters usually display their aggression in such traditional areas of female endeav-our as marriage and motherhood. One is reminded particularly of Blanche Sartorius, Raina Petkoff, Gloria Clandon and Candida. Shavian women who instead wish to channel celibate energy solely into the male sphere of the work-place (Vivie Warren and Proserpine Garnett spring to mind) are doused with authorial ambivalence. By way of contrast, Baker's *Edith* provides a clear and positive alternative for women unhappy with a society that saw them as mere adjuncts to their husbands, confining them to the home to perform the suitably feminine labour of housework and childcare. As a theatrical role, Edith also serves as one of Baker's contributions to the campaign to produce more varied, less stere-otypical women's parts. A successful unmarried businesswoman, Edith obviously enjoys the independence that self-employment and spinsterhood provide her. Neither employee, wife nor mother, she avoids the subjugation to a dominant male will that is so often presented in suffrage theatre as an inevitable aspect of those 'occupations'. In fact, in her business negotiations throughout the course of the play, Edith invariably bests the men. As such she stands in marked contrast to the other more conventional women of the piece, who as wife, widow, mother or fiancé, are presented as helpless victims of the vagaries of their respective male partners' wills.

Baker did not, of course, restrict her playwriting to polemical tracts designed for performance before suffrage sympathisers. When she appears in accounts of Edwardian theatre, her name is generally linked to innovative repertory companies in London, Manchester and Birmingham. To provide subject-matter for plays written for the wider audiences of the more experimental wing of the commercial theatre, she drew upon her own lower middle-class background; indeed the insistence of reviewers upon the manner in which Baker's work was informed by her life, class and gender should lay to rest the myth of the invisibility of the realist writer. Born in London, Baker began her career as a cashier but soon settled upon work as a stenographer and private secretary, appar-ently writing plays in her leisure hours (Clark 306).[3] She was

encouraged by the positive reception awarded her first piece, a
one-act play about cross-class alliance entitled *Beastly Pride* (originally *A Question of Caste*), initially performed in 1907 by the Croy-
don Repertory Theatre. Like all of Baker's plays, it was criticised as
'lacking in incident' (*Era* l April 1914, 14) as that was understood by
critics schooled on melodrama and the well-made-play. Its static
nature, however, helped focus attention upon the work's innovative lower-class reversal of plays like *Caste* and *Trelawny of the
'Wells'*, which allow that special circumstances can arise that will
permit women of lesser caste to be raised up through marriage
with men of higher class,[4] demonstrating the claims of social histo-
rians like Standish Meacham that 'women ... could more easily
move outside their class than men' (22). This amounts to what we
might call the 'case at hand' scenario, in which characters do not so
much oppose the social status quo as desire that exceptions be made
for their own particular situations. *Beastly Pride*, however, considers the contrary situation, that of a lower-middle-class daughter
who wishes to marry a working-class builder in her father's
workyard. Although the parents initially object to the would-be
fiancé's lower status they come to realise that their objections are
based on nothing but 'beastly pride' and the play concludes with
an invitation that he come to tea, such an invitation understood
among the working class of the period to signal the couple's engagement (Meacham 193). Unlike Granville Barker's period piece,
The Marrying of Ann Leete (1899; 1902) in which an eighteenth
century woman rejects her effete and declining aristocratic family
and willfully opts to return to her roots as it were by marrying the
gardener, John Abud, there is little sense in *Beastly Pride* of the
woman inevitably 'shinnying down the social ladder' to be where
the man is. In Baker's admittedly small-scale vignette of modern
life, the movement is towards the acceptance of the working man
into the woman's lower-middle-class family, the play charting a
woman's successful disruption of a male-dominated social hierarchy, albeit by means of the conventional device of matrimony.

But 'why should a new woman want to get married?' The question,
implicitly raised in *Diana of Dobson's*, is mockingly put by Sir
Richard Kato QC to feminist agitator Elaine Shrimpton in Jones's
1894 comedy, *The Case of Rebellious Susan*. A figure of ridicule, this
play's proto-suffragette is, according to Kato, totally unfit for marriage without preliminary instruction in both housekeeping and

cookery. When Elaine proclaims that 'There is an immense future for Woman –' Kato interrupts to finish her sentence according to the conventional wisdom of his day:

> At her own fireside. There is an immense future for women as wives and mothers, and a very limited future for them in any other capacity. While you ladies without passions – or with distorted and defeated passions – are raving and trumpeting all over the country, that wise, grim, old grandmother of us all, Dame Nature, is simply snapping her fingers at you and your new epochs and new movements. Go home! ... Nature's darling woman is a stay-at-home woman, a woman who wants to be a good wife and a good mother, and cares very little for anything else. (154)

In Jones's play the 'new woman' and marriage can only engage in a comic dialectic. During the Edwardian age, however, a number of women playwrights, among them Elizabeth Baker, began to take seriously Kato's cynical question to Elaine. In her first full-length play, *Chains*, Baker earnestly addresses the issue of marriage, expanding her investigation to consider, from her feminist vantage point, why men, as well as women, choose to marry. As such, her play takes its place among a sub-genre of late Victorian and Edwardian works that might conveniently be labelled 'condition of marriage' plays. Originating with Jones's social comedies of the 1890s, *The Case of Rebellious Susan* and *The Liars* (1897), the tradition culminates in such various Edwardian works as Shaw's *Getting Married* (1908), a round-table discussion of marriage by a number of its devotees and critics, Pinero's *Mid-Channel* (1909) and Galsworthy's *The Fugitive* (1913), both bleak studies of upper-class marital disharmony concluding with the suicides of their heroines. The 'marriage problem' (as it was referred to in a review in the NUWSS paper, *The Common Cause*, 15 April 1909, 11) was a matter of serious debate in the popular press as well. A work like *Modern Marriage and How to Bear it* by Maud Churton Braby (1909) found itself on book shelves alongside Hamilton's *Marriage as a Trade*. Editorials and Letters to the Editor on the issue were also rife in the period's various newspapers, with such a leader as 'Marriage: Choice or Necessity' (which could readily serve as a sub-title to Baker's *Chains*) making its appearance in *The Common Cause* in May 1912. 'The Marriage Question' as it was called at the time was indeed a matter of serious concern; in fact Hynes identifies it as the most central and inflammatory aspect of the woman's movement

for, in his words, 'it brought into question the entire social structure, government of men, the bases of sexual morality, and the
authority of the Church' (174). According to Kent, 'the assault on
marriage constituted a fundamental element of the women's attempts to gain freedom, equality, dignity, respect and power' (81).
Eschewing the society drama format favoured by other 'condition
of marriage' playwrights, Baker uses realism to anatomise, among
other things, the effect of what Hamilton calls the 'narrowing down
of woman's hopes and ambitions to the sole pursuit and sphere of
marriage' (*Marriage* 22).

Initially produced by the Play Actors at the Court Theatre for a
single matinée performance on 18 April 1909, *Chains* was revived
the following year by Dion Boucicault as part of Charles Frohman's
repertory experiment at the Duke of York's. The season, under
Granville Barker's artistic direction, proved a financial disaster,
closing after only seventeen weeks, but during that brief time and
in the company of such plays as *The Madras House* and
Galsworthy's *Justice*, *Chains* ran for 14 of the season's 128 performances. The last play introduced during the season, it was sur-
passed in number of performances by just three plays, Granville
Barker's and Housman's *Prunella* (17 performances), *Justice* (26)
and a revival of *Trelawny of the 'Wells'* (42).

There is not much evidence of the circumstances of the play's
composition and what little does exist is problematic. According to
Knoblock, Kingsway play-reader and dramatist in his own right,[5]
Chains was the product of his 'urging [Baker] ... to write a a three-
act play on a subject of her own experience – her own world' (90).
Knoblock writes that although he 'begged' Lena Ashwell to accept
the play for production at her theatre she refused because it
contained no part suited to her talents. Knoblock then claims to
have sent the play to Edith Craig who, he says, produced it under
the auspices of the Pioneer Players. Knoblock proceeds: 'I met Miss
Baker later on at some reception – but she did not remember me.
When I recalled myself to her, she seemed equally vague. I couldn't
help being a little surprised. It has taken me a long time in life to
realise that people resent being put under obligations to others'
(90). What could be interpreted as questionable behaviour on the
part of Baker becomes more explicable with the knowledge that it
was not Craig and the Pioneer Players but J. Farren Soutar and the
Play Actors, who first produced the play. The Play Actors included

Cicely Hamilton and Inez Bensusan on its Council, and was founded
in 1907 to mount Sunday performances of Shakespeare, plays in
translation and new works by English dramatists (Dickinson 160).
It would seem that Knoblock's and not Baker's memory was at
fault, rendering suspect as well his claimed role in the play's
genesis.

What is certain, however, is that the lower-middle-class world of
Chains reflected Baker's own position in England's social hierarchy,[6] her 'true-to-life' depiction of its living conditions earning her,
according to Barrett Clark, 'a position of honor among what was,
before the War, the "young" Naturalistic group' (306). The play,
hailed by P. P. Howe as the English repertory theatre's 'first veritable realistic play', examines the world of the lowly clerk, its
ideology of 'respectable' married life and the consequences of such
a system of beliefs upon 'a group of ordinary people' who are
realised, in Howe's view, quite 'without idealisation or caricature
or other deference to the conventions of the theatre. Their in-
comes are not multiplied by five in order – as is customary – to
placate the great public, which, in its theatre-going, hates anything
low' (146). H. Hamilton Fyfe, writing for the *World*, feared that
Baker's determination to present a lifelike picture of the clerk class
on stage might prevent her from becoming a popular playwright:
'The Many like Dukes. They prefer that the stage shall hold the
mirror up, not to Nature, but to the *Family Herald*. Such a vivid
study of actual life as Miss Baker offers us in *Chains* can only win
appreciation from an intelligent audience' (24 May 1910, 893). A
reviewer of the play's Manchester production, however, ap-
plauded *Chains* as a 'life-picture', noting that 'we [presumably
critics and audiences] no longer suffer gladly a bloodless auto-
matic Snobbium Gatherum on the stage' (*Manchester Courier* 2 May
1911). Of course, the *Courier* reviewer may have been speaking
more generally than was warranted. Certainly Marjorie Stratchey
for the *Englishwoman* was prepared to argue from just such an
elitist position, stating that 'with such a milieu – that of bank clerks
and successful plumbers – the truth of the picture inevitably brings
with it a certain amount of irritation and boredom' (1910, vol. 6,
224).[7]

The so-called 'ordinary people' of a play described by William
Archer as having 'absolutely no "story" ... no complication of
incidents, not even any emotional tension worth speaking of' (*Play-
making* 48), include Charley Wilson, a city clerk sick of the mono-

tonous routine of his life who yearns to throw caution to the winds (meaning emigrate to Australia) and is prevented by reason of his marriage to Lily, a woman conforming absolutely to Kato's ideal of the 'stay at home woman'. Running contrapuntally is the situation of Maggie Massey, a shop-girl newly engaged to a highly suitable man. Unlike Charlie, however, Maggie does finally rebel against a life circumscribed by oppressively narrow conventions; she refuses to marry. That, in the words of Archer 'is the sum and substance of the action'. Yet he adds, 'If any one had told the late Francisque Sarcey or the late Clement Scott, that a play could be made out of this slender material, which should hold an audience absorbed through four acts, and stir them to real enthusiasm, these eminent critics would have thought him a madman. Yet Miss Baker has achieved this feat, by the simple process of supplementing competent observation with a fair share of dramatic instinct' (*Play-making* 49).

The curtain first rises in *Chains* on the sitting room of 55 Acacia Avenue, Hammersmith. The name of the avenue would later puzzle Trewin, who notes that '"Acacia" appears, for some reason, to symbolise extreme dullness' (*Edwardian Theatre* 96). But its symbolism is more complex than this. It is in fact the first instance in the play of Baker's practice of layering realistic detail with a symbolism that is often ironically charged, her use of such a technique placing her in the company of fellow realist, John Galsworthy, who also 'masters the subtle marriage of naturalistic detail and "delicate" symbolism' (McDonald 143). Accordingly, Acacia, currently the actual name of twenty-three London streets (none in Hammersmith), is also a species of flowering shrub common to Australia, the fecund country of Charley's dreams. Visions of its lush vegetation torment Charley as he tries to make do in his dark, 'two-penny-halfpenny back yard' with its 'rotten', unproductive soil. For although Charley longs to be a fruit-farmer and would, most emphatically, 'give something for a piece of good land', in actuality he is a 'mere clerk'[8] whose experience of the blossoming acacia is limited to a name on a jerry-built street, and whose exposure to the art of horticulture is confined to leisure hour forays into the so-called 'garden' located off the sitting-room.

With its furniture 'a little mixed in style', its carpet-square of 'indeterminate pattern', its lace curtains, 'appalling wallpapers' (*Times* 18 May 1910, 10), family photographs and mantelpiece knick-knacks, this sitting-room, which is suitably 'feminised' by

Charley's stay-at-home wife, is a stage replica of any number of such sitting-rooms stretching in oppressive monotony throughout Hammersmith. It even contains a sewing-machine, the object which had come in the period to represent simultaneously a woman's femininity and servitude. And to lend a touch of genteel respectability, 'a big lithograph copy of a Marcus Stone picture' adorns the wall. Most likely a sentimentalised image of some aspect of eighteenth century aristocratic life, an iconography in which Stone specialised, it adds an ironic gloss to the larger stage picture of a clerk 'not even in the aristocracy of clerkdom' (*Times* 20 April 1909, 10), struggling, with the aid of his wife, to maintain their position among the lower reaches of the lower middle class.[9] The ironic intrusion of an idealised eighteenth century image into the 'real' world of early twentieth century petty clerkdom is suggestive of *The Marrying of Ann Leete*. Written on the eve of the 1900s as a comment on that time, but set at the close of the eighteenth century, it chronicles the decay of that old aristocracy so lovingly depicted by Stone, and the rejuvenation of life through Ann's marriage to yet another gardener. As she says to her father by way of explanation, 'we've all been in too great a hurry getting civilised. False dawn. I mean to go back' (82). Charley's wife, Lily, does not agree. Unlike Charley or Ann, she is content with her lot and dissolves into tears at the mere proposal of a new life married to a gardener of the 'new world'. She is Baker's stage version of the period's ideal (suitably civilised) wife, with *Chains* exploring the unhappy consequences for men as well as women of female conformity to that type.

When *Chains* begins, Lily, the only flower Charley seems able to cultivate in the oppressive conditions of suburban respectability, is at home laying the table for Saturday dinner. 'Obviously young', she has already settled into the housekeeping trade for which she has been trained, wearing the standard uniform of domesticity, 'a light cotton blouse, dark skirt and big pinafore' (211). Baker's rendition of Hamilton's regulation pattern wife, Lily is

> all home-loving, charming, submissive, industrious, unintelligent, tidy, possessed with a desire to please, well-dressed, jealous of [her] ... own sex, self-sacrificing, cowardly, filled with a burning passion for maternity, endowed with a talent for cooking, narrowly uninterested in the world outside [her] ... own gates and capable of sinking [her] ... own identity and interests in the interests and identity of a husband. (*Marriage* 45)

Her conformity to Hamilton's description is quite startling; in fact the play's crisis and resolution are wrought by the interplay between these various criteria for proper wifedom, as Lily's home-loving, submissive, self-sacrificing, cowardly and incurious qualities are brought into conflict with her need to reflect Charley's yearning for a new identity through a change of work and place, a conflict resolved by her timely announcement of impending motherhood.

At the outset of the play, however, Charley is readily identified as 'an ordinary specimen of the city clerk, dressed in correct frock-coat, dark trousers, carefully creased, much cuff and a high collar' (211), greeted on his return home from the office with a hurried kiss from his wife. But all is not happy. In another revealing 'clothing' incident by a woman playwright, Charley is made to express a 'feminist' hostility to restrictive dress:

> Charley [*looking at his silk hat*]. I should like to pitch the beastly thing into the river. [*He shakes his fist at it. Then he stretches his neck as if to lift it out of the collar and shaking down his cuffs till he can get a fine view of them, regards them meditatively.*] Pah!
> Lily [*anxiously*]. What's the matter with them? Are they scorched?
> Charley. Scorched! No, they're white enough. Beastly uniform!
> Lily. But you must wear cuffs, dear. (212)

It is a costume that Lily unquestioningly endorses. Charley, on the other hand, balks at the regulation dress of the clerk which figuratively as well as literally constricts his movements. But he wears it, capitulating to a dress code that results in the reprimand of a fellow clerk who dared to wear a red tie to the office.[10] For not only was such a tie considered too bright for normal wear, it was also marked with political significance, a socialist badge as it were. Accordingly, apart from those committed to disrupting conventions or in a social position to ignore them, 'members of the male population who depended for their living on the good-will of an employer had to reserve the red tie for the week-ends' (Newton 157). Charley takes advantage of that time to make 'a wonderful change into a loose, rather creased suit of bright brown, flannel shirt with soft collar, flowing tie and old slippers' (212).

Comfortably settled now in his sitting-room, he falls into conversation with his lodger, Fred Tennant, who announces his plans to emigrate to Australia. Like Charley, and in language reminiscent of Diana (*Diana of Dobson's*) and Helen (*The Apple*) Tennant complains of the dull 'grind' of work: '... who wouldn't have a little risk instead of that beastly hole every day for years? Scratch, scratch, scratch, and nothing in the end ...' (213). Significantly, however, while these clerks are preoccupied with their conditions of employment, Baker chooses not to re-create on stage – as Galsworthy does in his overtly clerk-centred drama, *Justice* (1910) – the clerk's office. For although 'to be a city clerk [may be] ... to be a kind of slave' the real slavery of *Chains*, as the *Times* reviewer goes on to point out, 'consists not in the work these city clerks do in the city, not in the routine of their occupations, not in their decent poverty, but in the narrowness, the ugliness, the vulgarity of the lives they lead at home' (18 May 1910, 10). Or as Fred Tennant puts it, 'Suppose I stay there [at the office]. They'll raise the screw every year till I get what they think is enough for me. Then you just stick. I suppose I should marry and have a little house somewhere, and grind on' (213-4). 'Like me' Charley responds. It is in fact the debilitating consequences of conventional marriage upon these people's lives, including the kind of work they do, that *Chains* addresses. And it is worth noting in this regard that Fred Tennant feels free to 'hook it' precisely because he is not married: 'Why did I ever go into the beastly office? There was nobody to stop me going to Timbuctoo, if I liked' (214).

When Lily is informed that Tennant is leaving she immediately assumes that he is going to be married. Once disabused, however, she sounds the voice of doom: 'I do hope you won't be sorry for it. It would be so dreadful if you failed' (215). Lily's sister, Maggie Massey, described as 'good-looking without being pretty', is more enthusiastic. Although she too initially assumes that Tennant is planning to marry, when she learns that he is emigrating purely on speculation she applauds his courage and initiative. As for 'the risk' that Lily harps upon, Maggie responds, 'He's a man. It doesn't matter' (215). At least as far as Maggie is concerned, men are initially freer than women, a position she clarifies in an Act II conversation with Charley: 'I can never understand why a man gets married. He's got so many chances to see the world and do things – and then he goes and marries and settles down and is a family man before he's twenty-four' (220). According to Charley, men marry out of habit, a habit supported in the case of innumerable lower-middle class men by monotonous and mind-numbing work. Women, on the other hand, Baker (like Hamilton) makes clear, view marriage itself as an occupation which, in the case of certain working women, can appear more desirable than other forms of employment. When Maggie first announces her engagement she prefaces it with the comment, 'No more shop for me in a month or two' (216). Her interest in marriage is quite obviously 'business-like;' her motivation primarily economic rather than amorous. In fact when Lily states (in a manner that suggests it is not always self-evident), 'You must be fond of him, dear', Maggie retorts

> ... No, I'm *not*, particularly. ... [*walking up and down*]. That's funny now. I didn't mean to say that. It just came. [*A pause*]. How queer! [*A pause*]. Well, it's the truth, anyway. At least, it's not quite true. When I came here to-day I was awfully happy about it – I am fond of him at least – I – well – he's very nice – you know. [*Irritably*]. What did you want to start this for, Lil? (216)

For Maggie, like Kitty Brant in *Diana of Dobson's*, marriage is simply a better career option. In fact her elation at leaving the shop is so great that the previous evening she claims, 'I took off my shop collar and apron and put them on the floor and danced on them' (216). At the same time that marriage apparently condemns Charley to a clerk's collar in perpetuity, it would appear to release Maggie for ever from hers. This is not to say that Maggie is over-joyed at the thought of marriage. Although pleased with the prospect of 'plenty of money' and a servant of her own that marriage to a 'rich man' affords, she too yearns for freedom and adventure in the colonies, envying (as Helen Payson does) a sister worker emigrating to Canada.

I should perhaps add here that despite the preponderance of the separate-spheres formulation during the period, it was not unusual for single women of the lower middle classes to be gainfully employed. According to Dina Copelman, parents of that class wanted their unmarried daughters trained for an occupation. She notes that among such 'generally stable but not affluent families, respectability was defined more in terms of maintaining an overall family income rather than keeping women out of the labor force' ('London's Women Teachers' 177). It should not, however, be thought that marriage secured every such woman a labour-free life. For Maggie, whose prospective marriage affords upward social mobility, removal from the work-place is a foregone conclusion, securing as it does increased status within the existing class hierarchy. It is a status beyond the reach of Charley and Lily, who, in order to maintain their present precarious position of respectability, require a contribution from Lily beyond that of mere domestic ornament. Her work takes place inside the home, a circumstance which preserves the appearance if not the reality of the separate-spheres ideology. To augment the family finances Lily undertakes what was conventionally thought to be suitable women's work: she makes do without a servant, takes lodgers and does her own washing. But becoming her own domestic servant as it were comes at a cost. Both the privacy and intimacy associated with middle-class married life in a home of one's own is, ironically, sacrificed simply in an effort to maintain said marriage and home. And when Lily in her efforts 'to make things smooth', suggests that they convert Charley's gardening room into a bedroom for an additional boarder, Charley's vexed response offers yet another challenge to the conventional public = work/ private = home dichotomy: 'An Englishman's home is his castle. I like that! Why, the only place where you can be alone is the bedroom. We'll be letting that next' (219). Charley's irritability at the prospect of converting his home into a public boarding-house is nicely contrasted with Lily's stoic complacence. For Lily, unlike Charley, is pragmatic in her attitude to the maintenance of their married life. And although Charley may register surprise that Lily's hands, soft when they married, are getting quite rough, Lily responds matter-of-factly, 'It's the washing, dear. It does roughen your hands' (218).[11] Seemingly content with her part as his wife, Lily transfers her hopes and longings to Charley, and when he expresses a reluctance to be head clerk some day – 'I don't know that I'm excited at the idea – a sort of policeman over the other chaps. I'd rather be as I am' (218) – she berates him for his lack of ambition. As such, Lily would appear to conform to Sue-Ellen Case's over-generalised description of female characters: 'when they do have a complex psychological base, [such characters] are usually frustrated and unfulfilled – like the Electra on whom their complexity is based, they wait for the male to take the subject position of action' (*Feminist Theatre* 122). In *Chains*, however, Charley does not want to take 'the subject position of action' that Lily desires, and the play goes on to explore the complex interplay between seemingly male/active and female/passive relationships and the extent to which a so-called passive position can be used to influence action. In other words, Baker addresses the much preached text of 'indirect influence', demonstrating in *Chains* its power to enslave men as well as women.

When the curtain next rises, we are in the midst of an evening 'singsong'. Present are Lily's brother, Percy, 'a good looking, somewhat weak youth of perhaps twenty-one or twenty-two' (219) and Sybil Frost, 'a pretty fair-haired girl, much given to laughing at everything' (219) (the part of Sybil was taken first by AFL member Doris Digby, and in the Duke of York's revival by AFL member Dorothy Minto, the Ernestine Blunt of *Votes for Women!*). Lily, with Maggie's connivance, is hard at work 'arranging' a marriage between Sybil and Percy, her efforts in this regard an instance of what Hamilton argues is a 'spirit of unconscious trade unionism among women' (*Marriage* 39). According to Hamilton, women's heavy involvement in the 'business of matchmaking' stems from their recognition of 'the economic necessity of marriage for each other.' Given a social system that makes marriage and livelihood synonymous for women, Hamilton goes on to insist that 'there must be something extraordinarily and unnaturally contemptible about a woman who, her own bargain made and means of livelihood secured, will not help another to secure hers' (39). Against such female proclivity, Charley rebels, producing a scenario that might be characterised as a microcosmic battle between the sexes, with Charley and Lily engaged in a curious tug-of-war over Percy's future, one that without male intervention bears a marked resemblance to Charley's own. When informed that Lily and Maggie have arranged his match, Percy denies it; refusing to see a shaping female hand in his destiny, he argues that 'we just came together – it was bound to be' (224). Charley perseveres, however, urging Percy to reconsider:

> *Charley.* You're too young to marry.
> *Percy.* I'm twenty-three. So were you when you were married.
> *Charley.* I was too young.
> *Percy.* Do you mean …
> *Charley.* [*impatiently*]. Oh, don't look so scandalised. No, I'm not tired of Lily. It's not that at all – but, are you satisfied to be a clerk all your life? (224)

From Charley's perspective marriage and clerkship are virtually indistinguishable. He cannot, however, convince Percy to delay a marriage that, with a recent promotion to £90 a year, he believes he can now afford. In fact, the connection between work and marriage is so precise that immediately Percy's pay increased to the point where he considers it feasible, he opts for marriage. Although the play makes clear that there have been other women in his life – 'he is a little bit of a flirt' given 'he's got nothing else to do with his evenings' (226)

– Sybil is conveniently present when he finds that his economic position can support a wife and three small rooms. And so conventional is Percy's outlook that he interprets Charley's cautionary intervention as 'crazed', a characterisation Charley challenges:

> ... Why am I crazed, as you call it? Isn't it because I know a little what your life is going to be? Haven't I gone backwards and forwards to the City every day of my life since I was sixteen and am I crazed because I suggest it's a bit monotonous? [*Going close to Percy and putting his hand on his shoulder solemnly.*] I'm not saying she isn't the right girl for you – I'm only suggesting that perhaps she isn't! (225)

In Baker's play, male camaraderie is powerless against the combined forces of societal convention and covert female machinations, Baker insisting that men as well as women are manipulated into the straitjacket of marriage. Percy admits that he too contemplated emigration at one time (a means of circumventing the vicious cycle of clerkdom and marriage) only to be prevented by his father's refusal to consent. He became a clerk instead, capitulating so far that he now rejects Charley's anti-marriage advice as 'rot'. Which is not to suggest that the play draws no distinction between men and women's compulsion to marry. In Act II at least Maggie takes it almost for granted that women must marry; if she were a man, however, she insists that she would never marry and settle down. On the contrary 'I wouldn't stay in England another week. I wouldn't be a quill-driver all my life' (220). Notice again how Baker insists upon the inevitable coupling of marriage and debilitating work as if it were a marriage in its own right. And while certainly much is made of the restrictive and exploitive nature of Charley's work (in Act II for instance he learns that his salary is to be reduced at the same time that his rent is being increased) the play links such circumstances inexorably to marriage. It is Charley's marriage and the obligations that society attaches to that state that keep him chained to his stool and desk. As Tennant answers Charley's plea for a similar 'chance to rough it', 'You're married. ... You're settled' (226). Tennant is free to leave because he is unmarried; poor Percy, on the other hand, has only just begun to forge the chains that already bind Charley securely.

Charley, however, unlike Percy, chafes under his chains, and in a scene that would tend to confirm Case's Electra/Orestes view of dramatic characterisation, is encouraged to break them by his seemingly more passive sister-in-law:

Maggie. I wonder what Lil would say if you did!
[*Charley stops dead and looks at Maggie.*]
Charley. If I *did*? What are you talking about.
Maggie. Why shouldn't you?
Charley. Why shouldn't I. Aren't there a thousand reasons?
Maggie. There's Lily, certainly – but …
Charley. She wouldn't understand. She'd think I was deserting her. [*A pause.*] But that's not all. I might manage her – I don't know – but – you see, I've got a berth I can stay in all my life … It's like throwing up a dead cert. And then …
Maggie. It *would* be a splash. (221)

But if Maggie would encourage Charley, in Case's terms, to 'take the subject position of action', Charley proves reluctant. He is, however, emboldened enough to at least raise the prospect with Lily, who reacts in a conventionally womanly way. She bursts into tears, insisting that his desire to emigrate is a mere pretence for leaving her. Deprecating his own proposal, Charley 'pets her like a child' and sends her to bed. Such a scene might seem, at first glance, a valid example of Case's critique of realism which, she explains, 'in its focus on the domestic sphere and the family unit, reifies the male as sexual subject and the female as the sexual "Other". The portrayal of female characters within the family unit – with their confinement to the domestic setting, their dependence on the husband, their often defeatist, determinist view of the opportunities for change – makes realism a "prisonhouse of art" for women …' (124). Of course Baker is deliberately constructing such a 'prisonhouse' in order to highlight its destructiveness. Far from endorsing or even merely recreating from a neutral viewpoint such a scenario, Baker uses realism as a means of questioning the legitimacy of its 'reality'. Furthermore, Baker's realist drama can hardly be said to 'reify the male as sexual subject'. A hesitant Orestes at best, Charley more accurately conforms to the Electra type. Unfulfilled and frustrated, enjoying action only vicariously through Tennant, he remains at the end of Act II trapped in the marital home, defeated by the action (the traditionally feminine tears and entreaties) of his wife. Within the parameters of realist drama, Charley is made, like Victor Bretherton in *Diana of Dobson's*, to suffer what is more conventionally interpreted as a woman's experience. As such the play can be usefully contrasted with Galsworthy's *Justice*. Out of the house and in the office, the clerk of this piece, William Falder, does succeed in taking some initiative. He forges a cheque that will allow him to rescue his suffering lover and her children from a vicious husband. Caught, however, before they can flee to the colonies, Falder is ultimately destroyed by law masquerading as 'justice'. His lover (a conventional portrait of victimised womanhood), unable to support herself and her children by sewing alone, succumbs to prostitution, a circumstance (the male characters of the play all agree) that effectively precludes her from further contact with Falder.

Much to Charley's disappointment, his connection with Lily is not so readily severed. In fact, Alfred Massey, Lily's father, reacts with blustering outrage to the merest hint of Charley's emigration. Although at the beginning of Act III, he is still comfortably ensconced on the saddlebag sofa of his own upper-working-class sitting-room in 'Sunnybank', Hammersmith – an 'unnecessary' scene change that provides, to borrow States's observation of Chekhov, 'a merciless commentary on human possibilities' (71) – he soon becomes severely discomfited by what he interprets as Charley's planned defection. For he too links marriage to inevitable confinement: 'You should have thought of that before you married. You can't run off when you like when you've a wife' (235). Massey accepts such a state of affairs unquestioningly, his complacency prompting Charley to speak out against the oppressive life he 'just settled down to' (235), a life shaped by patriarchal values. When Maggie asks her father why he didn't ask for a choice of work for instance (he readily admits that he disliked the plumbing that financed his house and family), he responds by describing a fairly typically pattern of employment, 'Me! Why should I do such a thing? Father was a plumber, and if it was good enough for him, it was good enough for me. Suppose I had thrown it up and gone to Canada for a lark? A nice thing for my family' (235). Charley rallies with an impassioned speech that questions the pervasive control of marriage over every other facet of his life:

> For Heaven's sake, can't you listen fair? My wife needn't go to her father for protection from me? I'm not a scoundrel just because I've got an idea, am I? [*A pause – nobody answers.*] But I'll tell you what, marriage shouldn't tie a man up as if he was a slave. I don't want to desert Lily – she's my wife and I'm proud of it – but because I married, am I never to strike out in anything? People like us are just cowards. ... We're not men, we're machines. Next week I've got my choice – either to take less money to keep my job or to chuck it and try something else. You say – everybody says – keep the job. I expect I shall – I'm a coward like all of

you – but what I want to know is, why can't a man have a fit of restlessness and all that, without being thought a villain? (235-6)

Despite his eloquence Charley is apparently bested in debate by the combined efforts of his in-laws, who unremittingly urge, albeit in choric variation, that marriage has its responsibilities. Charley falls another victim to the 'suffocating family closeness' documented in a number of accounts of Edwardian lower-middle-class family life (Copelman 177). He dutifully leaves the Sunday family social, wife in tow, their departure marked by Maggie's ironic rendition on the piano of 'Off to Philadelphia', a tune quickly replaced by the equally ironic but more 'appropriate' hymn, 'Count your many Blessings'. Such use of music to undermine or ironically comment upon the stage action is prevalent throught the play, the content of the songs becoming estranged by their placement within the text.

Running in tandem with the third act's explosive confrontation between Charley and Lily's family, is Maggie's more subdued struggle to reconcile herself to marriage. The act begins with a discussion initiated by Maggie in which she analyses her feeling for her fiancé, Walter Foster. As she quite frankly admits to her mother, it bears no relation to the overwhelming love Mrs Massey complacently declares she experienced for her husband. Mrs Massey dismisses Maggie's lack of appropriate feeling as jealousy of Walter's deceased first wife, an explanation that Maggie rejects. She states, instead, her desire to see Walter 'do something, and not worry about getting married' (228). Still behaving as a conventionally passive female, Maggie looks to her fiancé to act in a manner that she can vicariously enjoy: 'I should like Walter to go out and seek his fortune instead of getting it in a coal merchant's office' (228). But Walter, a 'prosperous-looking, rather stout' man of thirty-five, is content with clerkdom.

Prompted by her father's insistence that despite her cavalier manner she does indeed think about her impending marriage, Maggie proceeds to express herself in a manner that bears some resemblance to Diana's Embankment-bench exchange with Victor:

Maggie [slowly]. I think of the wedding dress, and the bridesmaids, and the pages. Shall I have pages, Mum?
Mrs M. Maggie!
Maggie. I suppose I shan't. I think of the house I'm going to have, daddy – and the furniture, and I'm going to have a cat and a dog –

Massey [*slyly*]. Nothing else, of course. Just a cat and a dog. Ha, ha!

Mrs M. Alfred, don't suggest. It isn't nice.

Massey. A cat and dog – ha, ha, ha!

Maggie. Don't laugh, daddy. I'm telling you the solemn truth – I think
most of all that I shall never, never, never have to go into a shop
again.

Massey. I wish old Foster could hear you.

Maggie. Why?

Massey. He'd say – 'And where do I come in?'

Maggie. Well, of course he'll be there. I wish – . (230)

Like Hamilton's Diana, Maggie must be reminded of the husband
who comes as something of an after-thought; it is the financial and
social benefits of marriage as a trade that are uppermost in the
minds of both women. And if she appreciates the pragmatic advan-
tages associated with legally sanctioned sexual intimacy, Maggie
also recognises its cost. Together with Georgiana in Hamilton's *Just
to Get Married*,[12] she displays a marked distaste for physical contact
with her fiancé:

Foster. ... Maggie, I – you haven't kissed me yet.

Maggie. I did – when you came in.

Foster. No – I kissed *you.*

Maggie. I'm sorry – I – I don't care for kissing in front of people. (232)

Under continued compulsion, Maggie kisses him. The link between
socially acceptable sexual contact and prostitution, already uncomfortably apparent, is rendered painfully obvious by Walter's
presentation of a brooch immediately following Maggie's kiss, the
'gift' requiring payment of yet another embrace which is broken off
abruptly by Maggie's impatient withdrawal of her hand. In an
exchange that recalls similar passages in both *The Apple* and *Diana
of Dobson's*, Maggie expresses a desire simply 'to go and – do
things' (232). Confessing, as Georgiana does, that her acquiescence
to the engagement was prompted by a compulsion to escape the
already unpleasant conditions of her life, she cries out for the same
freedom Helen Payson and Diana seek: 'I should love to be absolutely independent, quite – altogether free for a whole year' (233).
Walter's answer rings but a slight variation on the language of
Helen's male 'friend': 'You will be free when you are married to me,
Maggie. You can do anything you like' (233). Illustrative of much
contemporary feminist analysis of male attitudes in the period,
attitudes fostered by a separate spheres ideology which 'encour-

aged the view of women as sexual objects and perpetuated
women's powerlessness' (Kent 5), the men of these plays betray
an absolute inability to comprehend freedom for women as meaning anything other than a certain degree of leisure and physical
comfort coupled with compulsory sexual intimacy and financial
dependence.

It is a price that ultimately Maggie finds too dear. At the beginning of the final act, and within the confines of the 'prisonhouse' of
Charley's sitting-room, Maggie struggles for the sexual autonomy
that many identified as being at the heart of the feminist movement
(Kent 11); she announces that she has broken off her engagement.
Displaying the 'double-motived' interest in marriage that Hamilton
argues women possess, Baker's Maggie rejects the match because
it brought only one motive into play: 'I was just marrying – to get
away from the shop' (238). Although the play leaves no doubt that
social and economic factors enter invariably into women's marital
calculations, Baker, like Hamilton, draws a distinction between
marriage with and without love. The former may preclude freedom
(Maggie insists that 'nobody is free when they're married – more
especially the woman') but love reconciles one to the loss, with
Maggie going so far as to claim that she wouldn't want to be free if
she loved the man. To accept marriage without love, however, is in
Maggie's words, simply 'to throw up one sort of – cage – for
another' (239).

In a play supposedly characterised by inaction, Maggie acts. And
she does so in the face of her own contention that women should
play the role of supportive adjuncts to male crusaders: 'In the old
days the women used to help the men on with their armour and
give them favours to wear, and send them forth to fight. That's the
spirit we want now' (238). Unable, however, to prompt the men of
her time to an action she could, in true Electra fashion, vicariously
enjoy, she decides to take the initiative herself. Recognising that
her prospective marriage to Walter was merely an exercise in
caution, she opts instead for 'risk' and 'throws up a good match'.
Although Hamilton might characterise marriage itself as a dangerous gamble for women (*Marriage* 29), Maggie demurs. For her the
only risk associated with marriage is not marrying. High adventure
(a popular Edwardian preoccupation) lies elsewhere for women, a
point on which both Maggie and Hamilton would agree. And Maggie
is still ready to encourage Charley to his own display of self-
assertiveness. One wonders in fact whether Maggie wasn't driven

to break her own chains as a means of prompting Charley to similar action. As she says to him, '... I wanted to be safe and was afraid of risk. Then I made up my mind I wouldn't do that. I tell you because – if a girl can risk things – surely a man –' (241). Charley, however, doesn't get the point; he cannot see that her action constitutes a risk despite Maggie's insistence that 'A woman isn't tested in the same way as a man' (239). Indeed, Maggie's statement serves in context as a double indictment. It registers her triumph as opposed to Charley's failure while lamenting the fact that Maggie has been (to this point) enjoined from proving herself in the larger arenas traditionally associated with male endeavour.

Maggie's rejection of an advantageous match brings to mind Fanny Hawthorne's rejection of Alan Jeffcote's marriage proposal in Stanley Houghton's realist play *Hindle Wakes* (1912). A product of the Manchester School, Houghton's work celebrates Fanny's assertion of independence within what Allardyce Nicoll characterises as 'a stern father–rebellious son drama' (277).[13] It is not, however, like *Chains*, a critical study of marriage itself; the weekend affair between Fanny and Alan is rather the device by which Houghton can explore the clash of generational values. This is not to deny the force of Fanny's rejection, which has been characterised 'as a serious declaration of feminine emancipation' (Nicoll 278),[14] only to suggest how it differs from Baker's treatment of a similar incident. Firstly, there is no attempt in *Hindle Wakes* to examine the process by which Fanny reaches her decision. Present on stage only briefly in the first scene to start the plot on its way, she does not reappear until the final act when she breaks silence to make her announcement. If Baker is determined to show Maggie wrestling with the marriage question, Houghton is more concerned with dramatising Fanny's answer. And it is an answer, furthermore, that displays no double-motived interest. Fanny, who like Maggie can support herself on the money she earns at work (she is employed at a Lancashire cotton mill), rejects Alan purely on emotional grounds: 'You're not man enough for me' (325). The social and economic incitements to marry that occupy potential wives in both Baker's and Hamilton's plays are apparently a non-issue with Fanny. In fact, Houghton conveniently demonises such attitudes by locating them in Fanny's grasping, hypocritical mother. What renders *Hindle Wakes* 'feminist' in Nicoll's eyes is what most obviously divorces it from the women's plays examined here. For Fanny insists on her right to enjoy sex on the same terms as men, a proposal that genuinely offends her would-be fiancé:

> *Alan.* But you didn't ever really love me?
> *Fanny.* Love you? Good Heavens, of course not! Why on earth should I love you? You were just someone to have a bit of fun with. You were an amusement – a lark.
> *Alan* [*shocked*]. Fanny! Is that all you cared for me?
> *Fanny.* How much more did you care for me?
> *Alan.* But it's not the same. I'm a man.
> *Fanny.* You're a man, and I was your little fancy. Well, I'm a woman, and you were my little fancy. You wouldn't prevent a woman enjoying herself as well as a man, if she takes it into her head?
> *Alan.* But do you mean to say that you didn't care any more for me than a fellow cares for any girl he happens to pick up?
> *Fanny.* Yes. Are you shocked?
> *Alan.* It's a bit thick; it is really! (324-5)

Such a plea for sexual freedom might sound emancipated from the vantage point of the post 'sexual revolution' era. To many women in the Edwardian period, however, determined to distance themselves from a definition of their gender rooted in sexuality, *Hindle Wakes* could be construed as reactionary, insisting as it does upon Fanny's sexualisation. The nature of Edwardian feminist responses to the woman/sexuality nexus was prompted, as Jeffreys observes, by the view that the 'sexualisation of woman led to her being considered fit for no other career than that of sexual object and affected the opportunities of all women for education, work, and general self-development' (47). Accordingly, insisting in Hamilton's words that sex had 'assumed undue and exaggerated proportions' in women's lives (*Marriage* 35) and rebelling against what Christabel Pankhurst would come to characterise as 'the doctrine that woman is sex and beyond that nothing' (*The Great Scourge* 20), such women actively strove to break what they saw as the inhibiting, 'naturalised' bond between 'woman' and 'sexuality'. From such a perspective, Houghton's play would hardly seem liberating. Fanny's achievement of equal licence, while a response to the notorious 'double standard', moved, in the eyes of many committed feminists, in the wrong direction. Indeed, in this respect *Hindle Wakes* can be seen to harken back to the 'new woman' literature of the 1890s, already shunned for its linking of women with sexual promiscuity, and its concentration upon personal rather than political emancipation (Tickner 182-4). The feminist plays in this book, by contrast, equate female single life with sexual abstinence, and assuming sufficient money to sustain that status, a freedom otherwise unattainable. Sexual intimacy, on the other hand, signals female dependency, and bears the additional stamp of coercion and degradation where love is not a legitimating factor.[15] Once again, the divide between women writers of feminist plays and the work of sympathetic male fellow dramatists seems both real and substantial.

In *Chains* it is the sanction of marriage itself which most concerns Baker, and Maggie's active rejection of would-be wifedom – a decision signifying throughout the period 'a revolt against the prescribed feminine role' (Lewis 76) – is offered as an instructive contrast to Charley's acquiescence to a passivity more generally associated with heroines. Although he confesses to Maggie in the play's final act that he does in fact plan, despite family opposition, 'to cut and run', he is forestalled by Lily's own intervention. Remaining the epitome of the period's 'angel in the house' Lily nevertheless acts – ironically by means of the 'indirect influence' much lauded by anti-suffragists – to secure Charley's continued inaction. This stay-at-home wife manages to secure her future in said home, at the same time further aligning herself with the dominant ideology's 'accentuated (though not of course new) emphasis upon woman as mother' (Weeks 126) by announcing with decorous but calculated feminine coyness (she whispers in Charley's ear) the news of her impending motherhood. Like Maggie, Lily does not passively wait for the male to act but takes the initiative herself. Of course her motivation runs counter to that of Maggie who rejects conventional societal definition by refusing a suitable engagement; Lily avoids risk by forestalling any disruption to her marriage, using motherhood, as conservative forces advocated at the time, to ensure the perpetuation of the family as the stable social unit of society. Maggie responds to her sister's pregnancy with a phrase that lays bare Lily's machinations and her own contempt: 'So you've *got* him, after all' (243). She leaves the stage (a profoundly symbolic departure from a realist setting – a setting that 'says in effect, "It will all end here"' (States 69)) with the ironically cutting comment, 'I don't think I can wait for you, after all, Charley' (243). Charley, unlike Galsworthy's Falder, does not in desperation take his own life, he simply returns to said set wearing his 'beastly collar'. In one sense the conclusion of Baker's play brings full circle the pattern of rewriting *A Doll's House* from a woman's perspective. In *Votes for Women!*, Robins used Levering to provide a corrective to Ibsen's lumping together of the roles of spouse and parent. In *Chains*, Baker presents us with a male Nora reconceived through female eyes. Spouses and home can be left (albeit with some effort) but Charley, like Levering, proves incapable of slamming the door on his unborn child. Of course in this play it is the coercive nature of the period's glorification of motherhood and family that is laid bare. In the words of P. P. Howe, 'Paternity is the final chain' (149), a paternity manipulated by the dutiful wife to enslave her husband further. Thus ironically is Charley trapped by the very laws meant to ensure his domination. Such, Baker urges, is the cost to men of a patriarchal culture's reduction of women to 'regulation pattern' wives and mothers, her interpretation of such slavery as socially constructed a refutation of Shaw's biological determinism. According to Shaw, 'the bearing and rearing of children, including domestic house-keeping is woman's natural monopoly ... In so far as it is a slavery, it is a slavery to Nature and not to Man' (*The Intelligent Woman's Guide to Socialism and Capitalism* 176). In Baker's hands, the traditional figure of the femme fatale who ensnares men by the exercise of her female wiles becomes the happy homemaker so effusively celebrated by Kato, patriarchy's spokesman and feminist bogeyman.

Needless to say, reviewers displayed some difficulty in coming to grips with Lily's character (she was played by AFL members Gillian Scaife at the Court and Hilda Trevelyan at the Duke of York's) and their comments run the gamut from the *Stage*'s conception of her as 'a sweet, gentle, tender, and considerate little house-wife ... [a veritable] grown-up Wendy of Hammersmith' (19 May 1910, 16) to the *World*'s damning condemnation of her as 'the kind of fool-woman who drags a country down' (24 May 1910, 893). The critical reception of Maggie (played at the Court by AFL member Rose Mathews and at the Duke of York's by a young Sybil Thorndike, also an AFL supporter[16]) is more striking, and evidence of what has been termed a 'subject male gaze', so pernicious here that the parallels Baker carefully draws between Maggie's and Charley's metaphoric chains are wilfully ignored. The juxtaposition of Maggie's success with Charley's failure passes unwitnessed by reviewers who either tried to explain her by recourse to the popularised 'woman in revolt' theme or confessed themselves puzzled by this 'curious young person' who insists 'upon her brother-in-law's duty to desert everything for a restless whim' (*Sketch* 25 May 1910, 200). The fact, moreover, that Maggie remains enigmatic and unplaced – she does not disappear like a chameleon into the play's environment – invites a rethinking of recent analyses that identify as one aspect of realism an inevitable movement to closure which dissolves enigma 'through the re-establishment of order, recognisable as a reinstatement or a development of the order which is understood to have preceded the events of the story itself' (Belsey 53).

Not surprisingly perhaps, a greater consensus exists over Charley; most reviewers expressed sympathy with his frustrated rebellion although objections were lodged to what was deemed the 'exaggerated ... monotony of [Baker's] ... clerk-hero's working hours'. As the *Athenaeum* critic went on to explain, 'Most of us are victims of routine and parts of some machine. Even a farmer out in Canada has plenty of drudgery to go through' (28 May 1910 651). The *Times* objected to Charley's unrealistic expectations: 'There is a touch of slavery in all regular work, and domestic ties are "chains" of a sort for every one, and Queensland is not Utopia' (18 May 1910, 10). In a rather perverse reading of the play that demonstrates the difficulty of prescribing audience response, the *Sketch* insisted that Baker has a 'lesson to teach – the lesson that modern man, however much he may long for adventure, must stay at home and mind the wife and baby' (25 May 1910, 200). This reviewer conceived *Chains* to be an endorsement of the very life Charley seeks to flee, and in light of that view, concluded that Charley's longing to emigrate was 'somewhat unreal and a little far-fetched'.

Despite such doubts about Charley's motivation, however, he was nevertheless granted centre stage in a drama that was rapidly becoming 'The Clerk's Tragedy' (*World*), a term subsequently adopted by Howe and endorsed by Trewin, who goes on to describe the piece 'as a chilling little achievement' (*Theatre Since 1900*, 80). It is a view of the play prompted in part no doubt by Dennis Eadie's assumption of Charley's role in the Duke of York's revival.[17] Eadie had recently created, to great acclaim, the part of Falder in *Justice* and it is likely that the tragic figure of that piece shaded into critical perceptions of Charley as well.

Yet to construe *Chains* as the tragedy of a clerk ('too low a thing for the Elizabethans to have written' (147), says Howe) is to distort it. For the play is not so much about a clerkship as it is about marriage. As the *Times* noted, 'here we come to what, even more than clerkship, is the subject of Miss Baker's play – ... Wilson was married' (20 April 1909, 10). And despite male critical preoccupation with the husband, it is Lily's and Maggie's perceptions of marriage, as much as Charley's, that determine the shape of the play, perhaps even its genre. For when the play was originally produced by the Play Actors, it was billed as a comedy (*Era* 24 April 1909, 19, Wearing *The London Stage,* vol. 2, 742). Upon its revival at the Duke of York's, however, it was given the more generic label 'play', which (predominantly male) critics have gone on to translate as tragedy. As much as anything, however, this demonstrates the bias of its viewers. Certainly, if one takes the play as being about Charley's unrealised plans to emigrate, it assumes, in Cordell's words, 'the tragic force of frustration and defeat' (49) 'where inaction itself is the drama' (177). Adjust one's critical gaze, however, to include Lily and Maggie and the play is transformed from a tragedy about male paralysis to a comedy of female initiative. Lily, without deviating from the traditional pattern of the ideal wife, successfully closes the door on Charley's escape from lower middle-class suburbia, a door that Maggie, by dint of positively rejecting a 'suitable' marriage, pries open to possible adventure.

Notes

1 Sister WWSL member, George Paston's (Emily Symonds) one-act 'cockney' play, *Tilda's New Hat* (first produced at the Court Theatre 8 November 1908) also details the construction and disassembling through dress of the female sex object, and addresses the effect of both the adorned and unadorned female on male desire.

2 Jane Lewis has noted that during this period, shop assistants over the age of thirty faced major difficulties in finding a new job (*Women in England* 154).

3 According to the *Era*, Baker was a typist working for a City firm during the time she wrote *Chains*.

4 Other Edwardian plays that address that period's preoccupation with such cross class alliances include Pinero's *Mind the Paint Girl* (1913) which records with an ambivalent eye the union of a show-girl and a peer, and St John Hankin's *The Cassilis Engagement* (1907) which exposes the ruthless but successful efforts of an upper-class mother to forestall her son's marriage to a working-class woman. For discussion of these plays see Jan McDonald's chapter on Hankin in *The 'New Drama' 1900-1914* and Joel Kaplan's 'Edwardian Pinero'.

5 Knoblock co-authored with Arnold Bennett the highly successful *Milestones* (1912).

6 According to Hamilton Fyfe, Baker was the first playwright to really make something of the clerk as a character in drama. He adds that 'two or three of our leading writers for the stage began life, I believe, in Clerkdom, but they would not for the life of them make use of their knowledge in their plays. Like the gentleman with the dancing bear in *She Stoops to Conquer,* they "cannot abear anything that's low"' (*World* 24 May 1910, 893).

7 Pinero, a playwright fond of presenting the upper classes on stage, argued in an interview with William Archer that 'wealth and leisure are more productive of

dramatic complications than poverty and hard work', although he was prepared to assert that his play, *The Benefit of the Doubt* depicted suburbia and not Mayfair. To which Archer responded in terms similar to Howe, 'Suburban, perhaps; but they all lived at the rate of five thousand a year. ... And if there was no duke in the play, there were a knight and a bishop' (*Real Conversations* 21).

8 In the hierarchy of clerks, the Government clerk tops the lot, followed in turn by the bank clerk, the insurance clerk and so on all the way down to the 'mere clerk' (*Times*, 20 April 1909, 10). Geoffrey Best records that 'Junior Clerks in quasi-professional offices like banks, solicitors, railway companies – i.e. young men of eighteen to twenty ... generally began at between £70 and £80. How high they ever got would depend on their abilities and usefulness and on the extent to which the better jobs were reserved for better class men. ... He would have been an unfortunate and exceptional man who did not, in any of the rather classy establishments investigated by the Civil Service Inquiry Commissioners [in 1874], rise to between £150 and £200 a year' (89).

9 Best refers to R. D. Baxter's *The Taxation of the UK* (1869) for a description of the lower middle class as including a clerk earning £99 and renting at £15 per annum a house with no resident servant. Best adds, however, that in 1869 'a £15 a year house in London ... would look very lower lower middle class indeed, and would scarcely guarantee respectability' (90).

10 One is reminded of the farcical 'red-tie' incident in Pinero's *The Magistrate* (1885).

11 For a sentimentalised account of the extent to which household work and growing indifference to appearance can wreak havoc with a romance which is saved only by the timely intervention of Cupid, see Baker's one-act play *Cupid in Clapham* (staged by the Play Actors at the Court Theatre on 20 March 1910).

12 In Hamilton's play, following Georgiana's acceptance of his marriage proposal, Adam 'strides across the room to her and seizes her in his arms', demanding a kiss:

Georgiana (with a sudden impulse, pushing him away). No – I
Adam (astonished). You won't? What have I done? I didn't mean, Georgie –
Georgiana (recovering herself, laughing nervously). You nearly pulled my hair down – with your arm. You must be – careful. *(Going centre to chair, back to audience.)*
Adam (relieved). Is that all? I thought it was something serious. I'll be very careful this time. I won't even touch your pretty hair.
(He takes her in his arms and kisses her; she submits.) (31)

13 *The Price of Thomas Scott* (produced in 1913 by Miss Horniman's Company in Manchester under Lewis Casson's direction) is Baker's own examination of the conflict between parents and children. It charts a daughter's growing admiration for her father's adherence to his religious convictions despite the heavy cost to him and his family.

14 Trewin characterises it as 'at heart a Lancashire feminist variant on the inevitable Edwardian theme, marriage between the classes' (*Edwardian Theatre* 102).

15 I am not, of course, insisting that this was the only view of women's sexuality held by feminists at the time. As Kent has recently demonstrated, opinion was divided on this issue; it ranged the spectrum from Christabel Pankhurst's position on the one side to that advocated by the shortly-lived *Freewoman* on the other, that publication asserting an active female sexuality and addressing such issues as sexual pleasure and contraception. But the *Freewoman* earned the wrath of many feminists including moderates like Millicent Garrett Fawcett, and Olive Schreiner, noting that most of the articles were by men, suggested that it be renamed *The Licentious Male* (see Kent 216-17). Furthermore, 'in rejecting the model of Mary for female sexuality' Kent continues, 'most feminists were not

advocating sexual freedom or sexual promiscuity as symbolised by Eve'. They were, and Baker is obviously of their number, keenly alive to the interrelatedness of economic independence, freedom from reproduction and (sexual) liberation (Kent 218).

16 Sybil Thorndike claimed that her interest in women's suffrage came about as a result of Lewis Casson's urging, 'Your acting won't be much good if you don't think about the world in which we live and the conditions of the people'. Accordingly, 'Off I trundled with Lewis to the Free Trade Hall where Mrs Pankhurst and her daughter Christabel were speaking. I was entranced, first thinking what a lovely part Mrs Pankhurst would be to play. But, you know, she got me right from the start – quietly dramatic, dignified, and such well-chosen phrases. I thought, well, she'd convert anyone. Then up got Christabel; more violent, with wild arm movements, too much I thought, but exciting. Well, from then on with much instruction from Lewis, I began to think about Votes for Women' (quoted by Morley 37).

17 Eadie's performance as Charley was highly praised although the *Athenaeum* objected that he 'gives the idea of being rather too exceptional a clerk' (28 May 1910, 651), a view elaborated upon by the *Times* where it was insisted that 'There is refinement in every line of him, and, cleverly as he acts, he really does not for one moment represent a possible husband of the commonplace Lily Wilson' (18 May 1910, 10).

V

Githa Sowerby

'I've got something to sell that you want to buy'

Githa Sowerby remains something of an enigma. We know that she
was born at Gateshead, near Newcastle-upon-Tyne, and that she
began her career as a writer of children's books in collaboration
with her illustrator sister, Millicent. Her first efforts at play-writing
were, not surprisingly, also for children; a collection of *Little Plays
for School and Home* was published in 1910. Her later reputation
rests, however, entirely upon the success of one play, *Rutherford
and Son*. Although a number of contemporary writers stressed her
relative youth,[1] and Emma Goldman tells us that Sowerby undertook the play when she was 'barely out of her teens' (Goldman 130),
she was in fact in her mid-thirties when the piece was written. She
apparently composed the play 'for practice' (*Stage* 21 March 1912,
20). And if Baker and Hamilton struggled to produce their first
plays in time snatched from more immediately lucrative work,
Sowerby confessed to writing hers 'in odd moments idling in a
boat' (from the Raymond Mander & Joe Mitchenson Theatre Collection, [hereafter M&M], unidentified clipping). Unhappy with its
first act, she nearly discarded the work but was convinced to
complete it by friend and actor, Thyrza Norman, who went on to
perform the part of Mary in the play's first production. Although
there is no evidence directly linking Sowerby to the suffrage movement, Norman was an active supporter of the cause and member of
the AFL, appearing as Mme de Stael in the 1910 Aldwych Theatre
production of Hamilton's *Pageant of Great Women*. Norman was
married to J. H. Leigh, a wealthy businessman and amateur actor
who purchased the lease of the Court Theatre in 1904 in order, it
was said, to display Norman's talents in Shakespeare. Displeased
with the quality of the first productions, Leigh contracted with
Granville Barker to produce and perform in *The Two Gentlemen of
Verona*; as partial consideration Barker arranged with Vedrenne,

Leigh's manager, for a series of *Candida* matinées, the collaboration leading directly to the historic 1904-7 seasons that presented
Robins's *Votes for Women!* (Purdom 19). Leigh's theatre had also
been the venue for a 1908 production of *Mrs Bill*, a 'slight comedy of
pleasant people' written by Sowerby's husband, Capt. John
Kendall.[2] It was as part of a subsequent series entitled 'Mr Leigh's
Matinées' at the Court Theatre that 'unheralded, unparagraphed,
and unpuffed' (*Sketch* 7 Feb 1912 142), *Rutherford and Son* made its
first appearance on 31 January 1912 for four matinée performances. And as in the case of *Chains*, Edith Craig and the Pioneer
Players are erroneously linked to the play. But despite Holledge's
claim that Craig and her Society produced the work, it was in fact
staged by Kenelm Foss. And so enthusiastically was the play received – one journalist recorded that 'Every inch of available space
in the theatre was taken, and well-known people – critics, actors,
and managers – stood like a wall down the side of the stalls' (M&M
unidentified clipping) – that it was revived at Gertrude Kingston's
Little Theatre on 18 March 1912, subsequently transferring to the
Vaudeville, and running for a total of 133 performances.[3]

John Palmer, who had succeeded Max Beerbohm and Bernard
Shaw as dramatic critic to the *Saturday Review*, welcomed *Rutherford and Son* as the legitimate heir to Elizabeth Baker's *Chains*,
marking in both works the 'complete subordination of everything
to a persistent main theme' (30 March 1912, 391). Describing Sowerby
and Baker as 'aesthetic puritan[s]', he found in their plays a distinctly female voice: 'The conscientiousness and hard logic of a
woman applied to the theatre are able to go surprising lengths' (391),
an observation that is particularly interesting in light of Brander
Matthews's 1916 view that what he called 'the dearth of female
dramatists' was explained by 'the relative incapacity of women to
build a plan, to make a single whole compounded of many parts,
and yet dominated in every detail by but one purpose' (120).

Although there is no evidence that she participated directly in
the suffrage movement, Sowerby was nevertheless championed by
feminist writers. For anarchist and radical feminist Emma Goldman, she was the first 'woman dramatist of note' to appear in a
country where drama was still 'the stronghold exclusively of men'
(130). In the words of the reviewer for *The Vote*, the official newspaper of the Women's Freedom League, *Rutherford and Son* reached
the apotheosis of drama for the cause: 'No play has ever been
written that in the truest, strongest sense was so really a 'Suffrage'

play, although the word is never uttered and the thought never enters the minds of the people portrayed' (20 July 1912, 227). Maintaining that the play's (predominantly male) critics had to date only grasped one side of the play, this reviewer insisted upon an exegesis of 'the woman's side', her analysis betraying the increasing hostility which marked women's struggle for the vote at the time: 'As the hard, servile, weak, or worthless men are one after another weighed and found wanting, and as the threads are picked up and held firmly by one gentle woman, goaded into cruel strength by love of her little son and contempt for her wretched husband, we get glimpses of the hell this world has held for women – a hell created by the arrogance of men' (227). By its vivid depiction of such circumstances, the *Vote* argues, *Rutherford and Son* indicts the social and political system that keeps 'suffering women in thrall to ... men' (227). Apparently influenced in its composition by sister playwright Elizabeth Baker, and obviously appropriated upon completion by the suffrage movement to argue its cause, *Rutherford and Son* is best read as a continuation and a culmination of feminist drama in the Edwardian age.

Like *Chains* a product of drama's naturalist school, the play reproduces carefully selected features of the 'off-stage' environment in order to question the domestic, social and political assumptions upon which such worlds are built. *Rutherford and Son* is about a family business, a glass manufacturing concern located on the banks of the River Tyne in England's North Country. It is run by John Rutherford, a man so obsessively pre-occupied with the company that he rides roughshod over his children in his efforts to maintain it, crushing their spirits in the process and wreaking havoc with their lives. And in its depiction of the human suffering and waste wrought by the father in order to ensure his son's inheritance of the family business and the social status that implied, the play is pre-eminently Edwardian. Within the space of its three acts and in a work that some critics praised as equal to Pinero and better than Arnold Bennett, Sowerby manages to address many of the major issues troubling Edwardians. Waste, inheritance, capitalist enterprise, the status of women, cross-class alliance and marriage all come under Sowerby's purview as she exposes with unremitting grimness the agony of life in John Rutherford's house, built, as one might expect, 'far enough from the village to serve its dignity and near enough to admit of the master going to and from the Works in a few minutes' (333).

The play begins three months after the return of the eldest son (also named John) to the family home, cap in hand, wife and infant son in tow. Married 'secret-like' in the city, much to his father's displeasure, and unable subsequently to find work to support his family, John has been forced, at his wife's insistence, to 'crawl ... to the Guv-nor and ask ... to come back' (336) to a place in a house that still holds his sister, Janet, and brother, Richard (Dick). Upon returning to the Works, however, John happens upon an invention that will revitalise the ailing family business. Not prepared to donate it gratis to the company, he attempts to bargain for a price that will secure his quittance from *Rutherford and Son*. Unwilling to barter, his father steals the formula, prompting John to steal in turn what ready cash his father has on hand. When his wife, Mary, proves adamant in her refusal to accompany him, John sneaks away mumbling of emigration to Canada.

Such a plot places *Rutherford and Son* squarely within a factory drama sub-genre typified by Tom Taylor's *Arkwright's Wife* (1873), Jones's *Middleman* (1889) and Galsworthy's *Strife* (1909). Although these plays vary in their mix of melodrama and realism (as their dates would suggest there is a movement away from melodrama towards increased realism) they, along with Sowerby's play, demonstrate the range of dramatic effects possible from a capitalist's exploitation of a worker's invention. In *Arkwright's Wife*, the theft of an invention is ultimately legitimised in a work that becomes a picturesque piece of Tory history, celebrating Industry's victory over the Luddites. The *Middleman*, on the other hand, subordinates the fact of an inventor's exploitation to the ensuing struggle between a compromised daughter, her distraught father (the worker) and the capitalist employer who refuses to force his son to make amends. *Strife*, a play ostensibly about a bitter workers' strike against the Tenartha Tin Plate Works, is really concerned with the toll the struggle takes on the leaders of the contesting parties. That the leader of the workers received only £700 for a discovery which realised a £100,000 for the firm, becomes significant only as a partial explanation for his steely refusal to settle with the company. The information is in fact something of a dramatic red herring prompted, one suspects, by Galsworthy's fear that his character's intense hostility to the Tenartha Tin Plate Works would be unbelievable without the addition of a personal grudge; it is a miscalculation that serves only to diminish the character's stature.[4] In *Rutherford and Son*, the most starkly realist of this group of plays, the theft of an invention is pushed out of the factory altogether and into the home where it becomes a family matter, undermining (once again) the integrity of a separate sphere's ideology. And unlike the other exploited inventor plays which include scenes of the workplace or, in the case of *Strife*, at least a view of the '"Works" high wall', *Rutherford and Son*, like *Chains*, shows only the family home, focusing upon the consequences for what was traditionally heralded as the sheltered domestic establishment, when capitalist rapacity and patriarchy combine.

If Sowerby's 'living-room' with its red wallpaper, solid mahogany furniture, central dining table and strategically hung portrait of the family's most recently deceased patriarch, seems a bleak North Country reminder of the domestic setting of Granville Barker's *Voysey Inheritance* (1905),[5] her action – the return and departure of a wayward son coupled with the pyrrhic victory of his manufacturer father – brings to mind another Court play of the 1905 season, St John Hankin's *The Return of the Prodigal*. In spite of such similarities, however, both plays provide additional evidence of the distance that separated the work of Edwardian women playwrights from that of sympathetic male colleagues. Barker's play of family capitalism and patriarchal control resolves itself in terms of the son's coming of age, a process that culminates in the 'modern' union of a Shavian woman to a man who finds his purpose (and his humanity) in his patrimony. More telling are the points of contact between Sowerby's play and Hankin's. What Hankin ironically called his 'comedy for fathers' is set in a cloth manufacturing district in Gloucestershire. Its action is initiated by the return of Eustace Jackson to the bosom of his parvenu family. Five years earlier the failed Eustace had left on a paternal stipend to seek his fortune in Australia. His money spent the unscrupulous but charming Eustace stage manages his return to blackmail his father into indefinite support at the rate of £250 a year – for an extra £50 he offers not to write. While Hankin's play presents a witty attack upon capitalism fuelled by social and political ambition, Sowerby in a grimmer mood moves to indict patriarchy itself. Her returning prodigal, a neurasthenic weakling, brings with him wife and child – dependants whose relationship to old Rutherford becomes the playwright's subject. The collapse of son John, and the emergence of his wife as the tale's driver of hard bargains – its Eustace in fact – enables Sowerby to move beyond Hankin's blanket condemnation of an economic system to what she records as a mythic struggle between maternal obligation and patriarchal self-interest.

The magnitude of this battle is suggested by the presentation of old Rutherford himself, an outsized figure whose control over home and business assumes deitic proportions. The play's initial conversation, between daughter Janet (played by AFL member Edyth Olive) and Ann, her maiden aunt (played by AFL member Agnes Thomas, the Working Woman of *Votes for Woman!*), effectively makes the point:

> *Janet* [*glancing at the clock*]. He's not back yet.
> *Ann.* No.... If you mean your father.
> *Janet* ... Who else should I mean?
> *Ann.* You might mean any one.... You always talk about
> he and him, as if there was no one else in the house.
> *Janet.* There isn't. (334)

A thirty-six-year-old spinster compelled, from lack of education or other opportunity, to take up the traditional role of family housekeeper for her father and brothers, Janet is Sowerby's variation on the well-known type of the Victorian spinster, generally portrayed in the period as a pathetic or ridiculous figure of frustration and failure. The problem of 'redundant' women as they were known, an increasing phenomenon throughout the Victorian/Edwardian period,[6] was exacerbated by a societal structure that left many such women isolated and financially dependent. It cannot be said of Sowerby's Janet, however, as it is of 'Poor Honor', her dramatic counterpart in *The Voysey Inheritance*, that she 'is not unhappy in her survival' as that family's perpetual spinster (102).[7] For poor trod-upon Honor, like the six Huxtable daughters in *The Madras House* and Eustace's sister, Violet, in *The Return of the Prodigal*, acquiesces to her victimisation, accepting her lot in life with suitably feminine passivity. All, in Violet's words, stay, 'quietly at home, doing the duty that lies nearest ... and not crying out against fate' (199). Not so Sowerby's Janet who has become hard and angry, her bitterness a harsher version of that displayed by Hankin's prodigal son, whose emotional response to his father his gentle sister cannot fathom despite her own misgivings. Janet conceals her passionate hostility to her father behind 'an expressionless ... face and monotonous voice. All her movements are slipshod and aimless, and she seldom raises her eyes' (333). Like

many of her non-fictional counterparts, Janet is part of a family
whose economic and social position rendered paid female employment socially unacceptable, and she is forced, at her father's insistence, to waste her energy in idleness. Fond of aping 'gentlefolk',
Rutherford has forbidden Janet 'to do things like a servant' without
providing her with alternative satisfying work. She is expected, like
many unmarried daughters of the period, simply to subordinate
her will to her father's authority (Jalland 258). Insisting, however,
that she 'can't sit and sew all day' (334), Janet balks at being
elevated to the leisure class, her rebellion initially manifesting
itself in such a seemingly insignificant act as plopping a whole loaf
of bread down on the table despite her aunt's remonstrance: 'you
know weel enough that gentlefolk have it set round in bits' (334). In
a subsequent conversation, Janet compares herself unfavourably
to the family servant, Susan, pointing out the grave anomaly of her
situation as unpaid family help:

> *Ann.* Susan's not one of the family! A common, servant lass.
> *Janet.* Like me.
> *Ann* [*using the family threat*]. Just you let your father hear you.
> *Janet.* We do the same things.
> *Ann.* Susan's *paid* for it. Whoever gave you a farthing?
> *Janet* [*bitterly*]. Aye! (341)

Complete social isolation is an equally serious consequence for
Janet of Rutherford's attempts to raise the family to a station above
the commonfolk. Denied, by her father's decree, the companionship of the working class without (despite her father's intense
social ambition) realising the status of landed gentry, Janet is
caught, like Hankin's Violet, in a social no-man's-land. As she says
to her brother, her explanation of continuing spinsterhood echoing
Violet's account of the nouveau riche dilemma, 'No one in
Grantley's good enough for us, and we're not good enough for the
other kind' (341).

Her brother, John, has also suffered as a result of his social
elevation: 'he is the type that has been made a gentleman of and
stopped half-way in the process' (335), and as such he offers a
useful contrast to Houghton's Alan Jeffcote (*Hindle Wakes*), another Northerner raised from the working class by his father's
successful mill venture. Alan, educated at Manchester Grammar
School and Manchester University (John was given just a single
year at Harrow) does not, like John, speak affectedly or attempt to

conceal the fact that he is 'patently a Lancashire man' (305). John, who is much less confident of his social status, is accused by Janet of 'pretending' to a rank beyond him: '... you pretended – pretended you knew the folk ... Pretended you said "parss" for pass every day. I heard you. And I saw the difference. Gentlemen are natural. Being in company doesn't put them about' (342). Janet, who insists upon her own 'commonness', rejects all such pretence which has not, after all, succeeded in raising John into a higher social set. He is not made, however, to suffer the complete isolation of his sister who has become a veritable prisoner in her father's house. Allowed somewhat greater freedom than Janet, he has at least managed to marry although the union is condemned by his father as a misalliance. It is a view parroted by maiden aunt Ann in language that reveals the capitalist underpinnings of the play's central relationships: '... he looked higher for his son after the eddication he's given him.... Folk like him look for a return for their bairns. It's weel known that no good comes of a marriage such as yours' (335).

John's wife, Mary, is Sowerby's version of the London 'working girl', a character fast becoming a staple figure in Edwardian feminist drama. In language reminiscent of Hamilton's and Baker's plays, she recapitulates her own experience of work-day grind: 'Day after day in an office. The crowded train morning and night – bad light – bad food – ... It's been nothing else all along – the bare struggle for life' (336). Acquiescing to the conventional wisdom of the day, Mary assumed that marriage would lift her out of such a 'deadly' life. She was wrong. Compelled to work to support herself and her new husband (he 'couldn't find work'), she rebelled only when maternal obligations came to outweigh marital:

> I didn't mind when there was only ourselves. But when he [Tony, their son] was coming I began to think, to look at the other children – children of people in our position in London – taught to work before they'd had time to learn what work means – with the manhood ground out of them before ever it came. And I thought how that was what we had to give our child, you and I.... (336)

Like Vida Levering in *Votes for Women!* and Charley Wilson in *Chains*, Mary recognises a responsibility for her child that overrides all else. Accepting the legitimacy of the view (and note again the insistence upon an economic perspective) 'that we'd no business to marry and have a child when we'd nothing to give him when he came' (338) she insists that her husband return with her and their child to Rutherfords and the familial home that she comes to call a 'prison'. Yet despite the bleakness and austerity of the countryside which is reflected in the Rutherford household itself, where Mary finds herself completely ostracised (Rutherford refuses to speak to her and Aunt Ann insists that she is 'a stranger in the hoose'), she stays for Tony's sake: '... if I hadn't been Tony's mother, I wouldn't have come. Not for anything in the world' (335). It is a price she is willing to pay, and as the curtain rises on the first act we find this 'delicate-looking woman' seated in the Rutherfords' 'extremely uncomfortable' living-room, engaged in the suitably feminine activity that Janet dismisses. Mary sews butterfly bows on a baby bonnet as she, along with Aunt Ann and Janet, awaits the return of the master.

Young John returns first only to be accosted by Mary who, conventionally Electra-like at this point, looks to him to rescue her from what she has come to call an 'intolerable' life endured only for her child's well-being. Sick of her 'incessant nagging ... about the kid – and money' (338) and confident of his invention, John promises her future happiness with plenty of money. Despite her 'luke-warm' reaction, he assures Mary, in pared-down language similar to that employed by Helen's friend (*The Apple*) and Maggie's fiancé (*Chains*), that 'you shall do what you like and enjoy yourself as much as you want to – and forget all about those filthy years ...' (337). As for John himself, he naïvely believes that his invention will provide him with the means of buying his way out of a family business which seems possessed of almost supernatural powers to restrain and consume. In Mary's words, Rutherford himself is like an unholy god – 'no-one's any right to be what he is – never questioned, never answered back – like God!' (336) – while in John's overblown rhetoric the company itself becomes the insatiable Industrial god, Moloch:

> They built his image with an ugly head ten times the size of a real head, with great wheels instead of legs, and set him up in the middle of a great dirty town.... And they thought him a very important person indeed, and made sacrifices to him – human sacrifices – to keep him going, you know. Out of every family they set aside one child to be an offering to him when it was big enough, and at last it became a sort of honour to be dedicated in this way, so much so, that the victims gave themselves gladly to be crushed out of life under the great wheels. That was Moloch. (340)

Janet is struck by the description which so acutely reflects her own bitter experience of being 'dedicated – all of us – to Rutherford's. And being respected in Grantley' (340), the consequence of her father's greed and social ambition.

The father, an Edwardian Agamemnon who officiates over the sacrifice of his children to his professional concerns, 'is a heavily built man of sixty, with a heavy lined face and tremendous shoulders – a typical north country man' (342). (The role was initially played by Norman McKinnel, an actor who specialised in 'stern, despotic, old North-country business' (*Englishwoman* 1912, 219).) An athlete in his youth, Rutherford quelled a potential strike at his Works years before by descending to the coal yard himself in his shirtsleeves to shovel 'joost half as much coal again as the best of 'em' (340). It is a method of labour management young John rejects; he would have preferred it if 'the Guv'nor had sat quietly in his office and sent his ultimatum through the usual channels, [then] he would have been the owner of Rutherford's and the strike would have run its course' (340). Young John's favoured approach is the one adopted by John Anthony, Rutherford's counterpart in *Strife* (another McKinnel role[8]). By such means Galsworthy was able to dramatise the unbridgeable distance young John envisions between management's representative and that of labour. That is not, however, an issue in *Rutherford and Son*, which rather depicts the cost to individuals of Rutherford's absolute insistence upon maintaining the family industry. As such it is not surprising that Rutherford first appears on stage in the company of his foreman, Martin, 'a good-looking man of the best type of working-man' (342).

As Rutherford enters the family living-room, his dependants stop their quarreling. Initially cowed by his presence, John relinquishes his father's 'chair' and Janet 'after a moment's silent revolt' kneels to remove his boots. John is not prepared, however, to buy family peace at the cost of his invention. When Rutherford raises the subject, John refuses to disclose the formula without first obtaining his 'price'. Insisting upon their status as businessmen (both men repeat the phrase 'I'm a business man' in the scene), father and son proceed to discuss their familial relationship in terms of barter and sale. Young John states quite simply, 'I've got something to sell and you want to buy it, and there's an end' (345). Rutherford reacts with a patriarchal indignation ('To buy? To sell? And this to your father?' [345]) prompted by monetary considerations:

Rutherford.... This is what I get for all I've done for you.... This is the result of the schooling I give you.
John.... I suppose you mean Harrow.
Rutherford. It was two hundred pound – that's what I mean. (345-6)

John interprets his role in the family to be nothing but a cheap source of labour, a situation he resents. Just as Janet objects to acting as her father's unpaid handmaid (which Rutherford justifies as a due return for her support), John expresses his bitterness at being the firm's undervalued clerk/office boy. And although he agrees with his 'chained' fellow-clerk regarding the nature and conditions of the work, 'nothing but grind, grind, since the time you could do anything' (347), unlike Baker's Charley, John has 'had no salary' at all. Challenged on such grounds by his son, Rutherford insists upon his absolute control of family and firm: 'There'll not be two masters at Rutherford's while I'm on my legs' (346), an extreme position that marks the outer boundary of the period's 'family business' plays. In *Hindle Wakes* for instance, Jeffcote announces in the first act his intention of offering his son a partnership, while in *The Voysey Inheritance* Old Voysey is determined to include his son in even his illegal business dealings. Even *Strife*'s John Anthony, the unyielding Chairman of the Tenartha Tin Plate Works, makes room for his son as a director and his son-in-law as manager of the same. And although Undershaft disinherits his son according to the Undershaft tradition in Shaw's *Major Barbara* (1905), (a son quite unwilling to 'go into trade' in any case), he manages to bring his future son-in-law, the 'foundling' Cusins, into immediate participation in the family business by way of adoption (with a domesticated Barbara eager to tackle its housekeeping). No such familial partnership is envisioned by Rutherford who expects John to wait, unquestioningly, until he inherits the company upon Rutherford's death: 'You're my son – my son that's got to come after me' (346). When John answers that he, like Charley, but in a more feckless manner, wants to be quit of it all, Rutherford responds in language that recalls Alfred Massey's lecture to Charley in *Chains*:

Choose to do! There's no choose to do. The thing's there. ... Life's *work* – keeping your head up and your heels down. Sleep, and begetting children, rearing them up to work when you're gone – that's life. And when you know better than God who made you, you can begin to ask what you're going to get by it. And you'll get more work and six foot of earth at the end of it. (346)

The end of the act marks an impasse between John and his father. Although John insists that he will eventually get his price, Janet dismisses his claim as mere posturing, insisting that 'No one ever stands out against father for long – you know that – or else they get so knocked about they don't matter any more' (348). Her comment, which elicits a shudder from Mary, casts its ominous shadow over Janet's own future, embarked as she is on a collision course with her father and his values. As the curtain drops on Act I, we see her in the clumsy embrace of the family workman, Martin, a reluctant suitor whose kiss is passionate without tenderness, the first evidence of a secret affair managed in time stolen away from Rutherford. Theirs is another cross-class alliance, evidence of a daughter's covert rebellion against the family patriarch, but while it bears some affinity with similar liaisons in *Beastly Pride* and *The Marrying of Ann Leete*, in the bitter and unyielding world of *Rutherford and Son*, where the father sacrifices all in the name of the family firm, it proves incapable of comic resolution.

Act II, which takes place in the same 'dull and commonplace living-room' (*Era* 23 March 1912, 14) consists of a series of four duologues that chart the growing fragmentation of the Rutherford family. At the outset of the act, Rutherford suspects nothing of Janet's covert rebellion, and the opening sequence consists of Sowerby's well-wrought conversation between two men, Rutherford himself and his younger son, Dick, a local curate who like his brother seeks release from the Rutherford family. Offered a senior curacy elsewhere, the 'pathetic'-looking Dick requests his father's consent to accept the position. In marked contrast to his reaction to John's proposed defection, Rutherford responds to Dick's proposal with utter indifference. Judging his children solely in terms of their contribution to the family firm, he dismisses Dick with the comment, 'You can't make a silk purse out of a sow's ear – you were no good for my purpose, and there's an end. For the matter o' that, you might just as well never ha' been born – except that you give no trouble either way ...' (351). It is an unfortunate comment for Dick proceeds, albeit by indirection and without intention, to 'give' Rutherford a great deal of 'trouble', initially in the form of a parishioner, Mrs Henderson (played at the Court by Agnes Hill, yet another AFL member), come to plead with Rutherford to reinstate her son. Dismissed from the 'glass-house', as the Works are called, for stealing ten pounds from the company cash box (the first in a

series of 'thefts' that punctuate the play's action), the son himself
never appears. Instead his mother takes the initiative, arguing his
case in what becomes a burlesque anticipation of the abandoned
Mary's third act negotiation with Rutherford. But Rutherford turns
a deaf ear to the pleas of Mrs Henderson, responding in terms that
echo his earlier comment to Dick, '... lads that get their fingers in
my till are no use to me. And there's an end' (353). When Rutherford goes on to suggest that mother and son leave the community
to start a new life elsewhere, Mrs Henderson voices an independence from Rutherford's control that his own sons seem incapable
of mustering: 'And beggin' your pardon, though you are the master,
I'll joost take the liberty o' choosin' my own way' (353). Finally
balked, however, Mrs Henderson's fervency turns to vitriol, and
standing her ground against Rutherford's 'threatening manner', she
pours contempt upon his social aspirations: 'You think yourself so
grand wi' your big hoose, and your high ways. And your grandfather a potman like my own. You wi' your son that's the laughing-
stock o' the parish, and your daughter that goes wi' a working man
ahint your back!' (354). By means of a mother's drunken rage at her
son's employer, a daughter's secret rebellion against her father's
will is made known to him. And although Rutherford is initially
prepared to discredit Mrs Henderson's comments, Dick unwittingly provides corroborative details even as he tries to discount
them. In Janet's view, he betrays her; as she says to Mary in the
play's final act, Dick 'sneaked on me behind my back' (361).

In predictable fashion for a man who 'doesn't like women – never
notices them' (336) and who blames his dead wife for making his
son a fool,[9] Rutherford is more distressed at what he understands
to be Martin's defection than he is at his daughter's deliberate
subversion of family status. And when he summons to his presence
the man with whom he has 'worked together five and twenty years,
master and man' (356), the subject of Martin's liaison with Janet
never arises. Rather, Rutherford, in his obsessive concern for the
survival of Rutherford and Son, manipulates Martin's betrayal into
company profit. Rather than pay the 'price' that John demands for
the invention that will save the family firm from slow ruin in a
difficult market, Rutherford chooses to 'take' the formula by forc-
ing Martin into a reciprocal act of betrayal, this time the disclosure
of John's secret. It is a tactic sanctioned in Rutherford's mind by
what he conceives to be not so much Martin's sexual indiscretion
as his breach of trust. And although Martin proves a reluctant

Judas, insisting that 'It's Mr John's own; if it's ever yourn, he must
give it to ye himself. It's not for me to do it. He's found it, and it's his
to do what he likes wi'. For me to go behind his back – I canna do it'
(356-7), he is, unlike the leader of the workers in *Strife*, ultimately
persuaded by his employer's rhetoric. Martin becomes an unwit-
ting victim of one man's absolute dedication to the continuance of
a family business that, paradoxically, demands the sacrifice of the
family itself. In their struggle to avoid being so used, his children
work in devious, 'behind the back' ways that Rutherford, to counter, exploits himself. He counsels Martin to divulge John's invention for the good of the company itself. In a display of sophistry that
presents theft as faithful service, Rutherford convinces him that
such an act could not be construed as theft since neither he nor
Martin will gain by it: 'When men steal, Martin, they do it to gain
something. If I steal this, what'll I gain by it? If I make money, what'll
I buy with it? Pleasure, mebbee? Children to come after me – glad o'
what I done? Tell me anything in the wide world that'd bring me joy,
and I'll swear to you never to touch it…. If you give it to me, what'll
you gain by it? Not a farthing shall you ever have from me – no more
than I get myself' (358). John, on the other hand will receive his
patrimony; his invention will come back to him via his father's will.
On the basis of such argument, Martin capitulates, betraying
John's confidence 'for Rutherford's'. As such the scene can be dis-
tinguished from similar invention thefts in other factory dramas. In
Arkwright's Wife, *The Middleman* and *Strife* for instance, the theft or
exploitation of a discovery is unproblematically interpreted as
unjust loss suffered by the inventor and unwarranted profit gar-
nered by the capitalist/thief. In *Rutherford and Son*, on the other
hand, the profit motive becomes tangled with family matters and
what is theft in the eyes of one becomes an act of familial obligation
in the eyes of another, albeit that such family duty manifests itself
as business acumen.

   Family and business remain inexorably linked in the climactic
confrontation between Janet and her father at the close of Act II.
Eschewing the melodramatic posturing of a piece like *The Middleman*, Sowerby does not have Rutherford cry out against his daughter's seduction and condemn the man who compromised her. His
loyalties here are not to family but to gender and a business built
upon a gendered hierarchy, and he accuses Janet of stealing his
man away from him: 'You can't give him back to me. He was a
straight man. What's the good of him now?' (359). In fact, so strong

is Rutherford's characterisation of the affair as a theft perpetrated by Janet against him that she feels compelled to challenge the imputation, 'Confessed? As if I'd stolen something' (360). From Rutherford's perspective, Janet is the villain of the piece, using her female wiles to emasculate his servant, 'You've dragged the man's heart out of him with your damned woman's ways' (359). Unlike the fathers in *The Middleman* and *Hindle Wakes*, for instance, who favour cross-class alliances to resolve cases of sexual transgression, Rutherford rejects a solution which would compromise the social status he has imposed upon the family: 'I made a name for my children – a name respected in all the countryside – and you go with a working-man. To-morrow you leave my house' (359). His daughter's social and emotional well-being mean nothing to him; it is his reputation as the head of Rutherford and Son that preoccupies Rutherford: 'What ha' you got to lose? Yourself, if you've a mind to. That's all. It's me that's to be the laughing-stock – the Master whose daughter goes wi' a working-man like any Jenny i' the place – ' (359).

Admitting to a sexual aggressiveness foreign to the period's ideal of female passivity but linked to the stage adventuress and the 'new woman' of the 1890s, Janet insists that Martin 'didn't come after me. I went after him' (359). Of course, such a characterisation of the event must also be read as a deliberate attempt to shield Martin from her father's wrath, and at least in the eyes of one reviewer, Janet was 'seduced by the common but clever workman' (M&M unidentified clipping). She proceeds by way of further explanation, and in a manner that 'quite thrilled' contemporary audiences (*Sketch* 27 March 1912), to blame her father for condemning her to a life of idleness and isolation in his effort to ensure a superior status for the family and its business. 'Sitting the day long with ... [her] hands before ... [her]' is the price she is made to pay for family pride and capitalist ambition. Contemptuous of the pseudo-middle-class life imposed upon her by Rutherford – 'I've sat and sewed – gone for a walk – seen to the meals – every day – every day.... That's what you've given me to be my life – just that!' (360) – she insists upon her natural affinity with the married working women of the village: 'Me a lady! with work for a man in my hands, passion for a man in my heart! I'm common – common' (360). At this point in the play, Janet, like Maggie initially in *Chains*, still looks to define herself through subservient association with a male. Despite her earlier insistence that she initiated the affair, she volunteers to her father that 'Whatever Martin's done, he's taken me from you' (361), from a father whose devotion to capitalist enterprise coupled with his unyielding insistence upon patriarchal authority has produced a kind of monster 'that'd take the blood of life itself and put it into the Works' (361). In such circumstances the idealised family home of the Victorian/Edwardian period becomes a 'gaol' and the much lauded concept of filial obedience and devotion is inverted to display its chilling opposite, as Janet confesses to her father that 'you got me – me to take your boots off at night – to well-nigh wish you dead when I had to touch you ...' (361).

Sowerby avoids the Ibsenesque grand exit into the night that might well have followed such lines, her decision to eschew such 'physical visible externalisation', an indication, according to the *Englishwoman*, of the play's 'dramatic' rather than 'theatric' quality (1912, 217-8). Instead, the curtain simply drops at the moment of the daughter's denunciation of the father to raise on the same unremittingly austere set the following morning. Rutherford is gone and in a final act that again proceeds mostly by way of duologues, Janet, 'with a shawl about her shoulders' (361), sits talking to Mary. In a play that chronicles a series of betrayals by men, this scene of female camaraderie (itself evidence of the play's feminism[10]) serves as a quiet corrective. Mary, displaying an overriding loyalty to her own sex, confesses that she has long known but remained silent about Janet's affair, refusing to confide even in her husband:

Janet [after a pause]. You mean that you guessed?
Mary. Yes.
Janet. You knew all the time, and you didn't tell? Not even John?
Mary. Why should I tell him? (361)

In contrast to her tempered sense of obligation to John, one that is circumscribed by practical and commonsensical considerations, Mary promises her sister-in-law unmitigated support: '... if ever the time should be when you want help ... remember that I'll come when you ask me – always' (362). It is aid Janet does not anticipate needing, convinced as she is that 'we ... [will] win through to happiness after all, Martin and I, and everything come right' (361). For Janet, unlike Mary, is still behaving conventionally, looking to marriage for her salvation; she trusts Martin to free her from Rutherford and carry her down to a life among the commonfolk that in her enforced idleness she has exalted above her own deadly existence. It is a compelling vision, her description of her dreamed future an isolated moment of love and beauty in what is an increasingly ugly reality:

> I had a dream – a dream that I was in a place wi' flowers, in the summertime, white and thick like they never grow on the moor – but it was the moor – a place near Martin's cottage. And I dreamt that he came to me with the look he had when I was a little lass, with his head up and the lie gone out of his eyes. All the time I knew I was on my bed in my room here – but it was like as if sweetness poured into me, spreading and covering me like the water in the tarn when the rains are heavy in the fells. (361)

It is a romantic vision without the armature of romantic comedy. For this is no *Diana of Dobson's* and Martin is no make-do Prince Charming. Dismissed, like Janet, from further association with Rutherford and Son, Martin can envision no future without the Works. A working-man trained (like women, feminists of the period would argue, adopting much the same terminology) in subservience to the patriarch, he remains a 'slave in body and soul' (*Daily Telegraph* 12 March 1912). Despite Janet's passionate plea, 'What is there to mend except what's bound you like a slave all the years? You're free – free for the first time since you were a lad mebbee – to make a fresh start' (363), Martin places loyalty to the master above love for Janet and her passion for him proves powerless to break the incestuous triangle, 'He's had you, Martin – like he's had me, and all of us' (364). Despite the parallels between women's and workers' oppression insisted upon in her argument, Janet is unable to forge the kind of link that moderate feminists were beginning to establish with labour:[11] Her experience is closer to that of the WSPU whose early ties with socialism were broken by what was perceived to be its betrayal of the cause. Her faith in him unfounded, Janet refuses the money Martin offers to establish her in what could now only be a prostituted loveless life in a worker's cottage. Taking an initiative foreign to traditional portraits of passive womanhood, Janet hands him back to Rutherford, '... he needs you at the Works. Men forgive men easy where it's a woman, they say, and you could blame me, the pair of you' (365).

Contemporary critical reaction to the scene divided along gender lines. In the eyes of the male reviewer for the *Era*, for instance, 'the woman bitterly realises that the love she has brought the man cannot compensate to the simple, honest nature, for the self-respect he has lost by his breach of faith with master and master's son' (23 March 1912, 14). In the words of the female critic for *The Vote*, on the other hand, Martin is 'unfitted by his slavish devotion to his employer to be free man or lover, [and] he finds himself cast adrift because, having allowed himself to be made a thief and a slave, he proves too much of the one and too little of the other. One's heart aches for poor, sulky Janet, ruined by her love for this paltry soul who can give no thought to her anguish and whose fondness crumples under the strain like a child's tin sword' (20 July 1912, 227). Whether one sympathises with Martin's slavish character or not, there is no doubt that Sowerby, like Baker in *Chains*, paints a grim portrait of patriarchy's power to make slaves of men as well as women. Under such conditions free and equal marriage is impossible, a point lent visual credence by the separate exits of Janet and Martin. And despite one critic's attempt to impose a melodramatic denouement – he writes that Janet 'rushes out of the house apparently to commit suicide' (M&M unidentified clipping) – her un-Electra-like departure from a metaphoric House of Atreus is unheralded and downplayed, overwhelmed by the turmoil created by John's arrival and realisation that Martin has divulged his formula to his father.

Inveighing against his betrayal, John adopts Rutherford's language to describe Martin's breach of trust; Rutherford's 'Martin ... that I trusted as I trust myself' (359) is echoed by John's accusation, 'I never thought but to trust you as I trusted myself' (366). He has no use for Rutherford's sophistry, however. There is no doubt in his mind that Martin is 'a thief – you're as bad as he is – you two behind my back' (366). Arguments of future interest in Rutherford and Son fall on deaf ears. John, like Edward in *The Voysey Inheritance*, desperately wants to be rid of his patrimony. Forestalled by the 'theft' of his formula, however, from realising his escape through its sale, he opts for petty theft. Re-enacting Martin's Act I account of young Henderson 'wi' his hands i' the [master's] box' (342), John breaks into his father's cash-box for the £23 it contains, claiming, as Mrs Henderson argued in defence of her son and Rutherford asserted in defence of his action, that he is not a thief, '...Don't look at me as if I were stealing. It's mine, I tell you' (366). Unlike Mrs Henderson, however, John is not willing to argue the issue with Rutherford himself, and he prepares to leave the family home to avoid a confrontation that, following Janet's earlier clash with her father, we might be forgiven for expecting. John engineers an escape from the family business that Edward Voysey can only dream of. But in Granville Barker's hands, Edward's decision to accept his patrimony and engage in honest criminality lends him stature; we witness 'the transforming effect of the inheritance' (Kennedy Intro 13) on a man who had threatened to remain merely 'a bit of a prig' (157). And while it is clear that Edward will never realise his father's spirited individuality, shouldering his inheritance makes a man of him, albeit a lesser man his father. Conversely, in *Rutherford and Son*, John's flight from the family and its business, financed by insignificant pilfering, is the culmination of a process of diminishment. For Sowerby is not, like Granville Barker, concerned so much with the making of men as with the wasting of men and women when capitalism and patriarchy go hand in hand. We are invited to view John as 'a worthless but ill-used son' (M&M unidentified clipping) whose worthlessness is directly attributable to his father and his obsessive dedication of the family to its business.

In a reversal of the sexes, John, like Ibsen's Nora, walks out of the family home to the sound of a closing door, despite Mary's Torvaldian insistence upon his duty to their son. Of course, Sowerby's characters differ fundamentally from their Ibsenesque counterparts. Like her sister playwrights, Robins and Baker, Sowerby does not so much argue (as Eleanor Marx had) that 'Ibsen has failed us'[12] as that 'Ibsen got it wrong'. For she makes apparent in *Rutherford and Son* that Nora's much-quoted 'duty to myself' is as wrong-headed as Torvald's easy equation of 'duty towards your husband and children'. Like Robins and Baker, Sowerby elevates parental responsibility to a position far above either obligation to one's spouse or to oneself. In a world of patriarchal voracity it is a doctrine of maternal self-sacrifice that Mary pleads, 'Try and realise – we've no right to live as we like – we've had our day together, you and I – but it's past, and we know it. He's what matters now – and we've got to live decently for him – keep straight for him –' (367).

Needless to say John is not convinced, and when, at Mary's insistence that he explain how they will live, he pictures a return to cheap lodgings, their child in a neighbour's care and Mary back at the office, she proposes a radical disruption of the family, effectively ousting the husband/father as a figure of male-based authority. Displaying what Hamilton characterises as women's double-motived interest in marriage, Mary refuses to continue in a financially precarious marriage that threatens the well-being of her son.

Convinced that the harsh conditions of her working life made her child 'small and delicate', she refuses to endanger him further by once more attempting to combine motherhood and work. Perhaps conservative by to-day's standards, she would have been supported in her stand by many feminists of the period who agreed that young children needed their mother's full-time care.[13] Since marriage to John would not provide her with the means to stay at home with her child, Mary chooses to abandon any tie with her husband, remaining in the Rutherford 'prison' that has none the less improved her child's physical health. Although proceeding in an inverse direction, Mary like Janet proves a variation on the abandoned woman type. Deliberately adopting a role traditionally imposed upon passive female sufferers, their active decision to isolate themselves from male alliance reflects the increasing divisiveness and hostility between the sexes that had come to mark the battle for the vote in 1912, as the WSPU adopted, in the words of Emmeline Pankhurst, the 'argument of the stone' (Pankhurst 373).[14] And although Mary moves permanently into the house that Janet renounces, the patterns of their lives prove complementary. For if Janet rejects Martin's money because it is offered without love, Mary rejects John's affection because it comes without money.

As the play's final sequence unfolds, Rutherford and Mary, family patriarch and mother, negotiate grimly for the future. And such is the deterioration of relations between the sexes that maternity's spokesman makes no pretence to even a double-motived interest. Aping the language of capitalist enterprise, Mary proposes a 'bargain' to Rutherford, a bargain 'where one person has something to sell that another wants to buy. There's no love in it – only money – money that pays for life' (370). Like many feminists of the period, Mary adopts what Kent has characterised as the vocabulary of the public sphere 'in order to have [her] position heard and understood', 'the existence of separate spheres … [making] it literally impossible for men and women to 'speak' to each other' (85). In a telling condemnation of existing social and political structures, this mother is compelled to 'sell' her son to secure him 'a good house, good food, warmth' and 'a chance of life' that on 25s a week she cannot afford, but which Rutherford 'right or wrong' has the 'power' to supply. To one reviewer at least such 'bargaining of a mother for her child' bore the clear stamp of a woman playwright's hand (M&M unidentified clipping). Faced with the future loss of the family business without an heir to carry on – 'When you die,

Rutherford's will be sold – somebody'll buy it and give it a new name, perhaps, and no one will even remember that you made it. That'll be the end of all you work. Just – nothing' (370) – Rutherford, who is driven to speak with Mary for the first time in the play, accepts the deal. Confronting each other as adults, a concluding situation that has its roots in *A Doll's House*, Mary proposes a feminist variant of the Demeter/Dis division of Persephone; she will remain in possession of her child for the next ten years during which time 'he's to be absolutely mine' with Rutherford forbidden to 'interfere'. At the close of that period he will be handed over to Rutherford's 'to train up' for the family business. It is a calculated risk for Mary, who places her faith in a reformulation of the doctrine of 'separate spheres' to undo patriarchy itself. Her new agenda emerges when Rutherford expresses incredulity that 'you'd trust your son to me'. Rutherford still assumes his ability to appropriate reproduction as a privilege of male energy expressed through industrial productivity, what G. J. Barker-Benfield calls the fantasy of male self-making: 'Male energy was the icon to which man's vision of his relations with women, his appropriation of her power and that of nature, was captive. This accumulation of power, representing the three conquests of self, woman, and nature, betrayed in its own terms the fantasy of self-reproduction, the climax of male claims to self-making' (392). Mary, however, anticipates Rutherford's unmaking. Appealing to what she perceives to be the more formidable power of time, she explains that in the ten years her son will be apart from him, Rutherford will have become an impotent 'old man; you won't be able to make people afraid of you any more' (370). Not surprisingly, Rutherford insinuates an element of self-interest in Mary's bargain, and his observation that she has 'an eye to the main chance' (371) is echoed by at least one reviewer who called her 'a shrewd little baggage of a London-bred girl' (*Times* 2 Feb 1912, 9). Yet Mary is adamant that she will endure the deadly monotony that Janet cursed, '[I'll] sit and sew at the window and see the chimney flare in the dark; lock up, and give you the keys at night –' (371), only for her son's sake. It is maternal self-sacrifice and patriarchal interest that strike the deal that concludes *Rutherford and Son*. The play ends abruptly with the child's cry; it summons Mary away, leaving Rutherford alone in a 'very silent' room. The device, as theatrical effect, may owe something to the off-stage cry that accompanies Donna Anna's departure at the close of *Don Juan in Hell* (Court 1907).[15] Shaw, however, is concerned with biological imperatives, as Donna Anna's exit line – 'A father! a father for the Superman!' – makes clear. Sowerby's arguments are social and economic, insisting, in Mary's case, on the necessity of reorganising the world without 'fathers' at all.

Are we meant to locate a winner in the struggle between mother and grandfather for the future? The *Times* reviewer argues that the play's conclusion can be read in one of two ways, as the triumph of Rutherford's values over the next generation or as the successful manipulation of Rutherford by what he characterises as a (naturally) vindictive Mary, who 'will infallibly end by paying him back in his own coin of tyranny as he grows older and feebler' (2 Feb 1912, 9). To the *Times* reviewer, such complexity of response is a tribute to Sowerby's stagecraft. Other critics tended to endorse one or the other reading. For the *World* the final scene is tragic, depicting the sacrifice of 'yet another victim' to the Rutherford firm. John Palmer of *The Saturday Review* agrees; he writes that 'Rutherford's is victorious to the last dramatic scene where the mother of John Rutherford's grandchild bargains with her father-in-law for the inheritance. In this last scene Rutherford's, putting a period to the strife and misery of two generations, is already shaping the destinies of a third' (30 March 1912, 391). Goldman takes a different view. Although she originally found Mary's bargain 'unreal and incongruous' she was finally persuaded by Mary's argument that time itself would neutralise Rutherford's power. From Goldman's political perspective, 'The Rutherfords are bound by time, by the eternal forces of change. Their influence on human life is indeed terrible. Notwithstanding it all, however, they are fighting a losing game. ... Change and innovation are marching on, and the Rutherfords must make place for the young generation knocking at the gates' (137). Her interpretation was supported, albeit in less politicised language, by the *Times* March review, which concluded that 'The final triumph rests with the daughter-in-law' (19 March 1912, 5).

Critical reception was not simply divided over interpretations of the play's conclusion. Responses to *Rutherford and Son*, although almost uniformly enthusiastic, are marked, as the play is itself, by a separation along gender lines. This was perhaps to be expected given the increased level of 'sex antagonism' in the social and political arenas of the period, a situation that prompted Granville Barker to speak out against what he feared would become the curse of 'hatred between women as women and men as men.'[16]

Mainstream male critics viewed the play as primarily a study of character with little plot or incident, and praised it is for its 'power of character-drawing' (*Stage* 1 Feb 1912, 20) In the words of the *Daily Telegraph*, 'We care not so much for the story as for the characters' (12 March 1912). Construing the play as an account of the 'war of modern industry' (*Daily Telegraph* 1 Feb 1912), which in its focus upon 'the troubles of and combats of trade' would be appreciated by a 'business nation' (*Era* 23 March 1912, 14), such reviewers tended to agree with Palmer that the real protagonist (described in different reviews as 'villain' or 'hero') is the firm itself, a view which effectively renders Old Rutherford as much a victim as his children, and grants him in the eyes of one scholar at least, the status of a tragic figure (Chandler 215). It is worth noting in light of such views, that Sowerby originally entitled the play *The Master*.[17] Female critics, on the other hand, saw the play as a 'battle cry', and used it accordingly as a platform for feminist political debate. Goldman, for instance, read it in a spirit of revolutionary optimism, and while granting that Sowerby depicts 'the paralysing effect of tradition and institutionalism on all human life, growth, and change' (130) found, in what she maintained was 'the wisdom of Mary', the 'inevitability of the doom of the Rutherfords' (136). Marjorie Strachey, in her review for the *Englishwoman*, took the opportunity to argue for more specific change. She writes that from a suffragist point of view, Janet, 'by far the best-drawn and most interesting character in the play', represents a solution to the Rutherford's difficulties. Constructing an alternative scenario that calls to mind Baker's *Edith*, she reminds her readers that 'Rutherford has another child, whom no one dreams of as a business partner, but who inherits all her father's determination, vitality, and some, at least, of his capacity' (1912, vol. 14, 220). Adopting what could be characterised as a 'conservative' suffragist position, Strachey, herself a member of the law-abiding NUWSS, concludes, 'If only Janet had been brought into Rutherford's when she was a girl, where her powers would have been called out instead of stifled, and where she would have been useful and happy instead of wasted and embittered, what a different household that would have been!' (1912, vol. 14, 220-1). A more thorough-going condemnation of Rutherford, his world and values appears as we might expect, in the suffrage press. Writing for *The Vote*, 'CNB' sees the 'grim despair and unrelieved wretchedness' of *Rutherford and Son* as a woman's 'hell, created by the arrogance of men' (227). Unable to determine 'which of the male characters to dislike most', this reviewer identifies Mary as the play's 'one sympathetic character', a figure who is none the less held in 'thrall to "successful men", weak men, mean-souled and cruel men'. Generalising from Mary's experience, 'CNB' ends with what amounts to a new and markedly hostile battle-cry (one that anticipates Christabel Pankhurst's more vitriolic writing) in which she addresses her feminist sisters: 'Fear, hate, deceit, the fruits of subjection and coercion – how long will men and women be blind to the source of these fertile streams of degeneracy …?' Thus placed, Githa Sowerby's play seems to illustrate the dictum that political theatre is most potent when least overtly political. As such her work stands as dramatic evidence of the increasingly separatist nature of the period's battle between the sexes.

Rutherford and Son brings to an abrupt and premature close England's first wave of feminist theatre, an outpouring of both propagandist and commercial work that sprang initially from Robins's 1907 union of tract and society drama. A product of a movement rooted in the nineteeth century, newly awakened by the aggressive tactics of the WSPU, Edwardian feminist drama, like the larger cause of which it was part, was not merely reactive. Its authors did set themselves up in opposition to the traditional containment of women within the straitjacket of a 'separate-spheres' ideology. Theirs, however, was a creative endeavour; across the feminist spectrum and in the face of a male-determined iconography they sought to place images of women-defined women. The movement found common ground in a will to formulate its own definitions; for women, not men, to decide what was womanly. And here the theatre played a central role. Initially the entrenched conservatism of much turn of the century drama served as a provocation – especially when feminist playwrights responded to the stage women of their male contemporaries. Robins's challenge to people the drama with 'leaders, discoverers [and] militants fighting every form of wrong' was taken seriously by all of the authors discussed above. From the vigilant heroes of Hamilton's *Pageant of Great Women*, to the astutely political Vida Levering and Philippa Tempest, to Maggie Massey and Mary Rutherford battling on the domestic front, we see a new gallery of social and theatrical types in representative acts of self-determination. They are complemented by an assortment of male characters whose 'progress' marks the increasing hostility and divisiveness of the relationship between the sexes. Running the gamut from the congenial but feckless Victor Bretherton, through the irresolute Charley Wilson and arrogant Geoffrey Stonor, to the elder Rutherford, a destructive ogre with god-like pretensions, the men of these plays – brothers, lovers, fathers, husbands and bosses – all are measured and in some manner found wanting. Their insufficience, moreover, is presented as a function of their roles within an oppressive form of patriarchal capitalism.

In considering the arguments and themes of these plays, I have been concerned not only with the ways in which their characters and actions reflect the topical issues of Edwardian feminism, but with the dramatic strategies by which they were animated, drawing upon traditions of late nineteenth- and early twentieth-century stagecraft in a manner that makes them as pertinent to theatre history as to social history. Indeed, the selection and handling of particular themes and characters was as responsive (and reactive) to theatrical genre as it was to political ideology. As a result these plays may be read as women's challenges to conventions both social and aesthetic, often revealing unsettling links between the two. Ringing ingenious variations upon inherited forms, the women playwrights considered here exploit dramatic structures from civic pageantry to the well-made society play to squalid naturalism, constructing their actions to meet the exigencies of each type at the same time that such types were reshaped by the action they contained. By such means these dramatists, like their sisters in the cause, sought to replace prevailing stereotypes of women (social and theatrical) with their own self-defined versions. 'In the process', as Kent stresses more generally, 'they did not entirely reject cultural stereotypes. Instead they formulated their arguments in terms of and in relation to prevailing ideas as expressed in prescriptive, scientific, and political discussion' (58). In the case of playwrights, we must add theatrical discussion and existing dramatic representations. It was a project 'sustained [in] its momentum ... [by] the confidence that notions of masculinity and femininty were culturally constructed, and thus subject to change' (Kent 175).

Perhaps the most striking feature of feminist drama of this period is its 'intense sense of union and comradeship', a quality that Pethick-Lawrence identified as animating the suffrage movement as a whole (164). In the face of what they depict as, at best, male reluctance and, at worst, male betrayal, works like *Votes for Women!*, *Edith*, *Woman with the Pack*, and *Rutherford and Son* celebrate women's loyalty and friendship. As one contemporary enthusiast wrote of Robins's play, 'All the ages ... have sounded woman's loyalty to man, man's loyalty to man, but it remains to you, and a few women like yourself, to voice the great need of the present for woman's loyalty to woman' (quoted by Gates 260). Such faith in female camaraderie is also attested to by the manner in which these texts reached their public. In addition to the suffrage plays, written and produced under the umbrella of the all-women's AFL and/or WWSL, *Votes for Women!* began life as a commissioned piece for AFL member Gertrude Kingston while *Diana of Dobson's* was produced by AFL member Lena Ashwell. *Chains* was originally staged by the Play Actors, an organisation that had both Hamilton and Inez Bensusan (head of the AFL playwriting department) on its advisory council. In the case of *Rutherford and Son*, it was suffrage supporter Thyrza Norman who encouraged a frustrated Sowerby to complete the play which went on to transfer from the Court to Gertrude Kingston's Little Theatre for an extended run.

Although obscured by the passage of time, both plays and performances need to be reckoned with in reassessing the emergence of the repertory movement in modern England as well as the broader issues raised by Edwardian social history. The reception of these texts in their own day attests to the power they exercised over initial audiences and critics – an immediacy lost for a variety of reasons during the years of the Great War. After 1914, much of the energy expended upon the struggle for emancipation was channelled into a wider war effort, and patriotic plays uncritical of a warring nation replaced disruptive works meant to incite protest and foster change. After the awarding of a limited franchise in 1918, which was extended in 1928 to grant women the vote on the same terms as men, the narrowly political agitprop drama of the AFL and WWSL appeared redundant. The more broadly based drama of Edwardian feminists faced a different but equally dispiriting end. Sowerby, Hamilton and Baker all continued to write during and after the Great War. But their work, deprived of its suffrage context, lost much of its urgency and ingenuity. Indeed, their collective experience was similar to that described by Pinero, the period's most established playwright, who found it increasingly difficult to return to his pre-war work: 'it ... [was] as if an iron door had suddenly banged and shut out the operations of one's brain before the war' (Wearing 254). Yet for a rich if troubled decade, feminist drama of the suffrage era had joined what was a rising chorus of women's voices striving to fill the silence that was traditionally women's. *Rutherford and Son, Chains, Diana of Dobson's, Votes for Women!*, and a wealth of so-called suffrage plays, constitute evidence of a flourishing women's theatre in existence at the turn of the century, one that lent to contemporary debate an overtly theatrical shape, while using the theatre's ability to speak publicly of so-called private matters to raise the consciousness of its time. In its feminist manipulations of existing dramatic genres and styles, its restatement of character and shifts of thematic emphasis, it was a theatre that held at least a flickering light to what Robins's Vida Levering calls 'a good half of history.'

Notes

1 See for instance the correspondent for the *Daily Mail* who cites the *Westminster Gazette* as authority for his information that Sowerby was 'young, charming, and modest' (2 Feb 1912); another writer describes her as a 'young girl' (M&M, unidentified clipping).
2 *Mrs Bill* opened at the Court on 9 March 1908, for a run of 16 performances. Sowerby and Kendall (who published under the pseudonym 'Dum-Dum') were married on 8 July 1912.
3 According to Thomas Dickinson, the play proved so popular that it was translated into most of the languages of Europe, where it played frequently (*Contemporary Plays* 643).
4 *Strife* was criticised by the NUWSS's *Common Cause*, the reviewer objecting to the three women in the play as 'each belonging to a variety of the emollient type ... Yet these three women cannot be said to represent the typical mind of working women when their sons and husbands are on stike. Mr Galsworthy's strong imaginative grasp on features of individual character seems to have excluded a larger truth to nature' (29 July 1909 209).
5 Of course the bleak cheerlessness of the Rutherford living-room stands in contrast to the indulgent opulence of the Voysey dining-room.
6 The excess of women to men, as evidenced in nineteenth century census information, increased from 104.2 females to every 100 males in 1851 to 106.8 to 100 in 1911 (Jalland 255).
7 According to Granville Barker 'From her [Honor's] earliest years she has been bottle-washer to her brothers. While they were expensively educated she was grudged schooling; her highest accomplishment was meant to be mending their clothes. Her fate is a curious survival of the intolerance of parents towards her sex until the vanity of their hunger for sons had been satisfied. In a less humane society she would have been exposed at birth' (43).
8 McKinnel, Lena Ashwell's partner in the Kingsway venture, also played the policeman in the first production of Hamilton's *Diana of Dobson's*.
9 In Rutherford's words, 'Mr John's a fool. My son's a fool – I don't say it in anger. He's a fool because his mother made him one, bringing him up secret wi' books o' poetry and such-like trash –' (357).

10 The failure of fiction generally to explore women's relationships was descried by Virginia Woolf: 'All these relationships between women, I thought, rapidly recalling the splendid gallery of fictitious women, are too simple. So much has been left out, unattempted. And I tried to remember any case in the course of my reading where two women are represented as friends' (*Room of One's Own* 123-4).

11 The NUWSS established, in 1912, what it called an Election Fighting Fund to be used to finance Labour candidates seeking election to the House of Commons.

12 In a review written with Edward Aveling, Eleanor Marx argued that 'Ibsen has failed us' by not writing 'the really great modern play, [which] when it comes, will deal not with the struggle in two human lives only, but with that class-struggle which is the epic of the nineteenth century also' (*Marx's Daughters* 58).

13 Jane Lewis notes that among such women were Eleanor Rathbone, who succeeded Millicent Garrett Fawcett as President of the NUWSS in 1918, Ethel Bentham and Mrs J. R. MacDonald, who were leaders of the Women's Labour League, and trade unionist Mary MacArthur (Intro *Marriage as a Trade* 5).

14 By this time Emmeline Pankhurst was insisting, 'Until we get the power to make the law, we shall break the law'. Windows were smashed, street lights broken and pillar boxes vandalised. Throughout 1913 destructive militancy proceeded at an unparalleled pace; works of art were destroyed, empty houses and unattended buildings set ablaze, telegraph and telephone wires cut, and such bastions of male leisure and privilege as sporting clubs and golf links placed under siege. The Government stiffened its own position in March 1913 through passage of the Prisoners' Temporary Discharge Act (commonly known as the Cat and Mouse Act), which allowed those seriously ill from the effects of fasting and forcible feeding to be released only until they had gained sufficient strength to serve the remainder of their sentences.

15 Because *Don Juan in Hell* was originally staged separately from *Man and Superman* (it ran for 8 matinée performances at the close of the Vedrenne Barker seasons at the Court in 1907), the end of this episode did in fact mark the end of the play.

16 This was part of a speech delivered by Barker at a suffrage rally at the London Opera House in March 1912 (*The Standard* 16 March 1912 in vol. 17 of the Arncliffe-Sennett Papers).

17 See the typescript in the British Library's Collection of Lord Chamberlain's Plays.

Works cited

A. J. R., ed. *Suffrage Annual and Women's Who's Who*. London: Paul, 1913.

Archer, William. *The Old Drama and the New*. New York: Dodd, Mead, 1929.

—. *Play-making*. London: Chapman & Hall, 1912.

—. *Real Conversations*. London: Heinemann, 1904.

Arncliffe-Sennett Papers. [A collection of press cuttings, pamphlets, letters, etc. relating primarily to the Women's Suffrage Movement.] Compiled and annotated by Maud Arncliffe Sennett. 37 vols. 1906-36. London: British Library.

Ashwell, Lena. *Myself a Player*. London: Michael Joseph, 1936.

Baker, Elizabeth. *Beastly Pride*. ts. Lord Chamberlain's Plays. 1914/10. London: British Library.

—. *Chains. Contemporary Plays*, ed. Thomas H. Dickinson. Boston: Houghton Mifflin, 1925, 209-243.

—. *Cupid in Clapham. French's One Act Plays*. 3rd Series, ed. Percivale Wilde. London: French, 1927, 131-45.

—. *Edith*. London: Sidgwick & Jackson, 1927.

—. *Miss Tassey*. London: Sidgwick & Jackson, 1913.

—. *The Price of Thomas Scott*. London: Sidgwick & Jackson, 1913.

Barker-Benfield, G. J. 'The Spermatic Economy: A Nineteenth-Century View of Sexuality'. *The American Family in Social-Historical Perspective*, ed. Michael Gordon. 2nd ed. New York: St. Martin's, 1978, 374-402.

Belsey, Catherine. 'Constructing the Subject: Deconstructing the Text'. *Feminist Criticism and Social Change*, eds. Judith Newton and Deborah Rosenfelt. New York: Methuen, 1985.

Bensusan, Inez. *The Apple. Sketches from the Actresses' Franchise League*, ed. Viv Gardner. Nottingham: Nottingham Drama Texts, 1985, 29-39.

Bergeron, David M. *English Civic Pageantry 1558-1642*. Columbia: University of South Carolina Press, 1971.

Best, Geoffrey. *Mid-Victorian Britain 1851-75*. London: Weidenfeld & Nicolson, 1971.

Billington Greig, Teresa. *Towards Woman's Liberty*. Letchworth: Garden City, n.d.

Black, Clementine. *Sweated Industry and the Minimum Wage*. London: Duckworth, 1907.

Blease, W. Lyon. *The Emancipation of Englishwomen*. London: David Nutt, 1913.

Braby, Maud Churton. *Modern Marriage and How to Bear It*. London: Werner Laurie, 1909.

Brown, Janet. *Feminist Drama: Definition & Critical Analysis*. Metuchen: Scarecrow, 1979.

Campbell, Mrs Patrick. *My Life and Some Letters*. London: Hutchinson, n.d.

Case, Sue-Ellen. *Feminism and Theatre*. New York: Methuen, 1988.

Chandler, Frank Wadleigh. *Aspects of Modern Drama*. New York: Macmillan, 1914.

Clark, Barrett H. *A Study of the Modern Drama*. New York: D. Appleton, 1928.

Clarke, Ian. *Edwardian Drama*. London: Faber and Faber, 1989.

Copelman, Dina M. "'A New Comradeship between Men and Women": Family, Marriage and London's Women Teachers, 1870-1914'. *Labour and Love: Women's Experience of Home and Family, 1850-1940*, ed. Jane Lewis. Oxford: Blackwell, 1986, 175-193.

Cordell, Richard. *Henry Arthur Jones and the Modern Drama*. New York: Long, 1932.

Craigie, Pearl. [pseud. John Oliver Hobbes] *The Ambassador*. London: Unwin, 1898.

—. *The Flute of Pan* [novel]. London: Unwin, 1905.

—. *The Life of John Oliver Hobbes told in her correspondence*. Biographical sketch by John Morgan Richards. London: J. Murray, 1911.

—. *Repentance*. London: Chiswick, 1899.

—. *The Wisdom of the Wise*. London: Unwin, 1901.

Craigie, Pearl and Murray Carson. *The Bishop's Move*. New York: Stokes, 1902.

Dangerfield, George. *The Strange Death of Liberal England*. 1935. London: Paladin, 1970.

Davies, Hubert Henry. *A Single Man*, *The Plays of Hubert Henry Davies*, vol. 2. London: Chatto & Windus, 1921, 65–142.

Dickinson, Thomas H. *The Contemporary Drama of England*. London: John Murray, 1920.

Dolan, Jill. *The Feminist Spectator as Critic*. Ann Arbor: UMI Research Press, 1988.

Dugdale, Joan. *10 Clowning Street*, *Innocent Flowers*, ed. Julie Holledge. London: Virago, 1981, 173-188.

Foucault, Michel. *The History of Sexuality, Volume I: An Introduction*. London: Allen Lane, 1979.

Florence, Ronald. *Marx's Daughters*. New York: Dial, 1975.

Gates, Joanne E., ed. *Votes for Women by Elizabeth Robins: Harley Granville Barker's Prompt Book of the Court Theatre Production, 1907*. Jacksonville: Jacksonville State, 1989.

Galsworthy, John. *The Fugitive*, 275-326. *Justice*, 217-74. *Strife*, 99-156. *The Plays of John Galsworthy*. London: Duckworth, 1929.

Gardner, Viv. Introduction, *Sketches from the Actresses' Franchise League*. Nottingham: Nottingham Drama Texts, 1985.

Garland, Alison. *The Better Half*. Liverpool: Daily Post, 1913.

Garner, Les. *Stepping Stones to Women's Liberty: Feminist Ideas in the Women's Suffrage Movement 1900-1918*. London: Heinemann, 1984.

Glover, Evelyn. *A Chat with Mrs Chicky, How The Vote was Won and Other Suffragette Plays*, eds. Dale Spender and Carole Hayman. London: Methuen, 1985, 99-113.

—. *Showin' Samyel*. [London]: n.p., [1914].

—. *Miss Appleyard's Awakening, How The Vote was Won and Other Suffragette Plays*, eds. Dale Spender and Carole Hayman. London: Methuen, 1985, 115-124.

Goldman, Emma. *The Social Significance of Modern Drama*. 1914. New York: Applause Theatre Books, 1987.

Granville Barker, Harley. 'The Coming of Ibsen'. *The Eighteen-Eighties,* ed. Walter De La Mare. Cambridge: Cambridge University Press, 1930, 159-96.

—. *The Madras House*, ed. Margery Morgan. London: Methuen, 1977.

—. *The Marrying of Ann Leete,* 33-82. *The Voysey Inheritance*, 83-159. *Waste*, 161-239. *Plays by Harley Granville Barker*, ed. Dennis Kennedy. Cambridge: Cambridge University Press, 1987.

Granville Barker, Harley and Laurence Housman. *Prunella*. London: Bullen, 1906.

Hamilton, Cicely. *Diana of Dobson's*. London: French, 1925.

—. *A Matter of Money* [novel]. London: Chapman, 1916.

—. *A Pageant of Great Women, Sketches from the Actresses' Franchise League*, ed. Viv Gardner. Nottingham: Nottingham Drama Texts, 1985, 41-50.

—. *Jack and Jill and a Friend*. London: Lacy's, 1911.

—. *Just to Get Married*. London: Lacy's, 1914.

—. *Life Errant*. London: J. M. Dent, 1935.

—. *Marriage as a Trade*. 1909. Introd. by Jane Lewis. London: Women's Press, 1981.

—. 'Triumphant Women'. *Edy: Recollections of Edith Craig*, ed. Eleanor Adlard. London: Frederick Muller, 1949, 38-44.

Hamilton, Cicely and Christopher St John. *How the Vote was Won, How the Vote was Won and Other Suffragette Plays,* eds. Dale Spender and Carole Hayman. London: Methuen, 1985, 17-33.

—. *The Pot and the Kettle*. TS. Lord Chamberlain's Plays. 1909/26. London: British Library.

Hankin, St. John. *The Cassilis Engagement*, vol. 2, 117-226. *The Last of the De Mullins*, vol. 3, 1-87. *The Return of the Prodigal*, vol. 1, 115-213. *The Dramatic Works of St John Hankin*. London: Secker, 1912.

Hardwick, Elizabeth. *Seduction and Betrayal: Woman and Literature*. New York: Random, 1974.

Harraden, Beatrice. *Lady Geraldine's Speech, Sketches from the Actresses' Franchise League*, ed. Viv Gardner. Nottingham: Nottingham Drama Texts, 1985, 51-7.

Harraden, Beatrice and Bessie Hatton. *The Outcast*. TS. Lord Chamberlain's Plays. 1909/25. London: British Library.

Hatton, Bessie. *Before Sunrise, Sketches from the Actresses' Franchise League*, ed. Viv Gardner. Nottingham: Nottingham Drama Texts, 1985, 59-65.

Higgs, Mary. 'Three Nights in Women's Lodging Houses'. *Into Unknown England*, ed. P. J. Keating. Manchester: Manchester University Press, 1976, 273-84.

Hirshfield, Claire. 'The Suffragist as Playwright in Edwardian England'. *Frontiers* IX.2 (1987): 1-6.

Holledge, Julie. *Innocent Flowers*. London: Virago, 1981.

Holroyd, Michael. 'Women and the Body Politic'. *The Genius of Shaw: A Symposium*, ed. Michael Holroyd. London: Hodder & Stoughton, 1979, 167-83.

Holton, Sandra Stanley. *Feminism and Democracy*. Cambridge: Cambridge University Press, 1986.

Houghton, Stanley. *Hindle Wakes, Contemporary Plays*, ed. Thomas H. Dickinson. Boston: Houghton Mifflin, 1925, 289-327.

Howe, P. P. *The Repertory Theatre*. London: Martin Secker, 1910.

Hynes, Samuel. *The Edwardian Turn of Mind*. Princeton: Princeton University Press, 1968.

Ibsen, Henrik. *A Doll's House, Four Major Plays*, trans. James McFarlane and Jens Arup. Oxford: Oxford University Press, 1981, 1-88.

Jalland, Pat. *Women, Marriage and Politics 1860-1914*. Oxford: Clarendon, 1986.

Jamieson, Lynn. 'Limited Resources and Limiting Conventions: Working-Class Mothers and Daughters in Urban Scotland c. 1890-1925'. *Labour and Love: Women's Experience of Home and Family, 1850-1940*, ed. Jane Lewis. Oxford: Blackwell, 1986, 49-69.

Jeffreys, Sheila. *The Spinster and her Enemies*. 1985. London: Pandora, 1987.

Jennings, Gertrude. *A Woman's Influence, Sketches from the Actresses' Franchise League*, ed. Viv Gardner. Nottingham: Nottingham Drama Texts, 1985, 67-74.

Jerome, Jerome K. *Stageland*. London: Chatto & Windus, 1893.

Jones, Henry Arthur. *The Case of Rebellious Susan, The Liars, Plays by Henry Arthur Jones*, ed. Russell Jackson. Cambridge: Cambridge University Press, 1982.

—. *The Masqueraders*. London: French, 1909.

—. *The Middleman, Representative Plays*, ed. Clayton Hamilton. 4 vols. New York: Little, Brown, 1925.

—. *Mrs Dane's Defence, English Plays of the Nineteenth Century*, vol. II. Drama 1850-1900, ed. M. R. Booth. Oxford: Clarendon Press, 1969, 341-427.

Kaplan, Joel. 'Edwardian Pinero'. *Nineteenth Century Theatre*. 17.1-2 (1989): 20-49.

—. 'Have we no Chairs?' *Essays in Theatre*. 4.2 (1986): 119-33.

—. 'Henry Arthur Jones and the Lime-lit Imagination'. *Nineteenth Century Theatre*. 15.2 (1987): 115-41.

Kennedy, Dennis. *Granville Barker and The Dream of Theatre*. Cambridge: Cambridge University Press, 1985.

—. Introduction, *Plays by Harley Granville Barker*. Cambridge: Cambridge University Press, 1987.

Kenney, Annie. *Memories of a Militant*. London: Arnold, 1924.

Kent, Susan Kingsley. *Sex and Suffrage in Britain, 1860–1914*. Princeton: Princeton University Press, 1987.

Keyssar, Helene. *Feminist Theatre*. Houndmills: Macmillan, 1984.

Knoblock, Edward. *Round the Room*. London: Chapman & Hall, 1939.

Knoblock, Edward and Arnold Bennett. *Milestones*. London: Methuen, 1912.

Lewis, Jane. *Women in England 1870-1950: Sexual Divisions and Social Changes*. Brighton: Wheatsheaf, 1984.

Liddington, Jill and Jill Norris. *One Hand Tied Behind Us: The Rise of the Women's Suffrage Movement*. London: Virago, 1978.

Lyttelton, Edith. *Warp and Woof*. London: Fisher Unwin, 1908.

McCarthy, Desmond. *The Court Theatre*. London: Bullen, 1907.

McDonald, Jan. *The 'New Drama' 1900-1914*. Houndmills: Macmillan, 1986.

McLeod, Irene Rutherford. *The Reforming of Augustus*. London: Woman's Press, 1910.

McPhee, Carol and Ann Fitzgerald, eds. *The Non-Violent Militant: Selected Writings of Teresa Billington-Greig*. London: Routledge, 1987.

Marcus, Jane, ed. *Suffrage and the Pankhursts*. London: Routledge, 1987.

—. Introduction, *The Convert*, by Elizabeth Robins. London: Women's Press, 1980.

—. *Elizabeth Robins*. Diss. Northwestern University, 1973. Ann Arbor: UMI, 1973.

Matthews, Brander. *A Book about the Theater*. New York: Scribner's, 1916.

Meacham, Standish. *A Life Apart: The English Working Class 1890-1914*. London: Thames and Hudson, 1977.

Meisel, Martin. *Realisations*. Princeton: Princeton University Press, 1983.

Mitchell, Hannah. *The Hard Way Up*. London: Faber, 1968.

Mitchell, Juliet. *Women: The Longest Revolution*. London: Virago, 1984.

Monefiore, Dora. *From a Victorian to a Modern*. London: E. Archer, 1927.

Moore, Eva. *Exits and Entrances*. London: Chapman, 1923.

Morgan, Margery. Introduction, *The Madras House*, by Harley Granville Barker. London: Methuen, 1977.

Morley, Sheridan. *Sybil Thorndike: A Life in the Theatre*. London: Weidenfeld & Nicolson, 1977.

Mouillot, Gertrude. *The Master*. ms. Lord Chamberlain's Plays. 1909/25. London: British Library.

Natalle, Elizabeth. *Feminist Theatre: A Study in Persuasion*. Metuchen: Scarecrow, 1985.

Nevinson, Margaret. *In the Workhouse*. London: International Suffrage Shop, 1911.

—. *Life's Fitful Fever: A Volume of Memories*. London: A. E. Black, 1926.

Newton, Stella Mary. *Health, Art & Reason*. London: John Murray, 1974.

Nicoll, Allardyce. *English Drama 1900-1930*. Cambridge: Cambridge Univeristy Press, 1973.

Pankhurst, Christabel. *The Great Scourge and How to End it*. London: E. Pankhurst, 1913.

Pankhurst, Sylvia. *The Suffragette Movement*. London: Longman, 1931. Rpt. London: Virago, 1977.

Paston, George [Emily Symonds]. *Tilda's New Hat*. London: French, 1909.

Pethick-Lawrence, Emmeline. *My Part in a Changing World*. London: Victor Gollancz, 1938.

Phibbs, L. S. *Jim's Leg, Innocent Flowers*, ed. Julie Holledge. London: Virago, 1981, 169-71.

Pinero, Arthur Wing. *The Benefit of the Doubt*. London: Heinemann, 1895.

—. *The Collected Letters*, ed. J. P. Wearing. Minneapolis: University of Minneapolis Press, 1974.

—. *The Magistrate*. London: Heinemann, 1892.

—. *Mid-Channel*. London: Heinemann, 1911.

—. *The Mind the Paint Girl*. London: Heinemann, 1913.

—. *The Notorious Mrs Ebbsmith*. London: Heinemann, 1895.

—. *The Profligate*. London: Heinemann, 1891.

—. *The Second Mrs Tanqueray, Trelawny of the 'Wells', The Thunderbolt, Plays by A. W. Pinero*, ed. George Rowell. Cambridge: Cambridge University Press, 1986.

—. *The Weaker Sex*. London: Heinemann, 1894.

Purdom, C. B. *Harley Granville Barker*. London: Barrie & Rockliff, 1955.

Quigley, Austin E. *The Modern Stage and other Worlds*. New York: Methuen, 1985.

Raeburn, Antonia. *Militant Suffragettes*. London: Joseph, 1973.

Reeves, Magdalen Stuart Pember. *Round About a Pound a Week*. London: G. Bell, 1913.

Robertson, Tom. *Caste, Plays by Tom Robertson*, ed. William Tydeman. Cambridge: Cambridge University Press, 1982, 135-84.

Robins, Elizabeth. *Ancilla's Share*. London: Hutchinson, 1924.

—. *Ibsen and the Actress*. London: Hogarth Press, 1928.

—. *Theatre and Friendship*. London: Jonathan Cape, 1932.

—. *Votes for Women, How the Vote was Won and Other Suffragette Plays*, eds. Dale Spender and Carole Hayman. London: Methuen, 1985, 35-87.

—. *Way Stations*. New York: Dodd and Mead, 1913.

Robins, Elizabeth and Florence Bell. *Alan's Wife*, ed. J. T. Grein. Introd. William Archer. London: Henry & Co, 1893.

Rosen, Andrew. *Rise Up, Women!* London: Routledge, 1974.

Rubinstein, David. *Before the Suffragettes*. Brighton: Harvester, 1986.

St John, Christopher [Christabel Marshall]. *The First Actress*. TS. Lord Chamberlain's Plays. 1911/14. London: British Library.

Sharp, Evelyn. *Unfinished Adventure: Selected Reminiscences from an Englishwoman's Life*. London: Bodley Head, 1933.

Shaw, Bernard. *The Bodley Head Bernard Shaw Collected Plays with Their Prefaces*. 7 vols, ed. Dan Laurence. London: Reinhardt, 1970-74.

—. *Letters to Granville Barker*, ed. C. B. Purdom. London: Phoenix House, 1956.

—. *Shaw and Ibsen: Bernard Shaw's 'The Quintessence of Ibsenism' and Related Writings*, ed. J. L. Wisenthal. Toronto: University of Toronto Press, 1979.

—. *The Intelligent Woman's Guide to Socialism and Capitalism*. New York: Brentano's, 1928.

Showalter, Elaine. *A Literature of Their Own*. Princeton: Princeton University Press, 1977.

Sowerby, Githa. *Little Plays for School and Home*. London: Chatto & Windus, 1910.

—. *Rutherford and Son, Contemporary Plays*, ed. Thomas H. Dickinson. Boston: Houghton Mifflin, 1925, 333-71.

S[pence], E. F. *Our Stage and its Critics*. London: Methuen, 1910.

States. Bert. *Great Reckonings in Little Rooms*. Berkeley: University of California Press, 1985.

Steele, Valerie. *Fashion and Eroticism*. New York: Oxford University Press, 1985.

Stokes, John. *In the Nineties*. Hemel Hempstead: Harvester Wheatsheaf, 1989.

Stubbs, Patricia. *Women and Fiction: Feminism and the Novel 1880-1920*. 1979. London: Methuen, 1981.

Sudermann, Hermann. *Magda*, trans. by Charles Winslow. London: French, 1895.

Taylor, Tom. *Arkwright's Wife*. MS. Lord Chamberlain's Plays. Add. 53128B. London: British Library.

—. *Ticket of Leave Man, Plays by Tom Taylor*, ed. Martin Banham. Cambridge: Cambridge University Press, 1985, 165-222.

Tickner, Lisa. *The Spectacle of Women*. London: Chatto & Windus, 1987.

Todd, Janet. *Feminist Literary History*. Oxford: Polity Press, 1988.

Trewin, J. C. 'Cicely Hamilton'. *Dictionary of Literary Biography. Modern British Dramatists, 1900-1945*, vol. 10, ed. Stanley Weintraub. Detroit: Gale, 1982, 212-15.

—. *The Edwardian Theatre*. Oxford: Blackwell, 1976.

—. *The Theatre Since 1900*. London: Dakers, 1951.

Valverde, Mariana. 'Love of Finery: Fashion and the Fallen Woman in Nineteenth-Century Social Discourse'. *Victorian Studies*. 32:22 (1989): 169-188.

Vaughan, Gertrude. *The Woman with the Pack*. London: Ham-Smith, 1912.

—. [Selections from] *The Woman with the Pack, Votes for Women,*

22 December 1911: 187.

Vicinus, Martha. *Independent Women: Work and Community for Single Women 1850-1920*. Chicago: University of Chicago Press, 1985.

Wearing, J. P. *The London Stage 1900-1909*, vol II. Metuchen: Scarecrow, 1981.

Weeks, Jeffrey. *Sex, Politics and Society*. London: Longman, 1981.

Wentworth, Vera. *An Allegory, Sketches from the Actresses' Franchise League*, ed. Viv Gardner. Nottingham: Nottingham Drama Texts, 1985, 91-96.

Wilde, Oscar. *Lady Windermere's Fan*, ed. Ian Small. London: Ernest Benn, 1980.

—. *The Importance of Being Earnest*, ed. Russell Jackson. London, Ernest Benn, 1980.

—. *A Woman of No Importance, An Ideal Husband, Two Society Comedies*, ed. Ian Small and Russell Jackson. London: Ernest Benn, 1983.

Woolf, Virgina. *A Room of One's Own*. London: Hogarth Press, 1931.

Appendix: Cast lists

Votes for Women

First performed at the Court Theatre as a Barker-Vedrenne Matinée on 9 April 1907.

VIDA LEVERING	Edith Wynne-Mathison*
BEATRICE DUNBURTON	Jean MacKinlay
MRS FREDDY TUNBRIDGE	Gertrude Burnett*
LADY JOHN WYNNSTAY	Maud Milton
MRS HERIOT	Frances Ivor
ERNESTINE BLUNT	Dorothy Minto*
WORKING WOMAN	Agnes Thomas*
LORD JOHN WYNNSTAY	Athol Forde
HON. GEOFFREY STONOR	C. Aubrey Smith
ST JOHN GREATOREX	E. Holman Clark
RICHARD FARNBOROUGH	P. Clayton Greene
FREDDY TUNBRIDGE	Percy Marmont
ALLEN TRENT	Lewis Casson
MR WALKER	Edmund Gwenn

Diana of Dobson's

First performed at the Kingsway Theatre as part of Lena Ashwell's Repertory Season on 2 February 1908.

DIANA MASSINGBERD	Lena Ashwell*
MISS SMITHERS	Nannie Benett
MISS KITTY BRANT	Christine Silver*
MISS JAY	Muriel Vox
MISS MORTON	Doris Lytton
MISS PRINGLE	Ada Palmer*
MRS CANTELUPE	Frances Ivor
MRS WHYTE FRASER	Gertrude Scott
OLD WOMAN	Beryl Mercer
CPT. THE HON. VICTOR BRETHERTON	C. M. Hallard
SIR JABEZ GRINLAY	Dennis Eadie
P.C. FELLOWES	Norman McKinnel
WAITER	W. Lemmon Warde

*Members of the Actresses' Franchise League

Chains

First performed at the Court Theatre by the Play Actors on 18 April 1909 for a single performance.

MAGGIE MASSEY	Rose Mathews*
LILY WILSON	Gillian Scaife*
SYBIL FROST	Doris Digby*
MRS MASSEY	Marion Sterling*
CHARLEY WILSON	Ashton Pearse
FRED TENNANT	Gordon A. Parker
MORTON LESLIE	Leonard Calvert
PERCY MASSEY	Harold Chapin
THOMAS FENWICK	Sebastian Smith
ALFRED MASSEY	Clive Currie
WALTER FOSTER	H. K. Ayliff

Chains was revived at the Duke of York's Theatre as part of Granville Barker's Repertory Season on 17 May 1910.

MAGGIE MASSEY	Sybil Thorndike*
LILY WILSON	Hilda Trevelyan*
SYBIL FROST	Dorothy Minto*
MRS MASSEY	Florence Haydon
CHARLEY WILSON	Dennis Eadie
FRED TENNANT	Frederick Lloyd
MORTON LESLIE	Arthur Whitby
PERCY MASSEY	Donald Calthrop
THOMAS FENWICK	Lewis Casson
ALFRED MASSEY	Edmund Gwenn
WALTER FOSTER	Hubert Haraben

Rutherford and Son

First performed at the Court Theatre as one of Mr Leigh's Matinées on 31 January 1912.

JOHN RUTHERFORD	Norman McKinnel
JOHN (his son)	Edmund Breon
RICHARD (his son)	Frank J. Randell
JANET (his daughter)	Edyth Olive*
ANN (his sister)	Agnes Thomas*
MARY	Thyrza Norman*
MARTIN	A. S. Homewood
MRS HENDERSON	Agnes Hill*

Rutherford and Son was revived at the Little Theatre under the management of Gertrude Kingston on 18 March 1912 (subsequently transferring to the Vaudeville Theatre on 22 April 1912) with the following cast changes.

MARTIN	Harvey Braban
MRS HENDERSON	Marie Ault

Index

Index